DATE DUE

JE 3 '94			
SE 23 '94			
SE 29 '95			
DE 1 03			

DEMCO 38-296

EDUCATOR'S
Treasury of Stories for All Occasions

EDUCATOR'S

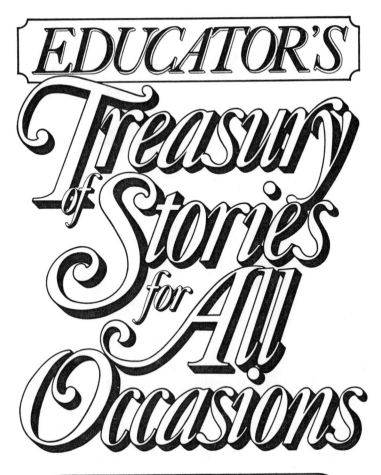

Treasury of Stories for All Occasions

501 Effective & Entertaining Anecdotes for Speeches & Letters

P. SUSAN MAMCHAK • STEVEN R. MAMCHAK

PARKER PUBLISHING COMPANY
West Nyack, New York 10995

PARKER PUBLISHING COMPANY
West Nyack, New York

10   9   8   7   6   5   4   3   2   1

Library of Congress Cataloging-in-Publication Data

Mamchak, P. Susan, 1944–
   Educator's treasury of stories for all occasions : 501 effective &
entertaining anecdotes for speeches and letters / P. Susan Mamchak.
Steven R. Mamchak.
     p.   cm.
   Includes index.
   ISBN 0-13-240805-8
   1. Public speaking—Handbooks, manuals, etc.   2. Educators—United
States.   I. Mamchak, Steven R.   II Title.
PN4192.T43M3   1993
808.5′1—dc20   92-17483
                                           CIP

ISBN   0-13-240805-8

Parker Publishing Company
West Nyack, NY 10995

Simon & Schuster, A Paramount Communications Company

Printed in the United States of America

...DEDICATION...

ABOUT THE AUTHORS

P. SUSAN MAMCHAK has served in many different educational posts, from substitute teacher to school disciplinarian to curriculum designer. She has also conducted workshops on teacher effectiveness, is a past member of Toastmistress International, and travels and lectures extensively. With her husband of 28 years, she is co-author of over a dozen books on education.

STEVEN R. MAMCHAK has been actively involved in education for over thirty years. He has worked with "disaffected" children as well as gifted and talented students, has hosted a weekly radio program on education, and is a frequent speaker to both educational and civic groups.

ABOUT THIS RESOURCE

You already know why you need this book. Perhaps, this afternoon, you need to explain new rules to the student body. Later, at the faculty meeting, it may be up to you to expand upon the new school board policy. Tonight, the parents of next year's incoming class may expect to be informed about the school their children will be attending. Or perhaps it's time to start working on that article for the newsletter or that presentation you have to make to the administration next week. So much to do—and so little time to do it in!

Of course, you want to do the best possible job you can in these important communication assignments. For example, you know that good communication is enhanced by the use of good examples—an essential part of good teaching as well as of good communication—but this is precisely where your problems develop. How do you get your hands on just the right example? And while it may be true that "a picture is worth ten thousand words," it does not follow that ten thousand words make a good picture. You need the *right* words. You need examples that are concise, effective, and to the point. And perhaps most of all, you need them *now*, because you don't have the luxury of hunting around or waiting for inspiration to strike.

That's why the *Educator's Treasury of Stories for All Occasions* provides over 500 stories and anecdotes you can use right now in your professional communications, whether oral or written, routine or special. We have provided material that will drive home the points you wish to make; give your audience something to think about in relation to what you have just told them; cause them to smile, perhaps, and get them on your side; break the ice and establish a rapport; sum up the essence of your communication; and provide incisive, dignified, appropriate, and dynamic examples, vitally related to today's education.

A glance at the table of contents will assure you that what is covered in this resource reflects the full range and scope of today's education and the professional educator's role in it. From the classroom to the principal's office, from parent and teacher interaction to the role of the school within the community, here is incisive material in a form you *can and will use.*

Use some of the material in Part One: First Steps and Little Acorns to set your audience at ease, to establish rapport, to open a speech, or to confirm the fact that you are an educator with an important message that deserves to be heard. Close your speech with one of the entries in Part Ten: Ending Up With a Good Beginning—something that will summarize what you have just told the audience and leave them highly inspired to carry your ideas well beyond the doors of the auditorium. For a group of parents, consult Part Six: Notes on the Great Adventure for stories about the joys and sorrows of family life. Educators, from classroom teacher to school superintendent, will find joy and food for thought in Part Nine: The Story and the Glory, which draws on the myriad facets of education. Or, you can try Part Three: Out of the Darkness and Into the Light, with its stories of the educational interplay within today's classrooms.

Whether you are speaking about an administrator (see Part Four: Principals and Their Principles), introducing a colleague (see Part Two: How to Remember "What's-His-Name"), speaking about a serious and troublesome problem (see Part Eight: Anything That Can Go Wrong), giving an after-dinner speech, (see Part Seven: When the Rubber Chicken Bounces) or at a PTA affair (Part Six: Growing Perfect With Practice), you will find what you need in this book. Because of the detailed table of contents and the very practical topical index, this is material that you can easily find and use.

Each entry bespeaks the authenticity that only decades of experience in schools can provide. We know that, for years to come, you will use this book as you use your other invaluable reference sources: to save you time and to help you say precisely what you had in mind in the most powerful and dynamic way.

Some of the following entries will make you laugh; some may bring a tear or two; *all of them will make you think.* As educators, isn't that what we most wish to accomplish?

P. Susan Mamchak
Steven R. Mamchak

TABLE OF CONTENTS

SECTION TWO: HOW TO REMEMBER "WHAT'S-HIS-NAME"—
              Introducing Yourself and Others **29**

SECTION FOUR: PRINCIPALS AND THEIR PRINCIPLES—
         A Closer Look at School Administration 81

SECTION SEVEN: WHEN THE RUBBER CHICKEN BOUNCES—
              Stories for the After-Dinner Speaker **155**

SECTION EIGHT: ANYTHING THAT CAN GO WRONG—
             Taking a Look at Troublesome Topics 179

**SECTION TEN: ENDING UP WITH A GOOD BEGINNING—
Material for Dynamic and Inspirational
Conclusions**

FIRST STEPS AND LITTLE ACORNS—ICEBREAKERS AND SPEECH OPENERS

Your name is announced, polite applause begins, and you step forward to face an audience who are about to listen to you speak. If you don't feel some nervousness at this point, then perhaps you are made of stone. What you will say over the next few moments will, to a large extent, determine the mood of your audience and the tone of the speech that is to follow. If you wish to plant that little acorn from which a mighty oak will grow, then these first steps are crucial. You must establish who you are, why you are speaking, and what you wish to accomplish—all within the first few sentences and paragraphs of your presentation. You can use the stories and anecdotes from this section to gain rapport, establish a mutual bond, set your audience thinking, or establish the point upon which you will elaborate. Certainly, you will find something to meet your needs.

That first step is never easy, but taken properly, it can lead to a destination that is well worth the trip.

1. Importance of a Good Beginning

The first year I taught, I ran across a veteran teacher who, it seemed, never had any trouble with his students, even though everyone knew that he had been assigned the toughest kids in school. In wide-eyed innocence, I asked how he accomplished this.

"The first day of school," he answered, "I stay in the Teacher's Lounge until a few minutes after the bell has rung. Then I slowly walk to this class who has never seen me before. By the time I get there, they are screaming and jumping around and throwing paper airplanes, and the room is bedlam.

"I take a deep breath and run into the room, slamming the door behind me as hard as I can. I stamp over to my desk and slam down my books so hard the blotter jumps. Then, I look up at the ceiling and scream. By now I have the attention of the class, and slowly I look out at them.

" 'It's a lie!' I shout. 'It's a dirty lie! If anyone asks you, you tell them I had nothing to do with putting that kid in the hospital! Do you Understand?!!!'

"After that, working out discipline for the year is relatively easy.

"You know," he concluded, "if you have a good beginning, half your work is already done!"

2. A Proper First Impression (I)

The young educator was due to speak at his first PTA function, and he was extremely nervous about making a good first impression. He showered twice, spent an inordinant amount of time combing his hair and otherwise grooming himself, and, finally, he stood in the middle of the living room, about to depart for the PTA meeting at school.

"Is my jacket clean?" he stammered to his wife. "Is my tie straight? Does my hair look OK? Do I have my speech?"

"Your jacket is perfect; your tie is straight; there's not a hair out of place; your speech is safely in your jacket pocket," his wife advised him calmly.

"Sorry I'm such a bother," the husband continued, "but I really do want to make a proper first impression in front of those parents!"

"In that case," smiled his wife, "I'd suggest you go back to the bedroom and look in the full-length mirror before you leave—you forgot to put on your pants!"

3. A Proper First Impression (II)

A farmer's son was playing with a football in the farm yard. He kicked the ball, and it sailed through the open door of one of the hen houses and came to rest in the hay on the floor.

Not a moment afterwards, a visiting rooster from the hen house across the way came strutting in. He looked around the place, and his gaze fell upon the football. He looked at it intently for a moment, and then, cackling and fluttering, he all but flew back to his own coop, where he immediately called all the hens together.

"Ladies," announced the rooster, "we are going to take a trip to the hen house across the yard. I was just there, and I got a chance to see the work that some of the hens over there are doing. I want you to see it, too, because I'll tell you—you are going to be impressed!!!"

4. Starting Off on the Right Foot

The PTA was holding a fundraiser for the school, and the program was all but over. Indeed, the principal was the last scheduled speaker. It was an exceptionally hot night in early June, and the parents had been packed into an un-air-conditioned and poorly ventilated gymnasium for almost two hours. As the principal rose to address the crowd, foreheads glistened and the heat that rose from the audience shimmered the air.

"Ladies and gentlemen," began the principal, "I always like to start out on the right foot, so I'm going to be honest with you. You know that tonight is dedicated to raising money, so I have prepared three speeches. If we raise over $700, I have a five-minute speech I'll deliver. If we make around $500, I have a twenty-minute address planned. If we raise anything under $300, then I have a wonderful talk to give that will last about an hour and a half.

"Now, let's take up the collection, count it, and find out which speech I'm going to give!"

5. Getting Acquainted

Just out of college and looking for my first teaching position, I went for an interview and was advised that the superintendent was running a bit behind schedule. I was ushered into a room and asked to wait.

There was another gentleman in the room, and we soon struck up a conversation.

"I hear this superintendent is real tough," he said. "Why would you want to teach here?"

With all the brash assuredness of my twenty-two-year-old knowledge and experience, I launched into my philosophy of education and what I hoped to accomplish in teaching. I also mentioned that I, too, had heard how tough this superintendent was, but I figured that I could handle him all right.

After about twenty minutes of this, the man leaned back and looked at me. "You know," he said, "with time and practice, you're going to make a fine teacher."

"Thanks," I answered, "but first I have to get through this interview with the old man."

"I'm certain that you'll do just fine," he smiled. "By the way, I never did introduce myself. I'm the superintendent of schools for this township, and I DO like to get acquainted with prospective teachers *before* the interview!"

6. *Uneasy Beginnings*

The forensics coach was telling his wife about the debate his students had held that afternoon with a neighboring school district. The coach of the opposing team had behaved horribly, the man told his wife, yelling and screaming and jumping up—accusing students of cheating and generally making a terrible disturbance and a thorough nuisance of himself.

"The end of the debate came," the teacher continued, "and I was making my way to the parking lot when I turned a corner and came face to face with this opposing coach. He glared at me, and I glared at him. He looked me squarely in the eyes and shouted, 'The principal of your school is an idiot!' I looked right back at him and said, 'The principal of *your* school is an idiot!' "

"My goodness," said the man's wife, "I do hope you didn't hit each other."

"Of course not," said the teacher. "We were so happy that we had finally found a point we could agree on that we shook hands, became friends on the spot, and I invited him to dinner tonight!"

7. *Nervousness of the Speaker (I)*

Thomas Edison invented the stock ticker, a device used to type out the current prices of stocks on a continuous strip of paper. It became the mainstay of stock exchanges throughout the world until the advent of computers. When it was first invented, however, Edison received an offer to buy the machine, and an appointment was arranged to talk about a fair price.

Edison agonized over how much he should ask, and he finally told his wife that he was going to ask for five thousand dollars, although he thought that the price was probably a bit high.

When the day arrived, the potential buyer got right down to business. "All right, Mr. Edison," said the man, "how much do you want for your invention?"

The suddeness of the attack so unnerved Edison that he became flustered. He was so nervous that the words stuck in his throat. Try as he might, his nervousness would not allow him to speak, and he sat there with his head hanging down and his arms limp.

Again the man repeated the question, and again Edison just sat there unable to say a word. Finally, the man leaned across the table and glared at Edison.

"Come now, Sir," said the man, "let's not be coy. If you won't begin, how does $100,000 sound to start?"

8. Nervousness of the Speaker (II)

These butterflies inside of me
    Are enough to make me weak;
Let alone the knowledge that
    Quite soon I'll have to speak.

Oh, how I hope and pray that when
    I get the first word said,
The others I've forgotten
    Will come back into my head.

And how I hope and pray as well
    That when my speech is done,
I'll be as welcome in this place
    As when it was begun.

Next time an audience awaits,
    I know I'd feel much better
If I spent the money for the stamps
    And sent each one a letter!

9. Nervousness of the Speaker (III)

The first-grade teacher had finished a short unit on public speaking, and now it was time for each first-grader to get up and deliver a short speech. Parents had been invited, and it was quite an affair.

Just before it was his turn to speak, little Bobby came running up to the teacher. "Mrs. Jones," he announced, "I have to go to the bathroom!"

"Bobby," said the teacher, "you don't have to go to the bathroom; it's just nervousness. The minute you start to speak, the feeling will go away."

Bobby got up to speak and delivered a flawless speech, smiling broadly every moment of the time. When he finished, he bowed to the audience and ran back to the teacher.

"Mrs. Jones," Bobby grinned, "you were right! When I started to talk, I didn't have to go to the bathroom any more!"

"You see," Mrs. Jones replied, "just as I told you."

"Gosh, Mrs. Jones," Bobby said, "you know everything. Can I ask you one more question?"

"Why certainly, Bobby," smiled the teacher. "What is it?"

"When everybody's finished with the speeches—can I change out of these wet pants?"

10. Desire for Proper Communication

The teacher found out that one particularly active and troublesome student had a cup of coffee each morning before coming to school. Thinking that this might be the cause of his behavior problem, the teacher wrote to the parents: "It is my considered opinion that you should refrain from allowing the consumption of caffein-based liquids by your offspring prior to his educational interaction with his peer group."

The parents wrote back that they would try to have him drink a second cup of coffee as she had suggested.

Again the teacher wrote: "Desist immediately. The influx of caffeine not only has a negative influence on his academic stature but also inculcates a hyperactivity which is detrimental to his social progress."

The parents wrote back that of course they could send in enough coffee to give a cup to each child in the class.

Finally, the teacher wrote: "Stop giving your kid coffee; it turns him into a little monster!"

To which the parents wrote: "No more coffee! If you had said so in the first place, we wouldn't be having this problem!"

11. Barriers to Proper Communication

Tonight, I want to make certain that we eliminate all barriers to proper communication and understanding, not like the woman I know who came home one afternoon to find her eight-year-old son staring into a mirror with his mouth open and weeping steadily.

"We got our teeth examined in school today," the boy told his mother, "and the nurse told me that I got a real bad disease. She said I got *flucky*!!!"

" 'Flucky?' " said his mother, "What's that?"

"I don't know," wailed the boy, "but she said I got it!"

Immediately, the mother called the school and presently was connected to the school nurse, to whom she explained her son's distress.

"He's very worried," the mother told the nurse. "He says you told him he has some rare disease called 'flucky.' "

"I have no idea what he's talking about," answered the school nurse. "I remember exactly what happened. The examination showed that he only had one small cavity. I distinctly remember telling him that considering the fact that he sometimes forgot to brush, he got *off lucky!*"

12. Using the Wrong Word

I think that it is extremely important that we begin by defining our terms. This fact was brought home to me several years ago in my own classroom.

My supervisor was visiting on a day when I had planned to have a debate within our class. The subject was to be that ever-popular focus of attention in schools, the cafeteria. Not only had we gone over the rules of debate, but I had also encouraged my students to do some vocabulary work and try to incorporate their newly learned words into their speeches.

Smiling to my supervisor, I bade the debate begin, and the first student took the floor.

"I think everyone should know just how TAWDRY things have gotten in our cafeteria," she began.

Tawdry? TAWDRY? I glanced over at my supervisor who now regarded me with one raised eyebrow.

I called the girl to me and asked what she meant by using the word *tawdry* to describe our cafeteria.

"Look," she replied, handing me a dictionary. "In there it says that *tawdry* means 'cheap and tasteless.' Well, if you've ever eaten in our cafeteria, you know exactly how tawdry that food can be!"

From that day forward, I have always defined my terms BEFORE I spoke!

13. Starting a Carnival/Fundraiser

Tonight, it is my happy duty to welcome you to our annual school carnival/our yearly PTA fundraiser.

A couple of years ago in my neighborhood, some of the neighborhood children got together and formed one of those "back-yard" carnivals which children have been doing for ages.

As I neared the "gate" to this affair, I noticed a hastily constructed lemonade stand which was staffed by the seven-year-old daughter of a neighbor. A sign, obviously written by an adult hand proclaimed "LEMONADE 10¢!" Below it, in smaller letters ran the legend "All Proceeds to the College Fund."

The child's mother was standing by, and as I plunked down my dime, I remarked, "I thought this was just a kid's thing; I didn't know you were sponsoring a college fund."

"Oh, yes," was the mother's reply as she put her hand on the child's shoulder. "You're our first customer. Only 999,999 more cups of lemonade, and she'll be all set for her first year at Harvard!"

Well, I don't know about saving up for Harvard, but your money tonight will certainly help our school.

I've got my first dime ready; how about you? Shall we begin?

14. The Tired Audience

Well, it's been a long night, and the only thing that's keeping you from your beds is me and my speech. I promise I'll make it short, but I do want you to know something before I begin.

When I was in college, I had a good friend who loved to go bear hunting. One afternoon, he had been stalking a bear for hours and was very tired. He sat down under a tree to rest for a while, and soon he was fast asleep. He began to snore, and he snored so loudly that several fellow bear hunters thought it was a grizzly and opened fire.

They never found my friend, but there is a rumor that one of those hunters has the mounted head of a snarling college freshman on the wall of his den.

How true that is, I don't know, but I have asked twenty-five bear hunters with very powerful shotguns to surround this school tonight. Considering how tired you look, I thought you'd like to know these things before I begin my speech!

15. *The Receptive Audience*

I had a child in class who was particularly shy and retiring, and I had been doing what I could to "draw him out." Finally, I convinced him that he should give a short speech before our class.

Prior to that speech, I did some work behind the scenes, talking to other members of the class and extracting the promise from them that they would receive John warmly and without whistles and catcalls. In other words, they promised to be a highly receptive audience.

I also got the librarian, the guidance counselor, and the vice-principal to attend and assured them of the need for much positive reinforcement.

John stepped up onto the small raised platform in front of the room. The place exploded. The children applauded and applauded. The visiting educators rose to their feet, and the class followed suit, cheering and applauding.

John took it all in, then lowered his eyes and went over to his desk and sat down.

"John!" I shouted as I ran up to his desk, "What about your speech?"

"I ain't gonna give it!" exclaimed John. "This is the best I ever felt, and I ain't gonna spoil it by saying the speech and giving them something not to like!"

16. *Using the Right Word (I)*

So much depends upon choosing the right words when we speak. I remember an elementary school where the heating unit in a first-grade classroom decided to die in the middle of January. As the temperature in the room dropped rapidly, the office was notified and the whole school scrambled to find an alternative space for the first-graders. In fact, the principal came down to address the first-grade class.

"Now, children," she said, "we're having trouble with the heat, but we will find you a new, warm classroom in just a little while. In the meantime, we are just going to have to bear with it."

With that the principal left the room and the teacher followed, talking to the principal in the hallway for a few moments.

When the teacher stepped back into the room, there were her twenty-plus first-graders, sitting at their desks as naked as newly-hatched chicks.

"Ms. Johnson," said one child to the sputtering teacher, "I don't think the principal knows what she's talking about. We got bare like she said, but I'm colder now than I was before!"

Yes, so much depends upon using the right word!

17. Using the Right Word (II)

We once did some work with very young children from a highly impoverished, "inner city" neighborhood. It was a preschool activity whose purpose was to prepare these children for school.

One of their teachers once read them the story of Cinderella. She did it with a great deal of enthusiasm, acting out many of the scenes. When she had finished, the children were asked to draw a picture from the story.

Quite a number of the children drew pictures of a little girl with a stick in her hand and a round object in front of her.

When we asked, we were told that this was Cinderella at the ball. She was up at bat and was about to hit a home run.

Yes, that made us chuckle, but it also made us think. Nowhere in these children's background was there a concept for the word *ball* other than that used in playing a game. Certainly, given their lives in the overcrowded inner city in which they lived, concepts such as "Prince Charming" and "lived happily ever after" were not a part of their vocabulary either.

What a comment these lack of words make upon our society. How long will it be before we start showing them the right words such as *educate* and *uplift* and *draw out* and *rise above*? How long before we realize that we need to help these children learn the right words that will lead them to a tomorrow where people can, indeed, live "happily ever after"?

18. Saying What You Mean

One of the school secretaries came into the principal's office and asked if he would like some coffee before they closed down the coffee maker for the day.

"Thank you," he said. "Whatever's there; milk, no sugar."

The secretary prepared the coffee and brought it back to the principal's office. As she came through the door, the heel of her shoe caught on a loose piece of carpeting and she suddenly lunged forward. She held on to the cup, but her forward momentum sent the coffee itself into space, travelling halfway across the office and landing squarely in the lap of the principal.

The secretary stared in disbelief at the coffee-covered principal who rose slowly to his feet.

"Ms. Jones," he said, gingerly shaking his wet trousers, "I believe this is all my fault."

"Your fault?" said the open-mouthed secretary.

"Yes," he continued, "I really should have told you that I preferred the coffee IN the cup. One must say what one really means!"

19. An Exercise in Bluntness

"I'm so disappointed," the teacher told her husband one evening. "Look at this pile of test papers from the midterm exams. My students did far worse than they might have; they made silly, careless mistakes. It looks like they hardly read the instructions. What a mess!

"Well, tomorrow I'm going to be perfectly blunt with them. I'm going to tell them that these papers are trash and that they should be arrested for littering!"

With that the irate teacher slammed down the considerable packet of tests and went off to attend to some other matter.

When she returned an hour later, the test papers were gone. She searched but could not find them. Beginning to panic since these were, after all, the entire midterm exams for all her classes, she asked her husband if he'd seen them. Then, she asked her eight-year-old son.

"Sure," said the boy, "I know where they are. You remember how you were telling Dad about how these were real trash and like littering?"

"Well, I was upset, I . . ."

"And, do you remember last week when you and Dad said I'd get no more allowance until I started to do my chores around the house? Do you remember what that chore was?"

"Taking out the garbage . . ."

"The 'trash' went into the incinerator," the boy smiled, "half an hour ago!"

20. Getting Others to Like You

A teacher I know relates the tale of a student who was transferred into the school from another district when his family moved into town. Like any student new to the class, she sought to introduce him to his classmates. She asked the boy if he would be willing to tell the class a little bit about himself and his family. The new student agreed.

He said all the things you would expect, listing the names of his brothers and sisters, talking about his dog and his hamster, and telling the class how he enjoyed skateboarding.

"There's just one other thing," the boy concluded. "I guess you should know that I don't do too well in my schoolwork. I guess I'm kinda slow like. I sure hope you guys will help me to learn. I don't think I can do it without you."

With that, the boy sat down, and the class flocked about him, slapping him cordially on the back and promising unending help with every subject.

Later, when they were alone, the teacher called the boy to her desk and placed a sheet of paper before him.

"This is your transcript from your other school," she said. "You're a straight A student. Why did you say all that about needing so much help?"

"Ma'am," sighed the boy, "if I'd told them I was a straight A student, I'd still be fighting my way out of the schoolyard. I want those kids to like me!"

21. Learning to Like Others

The new boy really started off on the wrong foot. Within the first few hours of his first day in our class, he had alienated almost every one of his classmates. He was bossy and pushy, he "mocked-out" several students, and he even reduced one girl to tears.

Just before lunch, I overheard one of the other kids ask this boy to sit with him and his friends during lunch period. Since the boy who asked was one of the most popular kids in class, I was somewhat taken aback. Personally, I spent lunchtime trying to figure out some methods of thwarting this potential menace before he became totally intolerable.

I needn't have bothered. When he returned from lunch, there was a complete transformation. The boy was helpful, friendly, and went through the remainder of the day with a huge smile on his face. At the end of the day, I spoke to the student who had invited the boy to lunch and asked if he had any clue as to the boy's change of heart and attitude.

"Sure," said the popular class leader. "At lunch, we told him that in order to get people to like him, he had to learn to like other people, and that was the secret of getting along."

"And that did it?" I asked.

"Yes, sir," answered the boy, "that and the fact that we also told him that if he didn't stop acting like a rat and be nice and smile for the rest of the day, we were gonna take him into the boy's room, stick his head in the toilet and flush it!"

22. My First Speech (Humorous)

I gave my first speech when I was in the first grade. I was seven at the time, and it was a day in which parents were going to come to school to watch us do some program. My job was going to be to welcome the parents and make them feel comfortable—that's the task the teacher assigned to me.

"I don't know what to say," I told my teacher.

"Just say something that would make you feel comfortable, something that would make you feel relaxed."

The day came and there I was, standing before a roomful of parents. I said, "Welcome, parents . . ." and suddenly I went blank. I had no idea of what to say next.

From the sidelines, my teacher stage-whispered, "Say something to make them feel comfortable, remember?"

I looked at my teacher; I looked out at the assembled parents.

In my best seven-year-old voice, I said, "The bathroom is over there. You gotta flush when you're done, and don't forget to wash your hands before you come back to class."

I sat down. My first speech had ended, and the highly receptive audience laughed and applauded.

Hey, I thought, this isn't so bad after all!

23. My First Speech (Serious)

The first speech I gave in my adult life occurred some two months after I began teaching. As a "new" teacher, I was being asked to "explain" my teaching philosophy and my plans for the school year at a PTA meeting.

Most of my free time for weeks prior to the meeting was taken up, it seemed, with preparing for the speech. I wrote what I thought was a learned and convincing speech, and I had gone to lengths to prepare slides, charts, and still photos to illustrate my points. I even edited to the point where the speech was only an hour long rather than its original three-hour length.

Came the night of the PTA meeting and I was introduced. I smiled, stood up, and everything went wrong.

I reached in my jacket for my speech and it wasn't there! I switched on the slide projector, and the bulb popped and hissed and went dark. The still photos fell to the floor, hopelessly out of order. I stood there silently before a silent audience.

"Folks," I said finally, "I was going to give you a fine, long speech and show you pictures and diagrams and everything; that's all ruined. All I can say now is that I really love your kids; I love teaching. This is my first job, and I make mistakes, but I'm learning every day. More than anything, I want your kids to learn and grow. I promise that I'll do everything I can to help them, because they mean so much to me. I guess that's all."

I sat down, and the applause was deafening. At that point, I began to learn that if you go where your heart leads, you can never get lost.

24. *Length of the Speech (I)*

We are told the story of a science teacher who was extremely knowledgeable about his subject and who loved teaching, but who had an absolute aversion to speaking before parents or any large group of adults.

The school conceived of a program where a teacher from each discipline would get up and "teach" a "mini-lesson" for the assembled parents. The idea was to show the caliber of teaching in the school. You guessed it—the teacher in question was assigned to speak for the science department.

In the program, his name was listed along with the subject he would teach on that evening. His subject was to be: The Antiquity of the Microbe.

When it came time, the speech-shy science teacher rose to the podium.

"The antiquity of the microbe," he said, staring out at the audience.

"Ladies and gentlemen: Adam had'em."

And he sat down!

25. *Length of the Speech (II)*

One administrator we knew had a unique way of giving what he termed an "inspirational" speech. He would take the name of the person being honored or the school or the activity and literally "spell" it out, going on at length about each letter of the name. If, for instance, he were speaking about Stephen's Elementary School, he might start out saying, "*S* is for Spirit, and let me tell you about the fine school spirit . . ." He was not known for his brevity.

Once, this administrator sent an invitation to the superintendent of schools to attend an affair at which he would speak. He and the superintendent shared a very positive relationship.

The administrator received the following reply: "Dear Sam, Thank you for your kind invitation to hear you speak on the 16th. Since you were kind enough to inform me that you will be speaking about the ALEXANDER R. ATCHINSON INSTITUTE FOR MEDICAL AND DENTAL STUDIES, you will understand why I will not be in attendance. When you're speaking about some place like CAL TECH, be sure to let me know, and I'll be there!"

26. The Importance of Outlook (Humorous)

It has been said that a school bus driver is a person who USED to like children. There was one bus driver in our district, however, who belied that point. An older man, retired and now supplementing his income, this gentleman was never without a smile and a gentle word, even when arriving with a busload of rollicking and raucous children, all of whom were screaming at top volume. Through it all this man remained calm and serene.

I asked him once how he did it: "How do you manage to stay so calm and happy with all these yelling and squirming children all around you? You must have some secret."

"I'll tell you," said the gentleman. "It's all a matter of outlook. You see, when a kid comes on my bus, I look at that kid and think of him or her as my very own grandchild. I couldn't get angry with my grandson or granddaughter, now could I?"

"This outlook, this point of view has really helped you?"

"I'll say," he continued. "As long as they're my grandchildren, everything is fine. You see, if I ever thought of them as other people's children, why—I'd have gone quietly insane and murdered the little monsters years ago!"

27. The Importance of Outlook (Serious)

I taught a boy once who was not doing well in school. Everything within me told me that the lad had the ability, and this was confirmed by test scores. Yet the boy continued to do poorly in all aspects of his school life. Finally, we called in the father.

The man listened to me and other teachers as we shared the opinion that the boy could definitely do better in school than he had shown so far. Then, the father spoke.

"You called me into school for this?" he said. "He's passing, ain't he? So what's the big deal? Listen, I was lousy in school myself. I hated school, and I never did any good. I told my son; I told him I never liked school, and I expected that he wouldn't either. I told him as long as he passed, I didn't care what he got. I told him to take it easy and enjoy the ride. It didn't hurt me none!"

Over the years, I have come to believe that we do not shape our images, but it is our image of ourselves that inevitably shapes us. That father had given his son an image that the son was trying hard to fit into. That father would have to live with what that outlook produced. So, unfortunately, would the son.

What image, what outlook have YOU given to your child?

28. Believing in Your Subject (Humorous)

I'd like to tell you about this girl I knew who was the spitting champion of our school. I grant you that the title was unofficial, and she never received public recognition for her accomplishment; but ask any kid in our school about Betty Jean and he would tell you that she could spit farther, longer, and higher than any other student who chose to give her competition.

One day, I was taking a shortcut across the campus when I turned a corner and came upon Betty Jean. She had a soda bottle in one hand which was about half filled with water, and she was standing about fifteen feet in front of a wall on which had been chalked various "bulls-eyes" at differing heights. The chalk, I might add, had been all but obliterated by the water that dripped from the school wall.

"Betty Jean," I said, "whatever are you doing?"

"Well, sir," Betty Jean explained, "Bobby challenged me to a big spitting match this afternoon after school. You know how it is when you really believe in what you're doing—you just GOTTA keep at it until you get it right!"

29. Believing in Your Subject (Serious)

There was an elementary school teacher who had one third-grade student who was having a horrible time with math. Try as she might, the child just could not seem to get the concepts being taught.

"It's no use," said the child, "nobody in my family is any good at math. I'm not either. I just can't do it."

"That's because I haven't given you my secret learning tool yet," said the teacher who reached into her desk and extracted something which she held in her hand.

"What is it?" asked the curious child.

"It's an Arithmetic Shell. Oh, I know it just looks like some regular shell from a beach, but this one is special. The Arithmetic Shell helps students to learn math. I don't give this to many students, but you're special. I want you to take this and keep it with you. Then, you'll have the ability to do all the math. OK?"

No, the child never went on to become a mathematical genius, but she did pass all her arithmetic tests from then on and did reasonably well in algebra and geometry and trigonometry in high school. With the Arithmetic Shell at her side, she went on to conquer the unconquerable.

Believing that you *can* is the first step in making it happen.

30. *Beginning a Speech on Student Behavior (Humorous)*

The first-grade class had been particularly noisy from the very first day. The teacher finally hit upon a plan to quiet her noisy charges if even for a short time.

"Did you ever hear the expression," she asked her class, " 'so quiet you can hear a pin drop'? Well, that's what we're going to do. I have this pin, and we are going to practice being so quiet that when I drop this pin on the floor, everybody, even those in the back of the room, will be able to hear it."

And, practice they did. For several weeks, at various times the teacher would get them to be quiet and see if they could hear the pin drop. It never worked—there would invariably be some distraction or noise produced by the class, and the pin drop would be lost to human hearing.

Finally, on a day when it was known that the principal would be visiting all the classrooms, the teacher tried it a final time. She got her class as quiet as quiet could be, lifted the pin and let it go.

PING! The eyes of the children grew wide in wonder—they had heard it!

And, as the visiting principal walked through the door of the classroom, twenty-seven first graders stood on desks, ran around the room, jumped up and down, and screamed at the top of their lungs, "We did it! We were so quiet! We did it!!!"

31. *Beginning a Speech on Student Behavior (Serious)*

Early on in my teaching career, I had a boy who was older than the other students in the class. Whether I wanted it or not, I had gotten advance notice about this boy. He had been in trouble from the first grade on, and all of his offenses involved violence. The other children gave him a wide berth. When they spoke of him at all, it was in undertones and whispers.

He sat in that seventh-grade class for the entire year. What did I do? I did nothing. When he sat in the back of the room, his chair tilted against the wall, thump-thump-thumping his head against the already cracked plaster, I ignored him. When he stood and yawned or burped loudly, the class and I went on without noticing. When he would let out with some vulgarity, if it was at all possible, everyone went on as if nothing had happened.

At that time, the boy was a good inch taller than I was and noticeably outweighed me. Often, he would stare at me with dark, sullen eyes that seemed to dare me to utter a word.

The year ended and the class and I let out a collective sigh of relief. The boy's family moved that summer, and I heard no more of him until six years later when I read the article about his arrest for murder.

He sat in my class for a year. All that time, I knew that here was a stick of dynamite waiting to explode. I went into teaching to help kids, and what did I do for this one? I ignored him. I did nothing and allowed the boy to slip into the world with only violence as a companion. I vowed then, that this would never happen again.

32. Beginning a Speech on Home-School Communication

Two attractive women were talking as they waited in the dentist's office. One explained that she was giving full time to raising her child, and the other explained that she was a kindergarten teacher in a nearby school system.

"I wish my daughter had you for a teacher," said the mother. "The way she describes her teacher to me, the woman must be ninety-seven years old, with a permanent scowl on her face, and she does nothing but yell and scream all day."

"Thank you," said the young teacher. "I wish all my parents were as nice as you. I've got one little girl who tells me that all her mother ever does is watch soap operas and yell and scream at her and her daddy. Isn't that terrible? That's all this child talks about—that and her dog, Ruff."

"Wait a minute," said the young mother, "we have a dog named Ruff. What's your student's name?"

"Rebecca."

"I'm her mother!" said the one.

"Kindergarten teacher!" exclaimed the other.

33. Beginning a Speech on Change and Changes (Humorous)

Change is a necessary part of life. I remember one elementary school teacher who told me about a little boy she had in class who had proven to be a little terror, always loud and raucous and rarely obeying anyone. She had spoken privately to the boy on several occasions, trying to get him to understand that he had to "change his ways," as she put it.

One day, the teacher came in early from recess to find the boy sitting alone in class and weeping heavily.

"Murray," she said, "what's wrong?"

"Oh, teacher," the lad wept, "I want to change; I really do, but I can't do it! I can't change!"

"Of course you can," said the teacher as she rushed to the boy. "I'll help you. We'll work at this together. It might take time, but your behavior will change. I promise it will!"

"What behavior?" scowled the boy. "I snuck in here during recess to put this frog in Anne Marie's lunch, only I forgot and sat down in this chair where we had put the glue we were using this morning. I'm stuck to the chair!

"That's what I was crying about. These are the only pants I got here. I want to change, but I can't!"

34. Beginning a Speech on Change and Changes (Serious)

I was just out of college and was starting my first teaching job. The school, at that time, had a policy of "teaming up" a younger teacher with an older, more experienced educator. I was assigned to a veteran teacher who had gone to "Normal School" rather than college and was only a year or so from retirement.

This wonderful woman taught me many things over my first hectic year in the classroom, but the thing I remember most was her advice about my planbook.

"Keep a good planbook," she told me. "Keep it up-to-date, and make certain that it's clear enough for someone else to take it and use it. When you get to the end of the year, it will be bursting with a record of all the classes you have taught."

"Then I keep it so I can use it next year?" I proposed.

"Absolutely not!" she told me. "Then you take it and throw the blasted thing away!"

"After all that work? Why?"

"Because," she assured me, "if you keep it, you'll use it as a guide next year, and the year after that, and the year after that. Pretty soon, ten years will have gone by, and you'll be teaching the same things in the same manner you did a decade ago. When that happens, son, you'll be one dead teacher. The administration might not catch it, but you'll know. You'll be up there going through the motions, but the spirit will have already left. When you stop changing, you stop growing, and you die."

I have thrown away my planbook every year since, and I have never regretted it.

35. Beginning a Speech on Economic Matters

The teacher gave each of the three students in the small math group a dollar.

"Now," she said, "let's suppose that you go into a candy store and you buy a candy bar for forty-nine cents. How much change would you get from the dollar? Write down your answer now, please."

The children figured and wrote, then the teacher asked, "Billy, what's your answer?"

"Fifty-one cents?" said Billy.

"Very good. Mary, what did you get?"

"Fifty-one cents, teacher," piped Mary.

"Excellent. And Harold, what's your answer?"

"Eleven cents," came the reply.

"Harold, that's wrong. How could you possibly come up with an answer like that?"

"Because," Harold stated flatly, "I don't eat cheap candy. The candy bar I want costs eighty-nine cents, and I don't see how I can be wrong just because I have a higher standard of living than these two Bozos!"

36. Beginning a Speech on the School (I)

Mom and Dad had done a wonderful job of preparing Billy for his first day of school. They told him what to expect and how to answer the teacher and all the fun activities he would do and the new friends he'd make.

When the first day of school came, mother made Billy's favorite sandwiches and even threw in an extra cupcake that he loved so well. Mom and Dad both walked him to school and waved to him as he entered the doors of the schoolhouse.

All seemed to go very well, and when Billy came home, he was full of stories to tell as well as a picture he had drawn for his mother.

When Dad arrived home from work, the stories were repeated with great enthusiasm. Mom and Dad simply beamed with delight.

"Well," said father, "if you enjoyed it this much today, just think of all the fun you're going to have tomorrow and next week and next month."

Billy looked up, and his eyes filled with tears. He dropped the picture he was holding and his chin began to quiver.

"Billy," said mother, "what is it? What's wrong?"

"Tomorrow?" the boy sobbed, the tears coming freely now, "next week? Next month? You mean I gotta go more than once?"

37. Beginning a Speech on the School (II)

Andrea's marks were falling rapidly, and half way through the marking period, the teacher decided to have a talk with the seventh grade girl.

"Andrea," the teacher said, "I think you know why I've asked to talk to you. I like you, Andrea, and I'm really concerned about your grades and your education.

"The answer is obvious when I look at your schedule. Outside of school you take ballet lessons, gymnastic lessons, piano lessons, and attend your church school one night a week. On top of that, you are a cheerleader, have a part in the school play, play clarinet in the band, sing in the chorus, and you are president of the Pep Club. All of this in addition to spending six and a half hours in school at your studies each day. The reason for your grades dropping is obvious. Let me put it plainly—you are going to have to cut out something!"

"I know, Ma'am," said the student, "and I've even talked to my mother about it."

"That's a good start," stated the teacher.

"In fact, there's only one difficulty, and maybe you could talk to my mother about it."

"What's that?"

"No matter what I say, Mom just won't let me cut out the six and a half hours of school!"

38. Beginning a Speech on the School (III)

It was seconds before the end of the school day when little Jimmy made his way to the teacher's desk.

"Ma'am," he said, "I know the bell is gonna ring soon, but do you think you could sorta write down an outline of what we learned today?"

"Why, Jimmy," replied the teacher, "of course I could. Do you want it so you can review what we did today?"

"Heck, no," said Jimmy. "See, the minute I get home from school, the first thing my mother asks me is what I learned today. Well, since I wasn't paying attention at all today, I figured I'd use the sheet you're writing, and I'd at least be able to hit the high points!"

39. *Beginning a Speech on Higher Education*

The principal and the head janitor were talking. "Did you ever think about going on to higher education after high school?" the principal asked.

"Yes, I did," answered the janitor. "My grades were very good in high school, and I considered going to college, but, as it often goes, one thing led to another, and I never did go on."

"What a shame," said the principal. "Do you ever think about what might have happened had you gone on?"

"Oh, yes—sometimes. I think my life might have been different."

"In what way?" asked the principal.

"Well, right now I'm a janitor . . ."

"Yes . . ."

"And if I'd gone to college, I'd be a custodial engineer."

40. *Beginning a Speech on the School Board (I)*

The president of the local Board of Education was invited to the school to address the civics class. She began to talk about the history of school boards, representative government, the trials and tribulations of school board members, and a host of other topics related to the work the school board does in the community.

It was not that she was uninteresting, just that she was thorough . . . and long. At half an hour into the speech the students began to fidget; at an hour into the speech the teachers started to fidget; at an hour and a half into her speech, several students were draped over their desks, and at least one teacher was having a fierce battle trying to keep his eyes open.

Finally, one student attempted to pass a note to a classmate. The note was intercepted by a vigilant teacher who gave a withering look to the notewriter and returned to the back of the room, where he unfolded the paper and read:

"When she asks who the SCHOOL BORED are, let's shout, 'Us, Madam, us!' "

41. *Beginning a Speech on the School Board (II)*

When Mrs. Jones decided that she would run for the school board, she discussed the matter with her eight-year-old son.

"George," she told the boy, "over these next few weeks, I might have to go out a lot at night. Of course Daddy will be here with you, but I probably won't be home before you go to bed."

"Why?"

"Because, George, Mommy is running for the school board."

On an afternoon two days later, Mrs. Jones looked out the window and saw her son lumbering down the street, trying to carry some object that was easily as tall as he was. She watched as he almost fell under the burden and righted himself with much huffing and puffing.

She ran out the door to her son and caught the object he carried just as it threatened to fall backwards on the lad. She looked at the object, and it was immediately clear what it was. It was a three-by-five-foot bulletin board, obviously ripped from a wall someplace. Indeed, the cork side still held push pins and stapled notices and messages.

"George!" she exclaimed. "What's this?"

"Look, Mommy!" smiled the boy. "Now you don't have to go running after the school board! I brought it to you!!!"

42. *Beginning a Speech on the Curriculum*

The teacher in the rural school district had designed an outstanding core curriculum centered on the role of agriculture in the development of the United States. Her students loved it; her principal loved it; even the local school board was called in to observe and was dutifully impressed.

One member of the school board was a local farmer who, while he had had very little formal education, had a great heart for the school children of the area.

"Excuse me for asking," said the farmer, "but what d'you call this thing that you're doing?"

"It's called a *core curriculum*," answered the teacher, "and anything that you can do to help would be greatly appreciated."

"A *core* curriculum?"

"Yes."

And the next day, that teacher received twenty-six bushels of the finest apples the county could produce.

43. *Beginning a Speech on Grouping*

Three veteran educators were talking about education during the "good old days" of their youth.

"I went to school in the East," said the first, "and we were grouped according to ability. We were called Airplanes, Cars, or Boats, depending on how well we did."

"I was raised in the Midwest," added the second educator, "and there we were ability grouped also, only our groups were called Cars, Tractors, and Hay Wagons."

"Well," said the third, "you have to understand that I grew up along the Pacific Coast, in California."

"So, what were your groups called?"

"Gucci's, Macy's, and K-Marts!"

44. *Beginning a Speech on an In-Service Session*

In a few moments, our annual In-Service Session will begin. Before it does, I want to tell you about my son and money.

I was trying to teach him the value of money and saving, so when he was old enough to understand, I required him to start a bank account. I supplied the initial ten dollars, but after that, he was on his own, and at least a part of each allowance or money he'd earned doing jobs around the neighborhood went into the account.

Then he spied that fabulous ten-speed bike which he wanted (at that time) more than anything else. He went to the bank to withdraw the needed amount, which was one hundred fifty dollars. When he got to his account, however, he found that all that was in there was eighty-seven dollars and forty-nine cents.

I asked him if he had learned anything from this, and he replied, "Yeah, I learned that the only thing you get out of it is what you put into it! Is that fair?"

I think that experience bespeaks every in-service session I've ever attended. I have taken from it in direct proportion to the time and effort I invested in it.

I am certain that today's in-service will be no exception.

Hey, I think that's very fair!

45. *Beginning a Speech on a Serious Matter*

A thousand years ago, when I was in high school, I had a friend name Beany. Beany loved to ride his bike. In a day when every boy was scratching to buy some wreck of a car he could call his own, old Beany could be found riding that bike day and night.

There was a street that was built on a hill near our school, and one of Beany's favorite things to do was to ride his bike to the top of that hill, get up to speed, and coast down the hill with his arms outstretched from his sides and his eyes shut tight.

When we asked him why he did such a thing, he would tell us that going down that hill with his eyes closed and arms out was the greatest thrill he ever experienced. According to him, it was pure joy.

During one afternoon of such pure joy, Beany could not see through his closed eyes the truck that had run the traffic light at the bottom of the hill.

Beany received a complete set of plastic teeth at age sixteen, as well as a broken leg that kept him home most of the summer. He also came away with a left arm that doesn't work right to this day.

I tell you about Beany, because there are times in life when it is the right thing to do to close our eyes and listen to the thrill of life that comes from within. But, there are other times, such as the situation we are talking about tonight, that absolutely require that we keep our eyes wide open and our hands firmly on the handlebars!

46. *Beginning a Speech on a Holiday Celebration*

I had given the assignment of preparing a research paper.

One boy had chosen to do some research on our school holidays. As he handed in his paper, I asked him if he had learned anything from it.

"I'll say," he replied. "I learned that Veterans' Day used to be Armistice Day; that Memorial Day used to be Decoration Day; that George Washington's Birthday is celebrated on President's Day which isn't on his birthday but the Monday closest to it, but it isn't Lincoln's Birthday either so that when we celebrate their birthdays it's not on either one of them.

"In fact, I've come to a conclusion."

"What is that?" I asked.

"That I'm going home this afternoon, get my Mom to bake a cake, have some friends over, and celebrate MY birthday before somebody moves THAT, too!"

47. *Beginning a Speech on the End of the School Year*

There was an assembly program scheduled for the last day of the school year. By the time all the classes had arrived and been seated, the children well knew that at the conclusion of the program, the bell would ring and their summer hiatus would officially begin. Consequently, the kids were sky high with excitement and not even repeated warnings from teachers could lower the volume of noise that rose in that auditorium.

Finally, the principal came up the podium, signaled for the volume on the PA system to be turned up full, and spoke to the restless, screaming audience.

"The Board of Education," he announced, "has just decreed that the school year will be extended by a month. Therefore, you will all report to your regular classes tomorrow morning!"

Eyes grew wide. Mouths hung open. The noise level dropped to dead silence as the assembled students stared at the principal.

"Now," said the principal, "while I have your attention . . ."

48. *Beginning a Speech on the Value of Work*

Mrs. Lyons was the mother of seven children, each a year apart. At one point, she had seven children in the same elementary school at the same time.

Even with such a burden, she was a tireless worker for the school, involved in many of the PTA activities and just generally being helpful wherever needed.

I spoke to her once and suggested that perhaps she could take it a little easier.

"Listen," she told me, "I've had seven children, and do you know what that's taught me?"

"What?"

"Without hard labor," she stated, "you don't get to bring home the baby!"

49. *Beginning a Speech on the Future (I)*

When little Billy had been reprimanded by the teacher for chewing gum in class, he had sulked for some time. In due course, however, he seemed to get back into the rhythm of the class.

That afternoon the teacher assigned the class a short composition about what they thought the future would be like.

"In the future," Billy wrote, "everything is going to be done by robots. Robots will even teach school. Robots will make great teachers. Machines won't get mad at kids, and I bet that old robot wouldn't even care if the kids chewed gum!

"So, just remember, Mrs. Smith. You can be replaced!"

50. Beginning a Speech on the Future (II)

The teacher began a discussion with the group about things that worried or concerned them. The teacher invited frankness, and she got it. Finally, one of the children asked the teacher what worried her.

Wishing to maintain honesty and openness, the teacher spoke plainly.

"Sometimes," she said, "I get worried about what's going to happen in the future. I worry about the possibility of getting sick and not being able to support myself. I wonder what the future will be like and what will happen to me. That's how I honestly feel at times."

"Mrs. Jones," said one boy, "can I tell you something?"

"Certainly, Harry."

"I don't think you got a thing to worry about," said the boy.

"And why is that, Harry?"

" 'Cause everything is gonna turn out just great for you," continued the lad. "Look at us, Mrs. Jones. We ARE the future, and we love you.

"Gosh, Ma'am, you can't get any better than that!"

HOW TO REMEMBER "WHAT'S-HIS-NAME"—INTRODUCING YOURSELF AND OTHERS

Whether introducing a new student to a class, a guest lecturer to a group of educators, or yourself to an audience of parents, the time will come when you must introduce *someone*. Merely rising and saying, "I give you Dr. Jones," is much too abrupt to effect a smooth transition to the speaker or person of interest for the occasion.

The stories in this section can be used to help you deliver a fitting and smooth introduction in a wide variety of situations. They are short, yet they bespeak the character of the individual being introduced. From introducing yourself in a humorous manner to introducing the teachers of a particular school, you will find something here for virtually every introductory need.

51. Introducing Yourself (Humorous)

I consider myself to be a cat fancier in that I have a particular affection for those little feline fluffballs and I have some knowledge of them. Because of this I was once asked to come to a first-grade classroom and talk about cats.

I brought with me Beau and Arrow, two loveable domestic shorthairs (that means "alley cat") who share my home. I introduced Beau and Arrow to the class after some instruction on how they should be handled, and I used them to illustrate my talk about cats, why they do what they do, and how we should treat and care for them.

The cats and the children behaved beautifully. Beau laid down and purred on cue as I explained that phenomenon, and Arrow frisked and rolled over to the delight of the class.

About a week after that incident, I was at a local store when one of the children in that class came running up to me with his mother in tow. "I know who you are!" he exclaimed.

"And I know who you are," I returned, "but I don't remember your name. Why don't you introduce me to your mother?"

"Mommy," the boy said, "this is the guy I told you about. This is Beau and Arrow's Daddy!"

So, in an ever-changing world, I, at least, have the benefit of knowing who I am. And now, you know it, too.

I'm the cats' Daddy!!!

52. Introducing Yourself (Serious)

My father, God rest him, never went any further than the eighth grade. At that time, his father was killed in an accident on the job. My father was the oldest of six children—the youngest was an infant—and the "compensation" they received was fifty dollars (remember the time we're talking about). So, at age twelve, my father set out to find a job to support his mother and five brothers and sisters.

He ended up at a local bakery shop where he snuck back to where the bakers worked, and he stood there until he was noticed. The owner of the shop came over to him.

"You're not supposed to be back here," the man said. "what do you want?"

"I need a job," my father said. "I want to learn, and you can teach me."

And, as one of the finest bakers in America (or so I will always believe), my father supported his brothers and sisters, married, had a family of his own, and even managed to send his son to college.

Allow me to introduce myself. I am someone who wants to learn—and you can teach me.

Together, we *can* learn, and together, we can build a future that will last.

53. *Introducing a Guest Speaker (I)*

Our guest speaker this evening is a woman whose reputation for brilliance and quick-thinking has preceded her.

There is a story told about her that once she was giving a lecture and had previously invited the audience to write questions on sheets of paper that had been passed out and to submit them for answers and discussion later. This worked very well, until she opened one folded sheet on which was written a single word—*Idiot*!

She read the one-word missive aloud and then gazed out at the audience.

"Ladies and gentlemen," she announced, "over the years, I have frequently received replies and questions where the sender has written the letter and then forgotten to sign his name.

"This, however, is the first time the writer has signed his name and forgotten to write the letter!"

54. *Introducing a Guest Speaker (II)*

Our next guest this evening is a man who has a fine reputation as a speaker of quality and note. Indeed, many people have said that he has moved audiences to tears and to laughter.

On one occasion, he was giving a speech at a local Elks Lodge. The affair was a memorial for deceased members, and as our friend remembered them, eyes all over the room began to fill up. In a few moments, audible sobs could be heard from all quarters, and a hundred hands scrambled for tissues. Everyone in the hall was deeply affected.

Everyone, that is, except one man who stood in the back of the room with a blank expression on his face. Throughout the entire speech, this man merely stood there, positively expressionless. Not a sigh, not a sniffle, not a tear.

When the speech was over, our friend sought out the frozen-faced individual.

"Excuse me, Sir, but I couldn't help but notice that while virtually everyone else in the place was reduced to tears by my speech, you didn't even raise an eyebrow. Did my speech not touch you?"

"Oh, it was a wonderful speech!" exclaimed the man. "I felt like weeping buckets!"

"Then why didn't you?"

"I couldn't," the man replied. "I'm not a member of this Lodge!"

55. *Introducing a Guest Speaker (III)*

Ladies and gentlemen, before I introduce our guest for this evening, I'd like to tell you about something that happened this afternoon.

We were testing out these amplifiers you see on stage when one of them gave out a horrifying shriek and died on the spot. We didn't know what to do, because we couldn't possibly get a replacement before this function tonight. Our vice-principal, however, suggested that I call the elementary school down the street, and they, very graciously loaned us that amplifier for our use this evening.

Therefore, before I introduce you to a friend who will give us an outstanding speech this evening, let me introduce you to something of which you have all heard.

[Walks over to the borrowed amplifier . . .]

This, you might well say, is our "guest speaker" for this evening!

56. *Introducing a Personal Friend (Humorous)*

Our speaker this evening is a personal friend of mine and an extremely intelligent man.

I remember that he once took me hunting. I complained that we did not know the area where we were hunting and might get lost. My highly intelligent friend stated that he had thought of that and had arranged for an experienced guide to come find us after our day of hunting.

"I told the guide to come to these woods at about three o'clock," he told me. "I told the guide that we would get off a shot at three o'clock and every ten minutes thereafter. That way he'd have no problem locating us and guiding us out."

Everything went well, and at precisely three o'clock, my friend fired off his first shot. He repeated his shot at 3:10, 3:20, 3:30, and every ten minutes after that. Soon, it was almost five o'clock, and still there was no guide. I began to get worried and told my friend as much.

"You know," he told me, "I'm getting worried, too. I keep shooting, but the guide still hasn't found us. If that guide doesn't show up soon, I'm going to run out of arrows!"

Therefore, allow me to introduce our speaker this evening, my friend who always hits the mark, Bill Reilly!

57. Introducing a Personal Friend (Serious)

I first met our speaker this evening when I was speaking before a group in another school district.

I had finished my speech, the meeting had ended, and people were flocking around me, almost all of them telling me what a wonderful speech I had given and how much they had enjoyed it.

All, that is, except one man who stood on the edges of the crowd and regarded me with a quizzical smile. When the crowd had thinned considerably, I went up to him and asked if he, too, had enjoyed my speech.

"In fact," he said, "I did. I think you are going to be a very good speaker, but there were a few things you could improve on, and I think you should know about them . . ."

With that, he told me. Not one thing was a criticism *per se*, and every point he made had reason and sense behind it.

"I want to thank you," I said when he had finished. "I will really think deeply about your advice."

"There are hundreds of people," he said, "who will tell you how good you *are*, but very few are willing to show you how to be as good as you *can become*."

What else could I do? We have been friends ever since.

It gives me great pleasure to introduce my friend . . .

58. Introducing a "Friend to Education"

Our guest tonight, Mr. John Smith, is a true friend to education. While he has never served on the school board or taught in our schools, his contributions to the children of this community are legendary, including donating the land on which this school sits.

In fact, just the other day I was discussing Mr. Smith and his many contributions in the main office of the school. A boy who had been sent down for disciplinary reasons sat in the office awaiting his talk with me as he sulkily scraped his shoes along the sides of his chair. Obviously, he took in every word.

Later, when it came time to speak privately to the boy, he asked me if it were really true that Mr. Smith had donated the land.

"And, for that," said the boy, "you call him a friend to education?"

"Why, certainly," I remarked. "What else would you call him?"

"Well," said the boy in trouble, "if it weren't for him, this school wouldn't be here, and I wouldn't be sitting in your office waiting to get suspended, so don't expect me to call him a friend!"

59. *Introducing a Person You Don't Know*

I must admit that while I am certainly aware of the fine record of our guest this evening, I do not have the pleasure of knowing her on a personal basis.

In fact, I feel rather like the first-grader who was asked to introduce the principal of the school at an assembly program.

"I'm supposed to introduce the principal," said the little girl, "but I don't know what a principal is, so I went down to the big office and looked. Now I can tell you.

"A principal is a person who sits at a big desk except when she is walking around the office saying, 'Why can't I find that paper?' or when she is drinking this black stuff that everybody says is terrible, but they drink all day long.

"So, this is Mrs. Jones, our principal, and that's what they pay her for!"

Obviously, I'm not going to project in the manner of that first-grader. Rather, I am going to look forward, as I know you all must be, to getting acquainted with our speaker of the evening, Ms. Claire Handley.

60. *Introducing a Colleague (Humorous)*

Our speaker this evening is a colleague whom I have known for several years.

One thing I can honestly say about him is that I have never heard him say a bad word about anybody, whether it was a student in his class, or another teacher in the school, or the administration. He has always had positive and uplifting things to say about everybody.

In fact, I remember once when the superintendent of schools came for a visit. My colleague and I were walking down the hall, when we came face to face with the superintendent. I had met the man once before, so I reintroduced myself and introduced my colleague to him.

"And, you, sir," said the superintendent, indicating my friend, "exactly what is your position in this school?"

Without missing a beat, my collegue replied, "Absolutely none! I'm neutral; I don't side with any of the factions in this place!"

61. *Introducing a Colleague (Serious)*

I remember that I had a rather bad toothache, and during the day, I had made an appointment to see the dentist directly after school. What I had forgotten was that it was the day I stayed for "extra help." I was headed out of my room, when fifteen kids showed up to go over the material of the past week.

I was in a quandary as to what to do, when a colleague came down the hall, understood the situation at once, and said to me, "Go on to your dentist. I'll look after these guys. We'll get on all right."

"But," I mumbled, "that's not right. It's not fair for you to have to . . ."

"Listen," he said, "too often, your colleagues are your problem. For once, I'd like to be a solution. Besides, we're colleagues, and that means sharing; if we can share our victories, we should be able to share our problems. Don't you think?"

That is why I am proud to call that gentleman my colleague . . . and my friend . . . and our chief speaker for this evening.

Ladies and gentlemen, may I present . . .

62. *Introducing an Award Recipient (Humorous)*

The first-grader came running home. On his way, he stopped just long enough to push over a neighbor child who was playing in her front yard. As he entered the front door, he spotted the baby in his playpen, took the rattle away from the child and tossed it just outside the baby's reach. On his way to the kitchen, he managed to pull the cat's tail, sending the animal scampering away with a howl. Finally, he burst into the kitchen where mother was working.

"Guess what?" said the lad. "I won an award in school today."

"Wonderful! What for?" asked mother.

"Most Friendly and Cooperative!"

Therefore, ladies and gentlemen, it gives me great pleasure to introduce someone who so obviously and richly *deserves* the award she shall receive tonight . . .

63. *Introducing an Award Recipient (Serious)*

When I think of our award recipient this evening, I think of a story a friend of mine told about his daughter. The child had fallen one evening and scraped her elbows and knees.

Mother came to the rescue, holding the child and kissing away the sting. She even gave the child a relaxing bath, wrapping her in fresh-scented towels, putting on a clean nightdress and singing her to her warm bed, surrounded by her favorite stuffed animals.

As the mother tucked the child in bed and kissed her good night, the child looked up.

"Mommy," she said, "do they give awards for love?"

The mother smiled at her daughter.

"Because if they did," the child continued sleepily, "yours would be made out of real gold!"

And, that's rather the way it is with our award recipient this evening. Indeed, it is her loving and caring attitude, manifested in the thousands of contributions she has made to this school district that has brought us to this place tonight.

It is with the deepest of respect that I introduce . . .

64. *Introducing a Dynamic Personality*

Our guest this evening is noted as a highly dynamic individual. Indeed, everyone who knows him understands what a highly charged, personable, and energetic fireball he really is.

I remember that I was once invited to his home for dinner. Just before the meal was served, we took a short walk along the street where he lived. We did this in spite of the fact that the weather had turned threatening and dark clouds loomed above.

Several neighbors were out in their front yards, and I was introduced to many, when a loud peal of thunder split the skies.

With a wink to me, Henry, always the dynamic and consumate actor, stood with his feet apart and addressed the heavens in a voice all the neighbors could hear.

"Come ye winds; come ye rains!" he intoned in his best stage voice. "Come ye lightning flashes; smite the earth!"

At which point, a gigantic flash of lightning zigzagged down and struck a tree in a nearby lot, knocking off a branch!

We stood there open-mouthed, as his wife, unaware of what had just happened, came to the front door and yelled in a voice to equal his.

"Henry!" she shouted, "Stop showing off and get in here! Your dinner's getting cold!"

65. *Introducing the Master of Ceremonies*

Our Master of Ceremonies this evening is a person I know well, and I can tell you that not only does he have charm and wit, but he is a highly intelligent and erudite fellow.

Why, just the other day, his son came home from school, looked at the dog and said, "Out, out, damned Spot!"

"Hey!" my friend shouted, "I don't allow that kind of talk in our home!"

"Dad," his son answered, "that wasn't me. That was Shakespeare!"

"I don't care where you got it," my friend said, "I don't want it in the house!"

"O.K., Dad."

"And, one other thing. . ."

"What's that?"

"I don't want you playing with this Shakespeare kid any more!"

66. *Introducing a Superintendent of Schools (I)*

Dr. Smith, our school superintendent was due to make a visit to our school. She arrived one rainy morning, and finding the front lot full, she parked on the side of the building and ran to the side entrance.

Unfortunately, it was locked, and Dr. Smith now faced the prospect of a long walk in a heavy downpour to the front of the building. Just then, she spotted one of our seventh-grade boys in the hallway. Dr. Smith tapped on the glass and got the boy's attention. Dr. Smith asked to be let in, but the boy refused at first, and it took a good five minutes before Dr. Smith could persuade the lad to open the door. Finally, however, the boy pushed the handle, and Dr. Smith came in from the rain.

"Don't worry," said Dr. Smith as she shook off the rain, "you won't get in any trouble for letting me in. Just think, you'll be able to tell everyone that you let the Superintendent into the building."

"Please, Ma'am," moaned the boy, "don't say that so loud! See, I'm cutting class, so I'm in terrible trouble with the teachers as it is. I can't imagine what they'd do if they found out that I was the one that let *you* into the school!"

67. *Introducing a Superintendent of Schools (II)*

One afternoon last fall, Dr. Smith spoke to the faculty of our school. Among other things, he regaled us with stories about school that he remembered when a local newspaper had asked him to write down some of his experiences for an upcoming special issue. We roared with laughter, and the entire faculty had an enjoyable time.

The next day, one of our student reporters for the school newspaper called Dr. Smith at Central Administration and told how he had heard about the many funny stories he had told and could he give some of them for an issue of the school newspaper.

Dr. Smith thanked the boy but told him that the local newspaper had wanted an exclusive, and he really couldn't let the students hear any of them until the special issue of the regular local newspaper had been published.

That weekend, hundreds of parents picked up the copy of our school newspaper that had gone home with each child and read the lead article:

"Last Tuesday, Dr. Smith, the Superintendent of Schools, had a big meeting with all of the teachers and the principal. They were all laughing, and Dr. Smith said that was because he was telling them stories that cannot be repeated to children."

68. *Introducing a Principal (I)*

Some of you may not know that our principal, Dr. Jones, is very athletic. In fact, that athletic ability is what led him into education.

You see, in his first year of college, he still hadn't made up his mind as to his future career. He did, however, join the college boxing team. Indeed, he had a rather good record and was never knocked out during the entire time he participated.

At the end of that first college year, Dr. Jones's boxing coach took him aside.

"Jones," he said, "you have a remarkable constitution. I've seen you take blow after blow and still hang in there punching away. No matter how hard you get punched, you keep coming back. You either have the hardest head I've ever seen or you enjoy getting slapped around!"

It was at that point that Dr. Jones knew that he was ideally suited to become a high school principal!

69. *Introducing a Principal (II)*

Our principal, Dr. Jones, often tells the story of the time she planned to visit several kindergarten and first-grade classes at the elementary school.

One first-grade teacher, anxious for her class to make a good impression, required the children to "dress up" on the day of the visit. With the cooperation of the class parents, the boys were dressed in pristinely laundered shirts and ties and wore their "good" shoes, while the girls were replete in pastel-colored dresses with shiny patent-leather shoes. Naturally, faces were scrubbed clean and every hair was in place.

In addition, because the teacher wanted the children to stay clean, the usual morning activities were drastically curtailed.

Finally, one little girl, in absolute desperation, raised her hand.

"Ms. Hutchison," she asked, "can I make a suggestion?"

"Certainly, Linda. What is it?"

"Honest, Ma'am," the child sighed, "don't you think it would be easier if we just blindfolded the principal?"

70. *Introducing a Principal (III)*

For some years now, I've been aware that our principal, Dr. Jones, keeps a special little notebook in his desk drawer. Often, I had seen him writing in it, frequently during or directly after some very trying and hectic times in the school. I wanted to ask him about it, but somehow there never seemed to be a right time.

Finally, there came a day when I had to go into his office, and there was the notebook, lying open on his desk. I couldn't resist. What treasures of wisdom might I be privileged to witness? I bent over it and looked.

What a disappointment! At first glance, it seemed to be nothing more than a list of dates, most of them in the future, with vague times, such as "after dinner," attached.

Just then, Dr. Jones came into the office, and I finally found the courage to ask him about the notebook.

"I don't get it," I said. "All I see are dates and times. What's it all about?"

"I'll tell you," Dr. Jones answered. "So many times around this place there are situations and problems that just make me want to tear my hair out, but I realize that if I'm going to be effective, I have to stay calm. That's when I go to this notebook. What I write down is the date and time when I can safely worry about the situation.

"It's a wonderful relief to know that I've scheduled a time when I can go to pieces in quiet and serenity!"

71. Introducing a School Nurse

Our school nurse, Mrs. Blunt, was in her office trying to catch up on some records when an obviously agitated and weepy first-grade boy came running in, breathing heavily.

"Son," said the nurse, "calm down! What's the matter?"

"It . . . it's Tommy!" the child blurted. "The teacher think's he's dead! I didn't even wait to be told, I just ran down here. You gotta come, quick!"

With that, the child was out of the office in a flash. Nurse Blunt grabbed her emergency kit and was right after him. With the child in the lead, they ran down the hallway, down a flight of stairs, through another hallway, up two more flights of stairs, and down half of another hallway to the classroom.

Student and school nurse burst through the door together, startling the class which was calmly gathered around a cigar box in which lay a very dead hamster.

Running to the box, the child gazed up at the school nurse.

"Here's Tommy, Mrs. Blunt," the child panted. "Come on! Why don't you give him mouth to mouth?"

72. Introducing an Administrator

A few months ago, our superintendent, Dr. Smith was driving back from a conference she had attended upstate when her car broke down. The garage said that it would be fixed by morning, so Dr. Smith took a room in a nearby motel. On a field next to the motel, a travelling circus had set up its tents, and, on a whim, Dr. Smith walked over and took in the show.

There was one fellow in particular who caught Dr. Smith's eye. This was a young man who did the most amazing feats of juggling you've ever seen. At one point, for instance, the man had six balls, three plates and four timber axes in the air at the same time and handled all of them effortlessly.

"You!" shouted Dr. Smith as she rose from her seat, "You're just what I need in Central Administration!"

And she hired him on the spot.

Therefore, I take great pleasure in introducing our new Assistant Superintendent of Schools . . .

73. *Introducing an Administrator from Another District*

Our guest tonight is Dr. Bennett, superintendent of our sister school district. Just recently, Dr. Bennett invited several of our administrators to visit his schools, and a group of us went. We had a very enjoyable time, but, in all honesty, one of our administrators was feeling a bit chauvinistic about our own district.

"Our gymnasium is much bigger," our administrator said, and throughout our tour he constantly bragged about how much bigger and better we were. "Our cafeteria is much larger; our art rooms have much better lighting; our halls are so much wider than these." And so on.

In the middle of the tour, I saw Dr. Bennett go up to a science teacher and whisper, "You know those homing pigeons in that project? Get three of them and put them in the closet in my office. I'll explain later."

When our tour was finished and we were back in his office, Dr. Bennett offered to get us our coats. As he opened the closet door, three startled pigeons fluttered out, flew once around the office, and headed off through the open door and down the hallway.

"Now," said Dr. Bennett to our bragging administrator, "tell me you have bigger moths than that in *your* school district!"

74. *Introducing a School Custodian*

When I think of our school custodian, Mr. Danny Shovins, I am reminded of a famous story about British author G. K. Chesterton, who was having a discussion with two fellow authors.

"Suppose you were marooned on a desert island with no possibility of being rescued," ran the topic of discussion, "and you could have with you one and only one book. What would it be?"

"Simple," said the first, "I would take the Holy Bible."

"Well," said the second, "as for me, I think I would want *The Complete Works of William Shakespeare.*"

"What about you, Chesterton," one of them asked. "What one book would you choose if you were marooned on a desert island?"

"Actually," said Chesterton, "I'd prefer a copy of *Thomas's Guide to Practical Shipbuilding!*"

That's why this story is perfect to introduce our school custodian, a man who is always ready with the practical answer to all our needs.

75. *Introducing a Teacher*

Thinking that some responsibility might help to straighten him out, the teacher assigned one child who was having all sorts of problems to a special role in an upcoming presentation the class would be holding for parents.

The lad was assigned the task of "introducing" the teacher to the assembled parents. So the boy would realize the extent of his responsibilities, she told him how important it was that he introduce her properly and how much what he said would mean.

On the day of the presentation, everyone was ready, and the teacher was going around to each child giving some final words of encouragement.

"And are you going to say some nice things when you introduce me?" she smiled at the boy.

"Mrs. Hadley," said the boy with a crooked smile, "I got nice things I can say and I got so nice things I could say, so before I get up there, maybe you and I should have a little talk about that test we took yesterday and what you're gonna tell my mother?"

Well, I don't have to worry about our guest this evening telling my mother, and I assure you that I have only the very nicest of comments to make about her.

Ladies and gentlemen, may I introduce . . .

76. *Introducing a "Special" Teacher*

"Mommy," said the little girl at bedtime, "am I special?"

"Oh, yes, my darling," said Mother, "you are very special."

"And is Daddy special?"

"He certainly is."

"And you're special, too. Aren't you Mommy?"

"If you say so."

"Mommy," said the little girl.

"Yes, darling."

"What's 'special'?"

Well, while that child may have been confused as to the meaning of the word, we have no such doubts. To us, "special" is our guest this evening, a teacher who has demonstrated, over the years, her special talents, her special abilities, and her special love for the children of our school district.

It is an honor for me to introduce . . .

77. Introducing a PTA Worker

Mrs. Judy Blaine is one of the most tireless workers I know. Indeed, the work that she has done for our PTA and for our school speaks eloquently for itself. Ask anyone around here, and they will tell you of the hours of volunteer time that she puts in working for the good of our students and our school.

I remember once close to the end of a particularly hectic day, Judy went for a cup of coffee only to find that the coffeemaker was empty and had been closed down for the day. She was standing there with her empty cup when I chanced to come by with a parent who was new to the district. Naturally, I introduced Mrs. Blaine as one of our PTA volunteers.

"Oh," said the new parent, "then you don't work here?"

I was about to interrupt and tell this new parent about all the things Mrs. Blaine did for us, when Judy held up a hand.

"Of course not," she said, turning over her empty coffee mug. "If I *worked* here, I'd be entitled to a coffee break!"

We know that Judy is entitled to much more than that, so please allow me to introduce . . .

78. Introducing a PTA President

Being the president of the PTA is hard work. There are long hours, and the work is often thankless labor since, as the saying goes, "You can't please everyone."

A few months back, the PTA was thinking of redoing the cafeteria, particularly the student eating area which has been battered by an endless line of active students over the years.

Mrs. Tanner, our PTA President, had asked a representative from a local supply house to come in and give some advice on what needed to be replaced and what could be done to "liven up" the cafeteria.

The representative took some time looking over the tables, the walls, and even the doorframes, worn in places by thousands of student hands.

Finally, the representative turned to Mrs. Tanner and asked, "Can you tell me what takes the most abuse around this place?"

"Sir," she answered, "I'm the president of the PTA and you ask what takes the most abuse? I do, Sir, I do!"

79. Introducing the Honored Retiree

Just before I introduce Mel Haskins, our honored retiree who is the focus of and reason for this evening's gathering, I'd like to share with you something that happened a few days ago.

In planning for this affair, I had the opportunity to speak with Mel about his life in education as well as getting a retrospect of his life in general.

"Mel," I said lightly, "are you sure you want to retire? Wouldn't you like to stay a few more years and see some of the changes that are going to take place?"

"I'll tell you," Mel said. "I've gone through enough changes. You may not believe this, but I actually lived in a time where a man and woman lived together *after* they got married. To us, *pot* was what your mother cooked in. *Designer jeans* were two women named Jean who were plotting how to marry the boss's son. And, in my time, a *meaningful relationship* meant being able to spend an entire evening with your little brother without punching him, even once!

"So you see, I've had enough changes!"

Therefore, allow me to introduce a man who has gone through many changes and whose life has brought about so many changes in others. Our honored guest this evening . . .

80. Introducing a Political Figure

There is a story told by Samuel Clemens, the great American author who wrote under the pen name, Mark Twain.

According to Twain, a man was running for political office in a small southern town where feelings always ran high on either side of any issue. It was little wonder, therefore, that every political speech or event was crowded by people from both sides of the political fence.

One night, the candidate was giving a speech at a bonfire rally when several supporters of the opposition candidate arrived. Not content with catcalls and name-calling, they began to throw things at the stage. One of the offenders had brought a huge, rotting cabbage with him, and this he threw squarely at the candidate.

The candidate stopped his speech, bent down and picked up the rotting cabbage and stared at it intently. The place quieted down.

"It is as I suspected," said the candidate in his best speaking voice as he stared at the cabbage. "The pressure has gotten so intense, my opponent has lost his head over the issues!"

Allow me, therefore, to introduce a political figure who never loses his head . . .

81. *Introducing a Parent*

It is always a pleasure to introduce one of our parents, and tonight is no exception. In fact, our guest tonight is a parent four times over, and all of them have passed through this school, the youngest one still here.

I asked Mr. Donner if there were anything he had learned from raising four children, and he replied that there was not enough time in the year to reflect on all he and his wife had learned.

"In fact," he told me, "all of parenting is just one big learning process. You just keep learning all the time."

"Could you give me an example of that," I asked.

"Well," answered this veteran parent, "just last week, my youngest son placed a can of soda too close to the edge of the table. It spilled, so I had him clean it up and gave him a short lecture about being careful with things that spill."

"But, how does that show learning and growth on your part?"

"Because," he said, "with my *first* child, I came into the room one day, and this two-year-old had taken an indelible marker and scribbled all over the living room wallpaper. At that point, I called my wife into the room, pointed at the wall, and exclaimed, 'Isn't it wonderful! He's only two, and he's already starting to write!'

"Believe me, the difference shows how much I've learned!"

82. *Introducing a Parent Volunteer*

I think we are all aware of the fact that Mrs. Keller is one of our most active parent volunteers. I think we are equally aware that all of this is accomplished in spite of the fact that she has seven children, five of whom are in this school.

I remember the day that Mrs. Keller came to volunteer for the first time. I went in to see the principal, and I said, "Mrs. Keller is outside, and she wants to sign up as a parent volunteer."

"Whom did you say?"

"Mrs. Keller," I answered. "You know, she's the lady with seven children."

"Good grief!" exclaimed the principal. "Sign her up before she decides to put her kids in private school. We couldn't afford to lose that much federal funding!"

Mrs. Keller has been with us ever since!

83. *Introducing a Board of Education Member*

When Mr. Young was first elected to the Board of Education, he was filled with energy. About a week after he had assumed his seat, he went to the Board President.

"What a wonderful day I've had," said Mr. Young.

"What happened?" asked the Board President.

"Well, you know that old school bus we've been wanting to get rid of? This morning, I traded it to the Hillsdale School System for two vans; then I traded the vans to Thomasville Schools for a maintenance vehicle; after that, I traded the maintenance vehicle to the Berrywood School System for a full sized tractor; finally, I contacted the Hillsdale School System and traded them the tractor for our old school bus!"

"Wait a minute," said the President. "If I have this straight, we got the same bus back; no money changed hands; we didn't make anything; we didn't lose anything; and everything stayed exactly the way it was."

"Yes!" shouted Mr. Young, "but just think of all the business I did for the school!"

84. *Introducing a School Board President*

Recently a civic group donated to our school a huge reproduction of the Declaration of Independence to be placed in our school library. Anxious to have our board of education see the contribution, I carefully wrapped the large reproduction and sent it by special messenger to the Board of Education offices.

A week later, I got it back and to my surprise, when I unwrapped it, there was the signature of the president of our board of education boldly written in black marker right along with those of Jefferson and Hancock!

I immediately called him and asked if he had put his name on what I had sent over.

"Oh, yes," the board president told me. "I figured that was an unusual way to send me a petition, but I read it, agreed with every word, and I signed it at the bottom where you had those names of the other board members!"

85. *Introducing an "Expert" (I)*

Our school had purchased a very sophisticated computer setup. I want to tell you, it worked beautifully. It did everything we expected of it and more. Very shortly, we came to rely on it.

That's why, when it broke down, we were devastated. Someone took the cover off the terminal, but the inside was so filled with integrated circuits and wires and such that no one could make heads or tails out of it. Therefore, we decided that we had to call the manufacturer.

"Please send over someone who is familiar with these things," I asked, and we waited for the repairman.

Half an hour later, a voice announced, "I'm here to fix the computer."

We looked up and saw a twelve-year-old girl. Of course, she wasn't that young, but she was young enough to make me feel ancient, and she was chewing gum as she spoke.

I was on the phone to the manufacturer immediately.

"Look," I said, "I don't want to sound crude, but I asked for a repairman to fix our computer. We need somebody older; with a little more experience in these things!"

"Sir," said the voice at the other end of the line, "our regular repairman is out sick today; that's why we sent the young woman. I really think you should let her work on the computer."

"Really, and why is that?"

"Well, Sir," said the voice, "she's the one who invented it!"

86. *Introducing an "Expert" (II)*

Two custodians new to the school system were polishing the cafeteria floor when the vice-principal walked by and stood watching for a moment.

"That's no way to wax a floor," the vice-principal told the two custodians. "You're using too much wax; you're holding the buffer all wrong . . ."

So it went on for a good ten minutes, and all the while the custodians said not a word. Finally, one of the floor-polishers shut off the machine and looked up.

"Excuse me, Sir," said one man, pointing to the door which led from the cafeteria to the parking lot, "is that your car on fire?"

Without a word, the vice-principal ran to the door, pushed it open and ran out into the parking lot. At once, the custodian went over and threw a lever, locking the door. The vice-principal, realizing that nothing was wrong with his car, began pounding on the door as the skies opened and a steady downpour began.

"Well," said the custodian to his fellow worker, "that man certainly knows a lot about floor-polishing. Now let's see if he's an expert in lock-picking as well!"

87. *Introducing a "New" Administrator or Teacher*

I'd like to introduce to you our new vice-principal. She comes to us with a great deal of experience and an outstanding list of recommendations.

Indeed, I was speaking with the superintendent of schools of her previous school district, and that man described our new administrator as a person of few words who got the job done and did it in such a manner that no one had a bad word to say against her.

In fact, I asked her how she accounted for the fact that she seemed to get on so well with everyone.

"It's a matter of breath control," she answered.

"Breath control?" I questioned. "What do you mean?"

"I breathe through my nose," she answered. "You try it."

I did for several moments and then asked, "But, what has that got to do with being amiable?"

"Simple," she said. "Perhaps you noticed that when you breath through your nose, it forces you to keep your big mouth shut. Believe me, that practice alone avoids all sorts of troubles."

88. *Introducing a New Idea or Concept*

Tonight we are going to talk about several new ideas and concepts that have been proposed for our school district. We want to make certain, however, that we all understand and appreciate the meaning and implications of these ideas.

We don't want to be like the psychiatrist who attended a man who was convinced that he was dead. Try as the psychiatrist might to reason with the man, the man merely kept reiterating that he was dead.

Finally, the doctor asked, "Tell me, do dead men bleed?"

"No," answered the patient, "dead men do not bleed."

With that, the doctor took a sterile needle and stuck the man's finger, drawing a bead of blood.

"Well," said the doctor, "does this give you any new ideas?"

"Oh, yes," said the patient.

"What?"

"Dead men *do* bleed!"

89. *Introducing a New Program (I)*

Tonight, we will be introducing a new program that, I am certain, will benefit all the students of our district.

I must tell you, however, that I feel a bit like the man who visited New York City for the first time. He had a few too many drinks, hopped into a taxi, and asked the cabbie to "show him the sights."

As the cabbie drove along the docks on the Hudson River, he noticed that the magnificent ship, the *Queen Elizabeth II* was in port, and he could not help remarking on it.

"That's the QE II," the cabbie said. "Why, do you know that if you took that ship and set it on its side, it would be as tall as the Empire State Building?"

"OK," said the visitor, "I'll try to set it up, but it looks so big, I think you're going to have to help me!"

Yes, the program we will introduce tonight is going to be magnificent, but like the gentleman in the story, we are really going to need your help if we are going to set it up right!

90. *Introducing a New Program (II)*

It is natural, perhaps, that people might ask why we need the new program that we are introducing this evening. In answer to that, I'd like to tell you about the training I received as a lifeguard.

My instructor placed me at the edge of the pool and said, "I want you to fall into the water, get out, and do it again—ten times."

I did it ten times.

"Now, I want you to lie face down in the water for as long as you can."

About a minute and a half later, I came up sputtering.

"Son," said my instructor, "you have learned a great lesson. A person doesn't drown from falling into deep waters; he drowns by *staying* in the deep waters!"

Sometimes we all need a little help getting out of the "deep waters" in which we find ourselves. I think the new program I am about to outline to you will go a long way toward putting our feet on solid ground.

Let's begin . . .

91. Introducing a Well-Loved/Respected Individual

When I asked our guest this evening why so many people thought so highly of him, I think he was a bit embarrassed. Finally, however, he told me a secret he had learned years ago.

"It is really very simple," he told me. "When you meet somebody for the first time, become genuinely interested in that person. Encourage that person to talk about himself or herself and listen closely, making a real effort to understand."

"And that method has never backfired on you?" I asked.

"Only once," he replied. "I met a gentleman who raised earthworms. I said to him, 'That must be very interesting work, could you tell me something about it?'

"He did. In fact, for the next three hours and twenty-two minutes, he did nothing but talk about earthworms. For days afterward, I dreamed of earthworms and found it difficult to walk on the grass lest I trample on one. I couldn't get earthworms out of my head!"

"So your tactic didn't work," I said.

"Oh, it worked fine," said our guest. "As far as that gentleman was concerned, he came away from the conversation convinced that I was a wonderful friend. I just hope he never realizes what an enemy *he* made!"

92. Introducing a School Crossing Guard

There is no one at this school who does not know Tess Denton, our school crossing guard. Every child and every teacher is well aware of the great effort she has put in not only with helping our students across streets, but also with educating us all about traffic safety. In fact, though it is a little known fact, Tess taught our principal how to parallel park.

I asked her about that, and she confirmed that the principal had asked her if she could teach him this delicate parking maneuver.

"Did he learn well?" I asked her.

"Oh, yes," she replied, "the principal now has his own unique method of parallel parking."

"And, what's that?"

"Well," she answered, "before, he used to circle the block seemingly for hours until he could find a space where he could just pull in foreward. Now, since he learned to parallel park, it's quite different."

"What's it like now?"

"Now, he simply backs in until he hits something; pulls foreward until he hits something; then tosses me the keys and says, 'Tess, will you park this blasted thing?'"

93. Introducing a Coach/Athletic Director

Recently, I was driving over in the Norwood section of town on a day when the heavens were trying to do a good imitation of Niagara Falls. I spotted one of our students, a cheerleader, standing in the rain beside what I knew to be her car. The car had one amazingly flat tire. I pulled up and asked the trouble.

"I have an appointment with Coach Harding," she said, "and I got this dumb flat tire. I don't even know how to change it, and I've *got* to see the coach about the plans for the Pep Rally!"

It is an educator's duty to help his students in all sorts of ways, so, with a deep sigh, I got out of my car and set about changing her flat tire.

Sheet after sheet of cold rain assailed me as I worked. It was a relatively easy task, but by the time I finished my shoes were ruined, my clothes were caked with dirt, and I was soaked through to the skin and shivering badly.

"There," I said finally, "it's all fixed. Perhaps you won't be late for your appointment with the Coach after all."

"Oh, I won't be late," she said. "The coach only lives across the street in the white house over there."

"What!" I sputtered. "You mean the coach lives right there, less than a hundred feet from where we are now? Why didn't you just walk over and get the coach to change your tire?"

"What," she replied with great indignation, "and have the coach get wet?!"

94. Introducing an Athlete

Martin Samuels is, without a doubt, one of the finest athletes this or any school has produced. Besides this athletic prowess, he also belies the image of the mindless brute who has nothing but brawn, since he is also a high honor student with an outstanding academic record. In fact, it is my understanding that he has always combined athletic talent with intellectual ability.

I was talking recently to Martin's elementary school physical education teacher. He recalls that in fifth grade, he had taken Martin's class to introduce them to the sport of archery.

Each child was given a bow and five arrows. The teacher explained the process and stood back. The physical education teacher then went to each child, explaining the finer points of the sport.

When he got to Martin, he stopped short. Martin had already fired his five arrows, and every single one of them was smack-dab, dead center in a bull's-eye—every single one!

"Martin!" exclaimed the teacher. "This is tremendous! You must have a natural talent! How did you ever manage to get five out of five bull's-eyes?"

"Gosh, Sir," said Martin, "it's real easy. First, you shoot the arrows, and then you walk down and draw bull's-eyes around each one!"

95. Introducing a "Special" Student

Bill Spooler is a very special student. His high intellectual ability has distinguished him throughout his school career, his athletic ability has distinguished him on the playing field, and his attitude of selfless giving for our school in his role as student council president has earned him a place in our hearts.

The fact is that Bill always was a challenge to his teachers. One of them recalls that when Bill was in fourth grade, he asked his social studies teacher a question.

"Ma'am," Bill asked, "suppose a man brings flowers and candy and stuff like that to a girl and asks her to marry him; and then later, he changes his mind and doesn't want to marry her. Can she sue him in a court of law?"

"What you're referring to," explained the teacher, "is called 'breach of promise,' and our state does not have provision in the law for that. So, the answer is no, in this state, the man in question could not be sued."

Nine-year-old Bill Spooler sat back and wiped the perspiration from his forehead.

"See," he said to the boy next to him, "I told you I had nothing to worry about!"

96. *Introducing a Volunteer Worker (I)*

Volunteer workers like Samuel Anderson are hard to come by. When Sam volunteers for something, he gives it his all.

Recently, he volunteered to help with a class trip. He was here at six in the morning, got kids and parents situated, hefted knapsacks and equipment, supervised and mediated disputes on the bus, hiked the nature trails, helped with the outdoor cooking, hiked some more nature trails, patched some scraped knees, helped load equipment and knapsacks back on the bus, tended tired and exhausted children on the way home, and finally arrived at the school just as the sun was setting.

One of the waiting parents who did not know Mr. Anderson wondered who he might be since this parent knew he wasn't one of the teachers.

"Pardon me," said the woman as she approached Mr. Anderson, "but how long have you worked here?"

To which Mr. Anderson replied, "Since the dawn of time, Madam; since the dawn of time!"

97. *Introducing a Volunteer Worker (II)*

Barbara Dean is a prime example of selflessness and giving. Her work as a volunteer at our school has proven invaluable for our students and our school. Indeed, I don't think we could get along without her. I once spoke to her about her tireless efforts.

"I had a grandmother," she told me, "who took me to her kitchen one day and sat me down at the table.

" 'I believe that little girls should get some homemade cookies,' she told me. Then she went over to the pantry, took down a plate, and set the empty plate in front of me.

"I stared at it for a moment and then looked up at my grandmother and said, 'But, you said you believed that little girls should get homemade cookies!'

" 'So I did,' said my grandmother, 'and I'll get them for you now, but you just learned a valuable lesson.'

" 'I did?' I said, 'What's that?'

" 'Why child,' said my grandmother with a grin, 'you just learned that it's not enough to believe it—you have to *behave* it as well!' "

98. *Introducing a Difficult or "Tender" Issue*

Two fourth-grade boys were discussing a project given to them by their teacher. Each student was to think up a number of questions, ask at least fifty people to answer those questions, and then they were to calculate the percentage of responses to each question.

"I'm having real trouble with one of my questions," one boy told the other.

"What's the question?" asked the other.

"It's this," said the boy. "What is it that has really great curves, gets everybody's attention, and when you look at it, it gives you this funny feeling in your stomach and you want to stand up and cheer and whistle?"

"That's easy," said the second fourth-grader. "It's when Dwight Gooden pitches a no-hitter."

"Of course," said the first, "but you'd be surprised at some of the weird answers I've been getting from those eighth-graders!"

99. *Introducing the Staff of a School*

The principal wished to introduce the custodial staff of the school to an assembly of parents. The entire staff was gathered on stage as he spoke.

The principal went on at length about the great job that they did, indicating the cleanliness and pristine condition of the building and classrooms.

"I am certain," concluded the principal, "that if heaven contains a place for people who do an outstanding job, this staff will be there!"

"Yeah," the head custodian murmured in a whisper that could be heard throughout the room, "and with our luck, it'll probably be a place that gets dirty!"

100. *Introducing Teachers to an Audience*

The teachers of the school had been assembled on the stage of the auditorium and were being introduced to a group of parents by the school's principal.

The principal went on at length and was effusive in his praise for the teaching staff. He remarked on their educational levels, the programs that they had created and ran so well, the hours that they spent preparing for class, their gentleness and understanding in handling student problems, and their fantastic cooperativeness in all aspects of school life.

At this point, the teachers on stage huddled together as if they were a football team.

"I don't understand," said the principal addressing the senior member of the staff. "Ms. Martin, what's happening?"

"I'm sorry," said the senior teacher, "but we're going to be leaving now."

"Leaving! You can't leave now!"

"Well," the teacher continued, "we hadn't intended to, but after your introduction, we got together and figured that if even half of your speech were correct, then we're not being adequately paid, so we're going on strike for higher salaries!"

Section Three

OUT OF THE DARKNESS AND INTO THE LIGHT—CLASSIC COMMENTARY ON THE CLASSROOM

The word *education* comes from two Latin words, *e* and *ducas,* and its literal meaning is "to lead out." One generally accepted implication of that definition is the leading *out* of the darkness of ignorance and *into* the light of knowledge. Although that can happen anywhere, for most of us it took place in the classroom, and that classroom experience has shaped our lives.

In this section, we'll investigate the myriad of classroom activities. Some may be serious, but the majority will definitely help to lead you *out* of the doldrums and *into* the light of laughter and remembrance. In a way, that's education at its best.

101. *How Children View Learning (Humorous, I)*

The teacher wanted to talk to her class about the value of an education. Gathering the children together, she began a class discussion.

"I have a very serious question to ask you," she said.

The class quieted and looked intently at her.

"How many of you," she continued, "would like to have a good job that pays you a fair salary?"

Every hand in class went up. Every one, that is, except for one boy who sat grim-faced with both hands at his side.

"Jamie," said the teacher, "are you telling me that you do *not* want a good job?"

"Heck, no!" exclaimed the lad. "I'm only eight years old! I don't want a job; I want to have fun!"

102. *How Children View Learning (Humorous, II)*

One child in the eighth-grade class was a regular entrepreneur. Not only did he have a "job" as a newspaper boy, but he did odd jobs around his neighborhood, made wreaths and knick-knacks which he sold at local craft shows, and had organized a lawn-cutting service, for which he often "hired" other eighth-graders whom he knew. In short, he was doing quite well for himself.

The problem was that with all the time he spent in his various endeavors, he sometimes lacked time to study for tests and often "forgot" to do his homework.

Therefore, the teacher took him aside one day and pointed out the decline in his grades. She also pointed out that his outside activities appeared to be interfering with his schoolwork.

"I'm afraid," she said, "that you are going to have to cut down on some of those out-of-school activities."

"Ma'am," replied the boy, "I can't do that. Don't you want me to learn?"

"Well, of course I want you to learn," stated the teacher.

"Then how can you ask me to give up those jobs?" questioned the student. "Do you want my schooling to interfere with my education?"

103. *How Children View Learning (Serious, I)*

School had ended for the day, and I was seated at my desk in the empty classroom when I became aware that someone was standing in the doorway. I looked up and saw a tall, muscular young man in his early twenties staring at me. He asked my name and when I had given it, he walked into the room.

"You probably don't recognize me," he said, "but you had me in class a lot of years ago. I'm Bill Jones."

Now I recognized him. He had been one of the toughest kids I had ever taught. As I recalled, we were joined in a battle of wills from the first day of school through the start of summer.

"When I was in your class," he continued, "you gave me a pretty rough time. You kept me after school a lot, got me in trouble with my parents, and forced me to read books and study. I really hated you. I used to dream about beating you up."

He had my attention now. I began to look out in the hall to see if anyone might be passing by. I think my hands started to sweat.

"I did a lot of stupid things after I got out of your class. Then one day, something dawned on me. Most people just got out of my way, and the only thing they cared about was that I left them alone. You were the only one who cared enough about *me* to fight to keep me from ending up a real mess."

He came forward, extending a burly arm.

"I'm doing OK now," he said, "and I just wanted to drop by and apologize, say thank you, and ask if you'd shake my hand."

104. *How Children View Learning (Serious, II)*

A teacher we know reports that one of her greatest rewards came on a day when they had invited a police officer to come and address the class.

During the officer's talk, he mentioned that it was wrong and illegal for anyone to force another person to do something against his or her will. Then, his speech was over and it was time for questions.

"You said that it's wrong to force somebody to do something they don't want to do," stated one child.

"Yes," said the officer, "it certainly is."

"Do you arrest people for that and put them in jail?"

"Sometimes we do."

"Are you gonna put our teacher in jail?" the child asked.

"What?" said the startled officer. "Why would I arrest your teacher?"

"Well," the child continued, "she gives us homework and makes us read books."

"But, what has that got to do . . ."

"Don't you see?" stated the student. "She's making us learn against our will. I don't want to do homework and math and stuff like that, but she's making us smart in spite of ourselves!"

105. The "New Kid" in Class

It was my custom that every time a "new kid" was assigned to my class, I tried to spend some time with him and get to know him a little better. Therefore, when Robby transferred in from another school, I waited for a convenient and private time and called him up for a talk.

After the usual chit-chat about how he was getting on in the school and did he need anything, I began to talk to him about the school from which he had come.

"I'm sure you must have felt sad about leaving your old school," I stated.

"Not really," he replied. "There was a lot of illness there."

"Oh, did you have any trouble?"

"Yeah," he answered. "I guess you might say that's why I left, because of illness and fatigue."

"You left because of illness and fatigue?"

"Right," he said with a deep sigh. "That school was really sick of me, and I was tired of giving excuses why I shouldn't be tossed out!"

106. The "New" Teacher

The new teacher arrived in the middle of the school year, and she quickly established her own discipline, a very wise thing to do. On the second day she taught, she overheard one of her pupils telling another that their new teacher was "a mean and crabby grouch!" Immediately, she took the child aside and gently asked what she had done that the child would call her that. With tears in her eyes, the student replied that she liked the new teacher but Billy Smith was telling everyone that the teacher was real mean and nasty.

Deciding to go to the source, the new teacher called for Billy Smith and held a private conference.

"I understand that you've been telling the other children that I'm a 'mean and crabby grouch,' " she said. "Is that true?"

"I . . . I . . . " stammered the boy, and then he lowered his head and said nothing.

Gently, the new teacher explained how bad it was to spread unkind remarks and how such a practice could hurt people.

"I don't want to hurt you," the boy sniffled on the verge of tears, and the teacher hugged him and told him that she was sure it would never happen again.

"You bet!" stated the repentant Billy. "I'll never tell anyone that you're a mean and crabby grouch."

"Thank you, Billy. I'm happy to hear that."

"Right!" stated the lad. "From now on, if they want to know how mean and crabby and grouchy you are, they're just going to have to find out for themselves!"

107. On Being a Teacher

The teacher had managed to get some very detailed maps of the local area, the kind that showed schools and hospitals and the like. She wanted to teach map skills, but during a recess period, she noticed two boys hovering over a map and dropping wads of paper onto it.

"What are you doing?" she asked.

"We're pretending that we're bombers," replied one boy, "and these spitballs are bombs. We're trying to bomb the school!"

"Boys!" said the teacher. "I know you're only pretending, but you must realize that even in real war, bombers are very careful *not* to bomb schools. It would be very wrong to bomb a school, do you understand?"

"We understand, Ma'am, but this is OK."

"Oh," said the teacher, "and why is it all right for you to bomb that school?"

"Because," answered one child with a wide grin, "we're not bombing the kids—we're only bombing the teachers!"

108. The Principal Visits the Class (I)

The principal visited the class of seniors and spoke about higher education. In fact, he spoke and spoke and spoke. His speech went on for a class period and then on into another. Even the upper classmen who had gained a great deal of maturity found it difficult to sit still as the principal droned on about the benefits of a college education.

As it neared the end of the second period of the principal's talk, one senior nudged a young man sitting next to him.

"You know," he whispered, "if that guy keeps talking any longer, we'll have graduated from college before he gets through talking about it!"

109. The Principal Visits the Class (II)

It sometimes happens that just the right (or perhaps we should say, "wrong") combination of personalities is placed together in a class, and that class becomes a true "wild bunch." Such was the case with one particular class, and at the end of a long line of strategies, the principal was called in to speak to the disruptive class.

"I'm not fooling around," the principal said, taking a no-nonsense approach. "This class has caused trouble all over this school, and your academic record is pitiful. Well, we're through fooling around with you. From now on, you will either behave yourselves and improve your grades, or you will be suspended from this school until your parents can guarantee your behavior. That's it. Any questions?"

"Just one," said a student in the class. "Do you think you might briefly outline any *other* options we have in this case?"

110. Excuses for Being Late (I)

Betty Jean came strolling into class a full hour late to school.

"Why are you late?" asked her teacher.

"You see this twenty-dollar bill?" said the child as she held it up for her teacher's inspection. "Well, this morning as I was coming to school I passed by the park, and there was the money, right by the big oak tree by the entrance."

Thinking that Betty Jean might be making up the story and that her parents may have given her the money, the teacher asked, "Betty Jean, are you certain this money was lost?"

"It was lost, all right," Betty Jean answered. "That's how come I'm so late for school."

"What do you mean?"

"I know it was lost," the excited child continued, "because I stayed there half an hour watching the guy who lost it search the park!"

111. Excuses for Being Late (II)

Ted had been late for school often enough that it was becoming a real problem. One day, the boy came running in a full half-hour late.

"Just a minute," the teacher said to the student. "Let's see. I'll bet you're late to school because on your way here you saw this lovable little puppy that was whining and crying. It looked hungry, so you shared your lunch with it. Then you noticed a tag on the dog's collar, and it was an address clear across town. Not wanting this poor little puppy to come to harm, you personally walked it home, where the grateful owner simply wouldn't let you leave until you had some cookies and milk. And that's why you're late for school, right?"

"Actually," said the boy calmly, "I'm late because my mother overslept, but I wonder if you could write down what you just said so I can use it next time!"

112. *Excuses for Being Absent*

"Mary," said the teacher, "your note for being absent yesterday states that you were attending your grandfather's funeral. I just want you to know that I'm very sorry."

"Thank you, teacher," said Mary.

"Mary," continued the teacher, "do you believe that there is life after death?"

"Oh, yes," said Mary with wide eyes.

"I'm very glad of that, Mary," said the teacher gently, "and do you know why?"

"No, teacher, why?"

"Because, Mary," said the teacher smiling, "I just got a note from downstairs that the grandfather whose funeral you attended yesterday is in the office waiting to take you to your dentist appointment!"

113. *Excuses for Not Having Homework*

"I have heard every excuse there is for not having homework," the teacher told his class. "I no longer believe that it blew out the window of the school bus; I no longer believe that your baby brother threw up on it; and, I most certainly will not believe that your dog ate it!"

"Sir," said a boy who had recently arrived from Florida, "would you believe that I have a pet alligator who loves to eat paper?"

"Most certainly not," stated the teacher, "not unless I see the beast."

"In that case," said the boy, "can I bring in Clyde for show and tell and feed him your marking book?"

114. Excuses for Failing a Test

After a test one morning, the class went out for recess. When they returned, the teacher noticed that an apple that had been on her desk was missing.

"Someone took the apple," the teacher told the class. "Now, I want whoever took it to be brave and honest. Who took it?"

One little fellow raised his hand and, with a shaky voice, said, "I was hungry, teacher, and it looked so good that I took it without asking. I'm sorry. Are you going to punish me?"

"I'm not going to punish you, Henry," said the teacher. "You see, you told the truth; you were honest, so I'm going to give you an *A* in my mark book for your honesty."

With that, a child in the back of the room raised his hand.

"Teacher," he said, "you know that test we took this morning? Well, I didn't study for it at all; I never even looked in the book. That's the honest truth, and I want you to know that before you correct the papers."

115. Interesting Answers on a Test

The science teacher was going over the various systems of the human body. This particular day, he was teaching about certain glands and their functions.

As he taught, he noticed that a few students weren't paying much attention, so just before the end of the period, he gave a pop quiz.

The quiz contained one question: Tell me all you know about the salivary glands.

Later, he was going over the papers and came to the one handed in by a girl who he knew had not paid any attention to what was going on.

"I don't know much about the salivary glands," the answer read, "but there is a good reason for this. Nobody knows much about the salivary glands, because they are so secretive!"

What could he do? The teacher gave her an *A*!

116. Students and Their Textbooks

The child had been out of school for some time due to an extended illness but was scheduled to come back soon. One evening, the teacher visited her student's home to see for herself if the child needed any extra help staying on level with his class.

Mother and father were delighted, but Billy, the soon-returning student, was decidedly uneasy.

"Oh, yes, Ma'am," Billy affirmed. "I've been studying every day. In fact, every chance I get I read my textbook. I read it night and day!"

"Well," said the teacher, "that's very good. Suppose we get your textbook, and you can show me what you've been going over."

"Timmy!" the boy called, and his three-year-old brother appeared.

"Timmy," continued Billy, "I want you to go get me my textbook."

"What's a tackbook?" asked the little brother.

"Textbook!" corrected Billy. "You know. Just go get me that book that I study from; the one that I'm reading *all the time!*"

"Oh, that one!" Timmy exclaimed. Then, in the loudest possible voice, little Timmy shouted, "Hey, Ma! Where did Billy leave the Superman comic book?"

117. The Mischievous Student

Molly was an extremely mischievous student who had given the teacher many a restless hour. She came up to her teacher's desk at the close of school one day.

"Ma'am," said Molly, "I know I haven't always behaved properly, and I know that sometimes I've made you mad. Well, I just want you to know that I care for you very much, and if I have done or said anything to upset you, I am deeply, deeply sorry, and I apologize from the bottom of my heart."

"Why, Molly," said the teacher, "what a beautiful thing to say. You have a gift with words, Molly, and I only wish that I could say something warm and meaningful like that. I don't think I could."

"Sure, you could, Ma'am," said Molly. "In fact, it would be real easy if you were as good a liar as I am!"

118. The Shy Student

The teacher overheard two of her students talking during a play period. One was a very gregarious little girl, while the other was the shyest boy in class. In fact, through the whole conversation, the boy sat with head down, studying his shoes.

"You love me, and we're gonna get married and live happily ever after, aren't we?" asked the girl.

"Yep," said the boy.

"We'll live in this great big castle and have lots and lots of children, won't we?" the girl insisted.

"Yep," came the reply.

"And, you'll buy me furs and jewels and lots of cars, right?" continued the girl.

"Yep," the boy said once again.

Just then, the girl looked up and saw the teacher listening.

"Oh, Ms. Jones!" exclaimed the girl to the teacher. "Isn't he wonderful? How does he think up all those wonderful things to say?"

119. The Class Clown

Perhaps there is something wrong with me, but I have a particular affinity for "class clowns." Most of the time, I have found their humor truly funny; and once they have learned to put some control on themselves, they really become producers.

I remember one boy whose name was Sam. One day, Sam asked to visit the boy's lavatory, and I gave him a pass. Not a minute later, he came running back and shouted, "Quick, give me some tape and a sheet of paper!" I did.

A minute later, he was back again demanding, "A black marker, please! I need it desperately!" I gave it to him.

Then it occured to me that for all I knew, Sam was out there writing on every wall in the school. I became alarmed, and getting the hall duty teacher to cover my class, I followed him into the boy's room.

The school had just that day installed hand dryers in the lavatories—you know, those devices you push and a jet of hot air blows on your hands until they are dry.

There was Sam, standing next to the first blower, taping the paper I had given him to a spot just above the dryer. Sam stood back to admire his work and I read: "PUSH HERE, AND LISTEN TO A RECORDED SPEECH FROM OUR PRINCIPAL!"

120. Children and Television

The class was discussing television and its impact. The teacher had voiced the opinion that she thought that watching too much television might have a bad effect upon children. As you might expect, the class disagreed.

"We should be allowed to watch whatever we want!"

"Television teaches us things!"

"Television is good for us!"

"I'm afraid that television tends to get you out of touch with reality," protested the teacher.

"Nonsense! Never!" replied the children.

Just then, a thunderstorm that had been threatening for some time broke heavily just above the school. Peal after peal of thunder rattled the window-panes and the room was illuminated with bursts of blue-white light. So sudden was the onslaught, that several children began to wimper.

"Mrs. Smith," said one boy in a fragile voice, "I don't like this!"

"I'm scared!" chimed in another.

"I know what let's do!" exclaimed a third. "Let's change the channel!"

121. Helping Children Learn to Read

"How did you ever manage to get Billy Jones to read?" one teacher asked another. "I had him last year, and he wouldn't go near a book. Now, every time I see him he has a book in his hand. How did you do it?"

"I had the same problem with him," explained his current teacher, "so one day I decided it was time for some 'special' reading tactics."

"What did you do?"

"I got a book which I knew he'd like," she said, "and I waited until I had Billy alone. Then I picked up the book and tossed it on my desk with disgust.

" 'This is terrible,' I said to no one in particular. 'I'm going to have to send this book back!'

" 'Why?' Billy asked as I knew he would.

" 'You won't believe this,' I told him, 'but this book contains a whole section on absolutely foolproof plans for getting out of doing homework. Why, if any of my students read this, they might get out of doing homework ever again!'

"Then I gave him the book and asked him to take it back to the library. It was the first book he read all the way through, and he's been reading ever since!"

122. The "Daydreaming" Student (I)

As I taught the class, I noticed one student who was daydreaming, her eyes fixed on eternity and a smile on her lips.

I touched her shoulder and said, "Having a nice dream?"

"Oh, yes," said the girl, blinking awake. "I was dreaming about the test we took this morning. You were handing back the test papers, and when you got to mine, you were smiling, and I could see a big gold star on the paper."

"Really," I smiled, "and what grade did I say you had gotten on the test?"

The girl replied, "You said, Lizzie, you tell me what grade to put on this paper—after all, it's your dream!"

123. The "Daydreaming" Student (II)

The lesson was going so well that I didn't stop when I noticed that one of the students was daydreaming in his seat. Rather, as the class was leaving, I asked that student to remain.

"Kevin," I said, "I really don't think you should be daydreaming during class, do you?"

"But, Sir," said the student, "it was such a wonderful dream. I was in a big stadium where the Dallas Cowboys were about to play a game. All of a sudden, the Dallas Cowboy Cheerleaders came out, and they grabbed me out of the stands! Then, they all stood around me in those little, tiny costumes—all those beautiful women!"

"Some dream," I had to remark.

"Then," the student continued, "these beautiful women gathered around me, and they asked me to do something so wonderful, I couldn't believe it!"

"And what was that?" I asked with one raised eyebrow.

"It was fantastic!" he exclaimed. "I got to kick off for the game!"

124. The Teacher's Desk

I knew one teacher who had a glowing faith and was an ardent churchgoer. In fact, she brought her Bible to school and would spend some quiet time each day reading it. Each morning, she would put it in the top drawer of her desk, close at hand.

One day, a child in class reported that someone had stolen a dime that was on her desk. The teacher called the class together and spoke to them.

"It is wrong to steal," she told them. "When you take something without permission that isn't yours, that's stealing. It doesn't matter if it's a dime or ten dollars; stealing is wrong. Remember, also, that the Bible says, 'Thou shalt not steal.'

"Billy," she said to a student, "go over to my desk and get my Bible, so I can show the class what it says about stealing."

As Billy headed toward the desk, the teacher continued, "You'll see that we should always be honest."

Just then, Billy spoke up from the teacher's desk.

"OK, you guys," he shouted. "Who stole the teacher's Bible?"

125. *The Newly Married Teacher (I)*

The first day back from summer hiatus, a female teacher whom everyone knew to be unmarried, startled the faculty by bursting into the teacher's lounge and distributing candy and cigars, each cigar wrapped with a band that proclaimed, "It's a Boy!"

Finally, one of the stunned teachers spoke up.

"This couldn't possibly mean what it's supposed to mean?" he asked. "Could it?"

"It means exactly what it says!" exclaimed the jubilant teacher.

"But . . . but . . ." stammered the other teacher.

"It's a boy, all right!" the young woman exclaimed as she displayed her brand new wedding ring. "He's five foot ten, weighs 165 pounds, and I got him!"

126. *The Newly Married Teacher (II)*

The teacher was married during the mid-winter break, and when school had returned to session, she told the class all about her wedding and showed them her gleaming new wedding ring. She also told the class that from now on, her name would be *Mrs.* Jones.

"Mrs. Jones," said one boy, trying out the new name, "do you play baseball?"

"No, Billy, I don't."

"Mrs. Jones, do you follow the teams in the NFL?"

"No."

"Mrs. Jones, do you like to go fishing?"

"No, Billy, I don't like to go fishing at all."

"Good grief!" said Billy to a classmate. "I don't know what the heck the guy sees in her!"

127. The Pregnant Teacher (I)

The teacher was obviously pregnant, and she had been getting so many questions from her first-grade class that she decided to have a talk with them.

"You see," she explained gently, "I'm going to have a baby. Right now, the baby is growing inside of me. That's why my tummy is so big."

The teacher spoke to the class on what she perceived to be their level of understanding and tried to explain what was happening.

Later, two boys from the class were talking.

"Do you believe what Mrs. Hendly told us this morning?" one asked.

"Of course not!" stated the other. "But I'll tell you this: If she gives us a quiz on this, you'd better put it down the way she said, even if it does sound crazy—otherwise, she'll take off credit!"

128. The Pregnant Teacher (II)

The teacher's pregnancy was beginning to show. One day, therefore, she spoke to her class.

"If you have noticed some changes in me," she told them, "it is because of the happy fact that I am pregnant. Do you all understand what that means? Do you know what 'pregnant' means?"

Twenty-seven heads nodded in understanding, and the teacher went on to other things that had to be done.

Later that day, a little girl took the teacher aside.

"Mrs. Langley," said the little girl, "I don't want you to worry. My mommy was in the same condition you're in, and now she's fine."

"Thank you for telling me that," said the teacher. "So, your mother is just fine now?"

"Oh, yes!" said the girl. "When she got fat like you, she went to the health club and they exercised her skinny again. Do you want the number?"

129. The Pregnant Teacher (III)

Just before the pregnant teacher was to go on maternity leave, she gathered her class together and, on the level of their understanding, tried to explain what was happening to her and why she would be gone for a while.

"So you see," the teacher concluded, "all babies come into the world this way through their mommies, and all mommies have their babies in the same way."

"Mrs. Opner," asked a child, "are you sure that *all* mommies have babies in the same way as you are?"

"With little differences, yes, they do."

"All mommies do it the same way as you do?"

"Yes, as I said."

"How about that!" exclaimed the boy. "My Mom was a pregnant teacher, and I never knew it!"

130. Animals in the Classroom

It was "Show and Tell" time again. Little Franny had brought in her puppy and gave a very nice presentation. Then, it was time for questions from the class.

"Is it a boy dog or a girl dog?" asked one student.

Franny immediately picked up the dog, turned it on its back and offered the tail end for her classmates' inspection.

"It's a boy dog," said Franny, "see."

"See what?" asked a student as the teacher began to move in. "How do you know it's a boy?"

"I don't know," answered Franny, still holding the upside-down puppy, "but this is what Daddy did when we got him, and he said it was a boy. I think it has to do with the way the fur grows on his paws!"

131. Wasps on the Ceiling

I have an aversion to insects; I simply don't like them. I particularly don't like things that sting.

It was mid-September of my first teaching year and warm enough to keep the windows open. I was teaching a lesson when I noticed a small hubbub and saw several students looking up.

"Look!" exclaimed one. "We have wasps on the ceiling!"

I ran back to the area, and there they were. In a corner of the ceiling, a swarm of wasps went busily about their tasks.

All at once there was a cry, and a little girl sitting close by began to visibly shake.

"I'm allergic to stings," she wailed. "Please, don't let it get me!"

As if on cue, one of the wasps swooped down and alighted on her shoulder. The child went stark white as she sat frozen in terror. My stomach was turning over, and the hair on my arms literally bristled. I looked at the wasp; I looked at the girl.

My hand shot out almost of its own accord. It surrounded the wasp, pulled it from the child's shoulder, and smashed it flat on the windowsill.

"Come on!" I yelled to the class as I pulled the girl from her seat. "We're getting out of here!"

It really wasn't until some time later that I realized that I had a wasp sting on the palm of my hand. Yes, it hurt; yes, it throbbed; and, yes, now, I was a teacher!

132. Showing a Movie in Class

Back in the days before VCRs, we showed movies in class via the old projector and screen method. The films that we showed would have to be ordered weeks and sometimes months in advance through local libraries or film supply houses. They were delivered to the school, we showed them, and then we mailed them back.

Once, in those days, I had ordered a film on Shakespeare for young audiences. I took the film directly from its mailing container and put it on the projector. The lights went out; the switch was thrown.

Someone blundered. The film can was clearly marked as the film on Shakespeare I had ordered, but when the film itself began to roll, it was obvious that the film had been changed, since there, in living technicolor, were five young ladies clad in the briefest of black bikinis with gold tassels in appropriate places!

The sixth-grade class began to hoot and howl. I fell on the 'off' switch.

"Did you see that!" exclaimed one sixth-grader. "That was great!"

"I'll say!" shouted another. "Just wait until I tell everybody!"

"Tell them what?" I exclaimed in frustration.

"You mean you didn't see?" said the boy. "They were wearing our school colors!"

133. Taking Responsibility

The teacher wanted to teach her class the virtue of responsibility. She asked for volunteers to pass out the books, and one boy took on the chore and did it quite well. When he was finished, the teacher took a piece of candy and very obviously placed it on his desk.

"This is for you," she said so the others would hear, "because you took *responsibility* for what you did just now."

Later that day, the teacher returned from lunch to find the room a mess. Every desk was turned upside-down, and books and papers were lying everywhere. In the middle of the disaster area, three boys sat on the floor, grinning widely.

"And just who is responsible for this mess?" the teacher bellowed.

"We are!" the three students exclaimed together.

"Ma'am," said one of them with a huge smile, "can we have our candy now?"

134. The Use of Improper Language

It was not that the boy used obscenity, for he never did, but his speech was often filled with small vulgarities. Particularly when he was excited or frustrated, one or more would fill his speech.

One day, while working on a difficult math problem, he told his teacher, "Hell, Ma'am! I can't do this damn thing!"

No matter what the teachers did, the boy could not seem to break his speech pattern, so one teacher decided to call home and enlist the aid of the parents.

After she had introduced herself, the teacher very delicately explained some of the things the boy had been saying.

"You mean," questioned the shocked parent, "that he uses the 'D' word and the 'H' word?"

"I'm afraid so," said the teacher.

There was a long pause, as the teacher could hear the parent's breathing rate increase audibly. Finally, the parent burst forth into the phone.

"Damn it all!" said the parent. "I don't know where the hell the kid gets it!"

135. Examinations and Testing (Humorous)

The test was a complete surprise to the class. Most students did about as well as the teacher had expected. One boy, however, did extremely badly on the test. This was surprising, since a check of the teacher's mark book revealed that the boy's homework had been flawless and regularly turned in. How could he do such good homework and then fail a test on the same material so badly?

Then, it dawned upon the teacher that if the boy had cheated and copied his homework from someone else rather than doing it himself, that would explain everything. She decided to talk to the boy.

When she had some privacy with the boy, she stated, "Robby, I'm going to ask you a question, and it is very important that you answer. Now, from whom did you copy your homework?"

The boy fiddled and squirmed, and finally he looked directly at the teacher.

"Gosh, Ms. Simms," he said, "I copied from so many kids, I don't remember who I got the homework from. Honest, Ma'am, if I'd have known you were gonna give a quiz on cheating, I'd have kept notes!"

136. Examinations and Testing (Serious)

"It's no use, Mrs. Bradley," said the student. "I just can't get this stuff. I'm gonna fail the test for sure."

"No, you're not," stated the teacher, "because I'm going to help you study for it."

Mrs. Bradley did just that. For the entire week, she met with the girl during recess and lunchtime and after school, slowly and painstakingly going over the material and explaining over and over and over again, until light dawned in the child's eyes.

Test day came and went, and the following morning the teacher handed back the corrected tests. The young student got a very respectable *B*!

"Gosh, Mrs. Bradley," said the student later on, "thanks for helping me pass this test. Thanks for doing all this for me."

"In all honesty," said the teacher, "part of it I did for you, but I also did it for myself."

"For yourself?" the child wondered. "What do you mean?"

"Didn't you know," asked the teacher, "that you are my test?"

137. Cleanliness in the Classroom (I)

The teacher had the students clean the classroom in preparation for a visit by parents the following day. In fact, the students worked most of the afternoon, picking up and dusting and polishing.

"Remember, class," the teacher intoned, "cleanliness is next to godliness!"

The work continued for several minutes more, when the teacher again exclaimed, "Cleanliness is next to godliness! Remember that!"

Five minutes later, the busy students again heard the teacher proclaim, "Cleanliness is next to godliness!"

At which point, one girl stood up from her dusting chores and proclaimed, "In that case, couldn't we just pray and ask God to move to another location for one day?"

138. Cleanliness in the Classroom (II)

In preparation for the guest speaker, the teacher insisted that the children clean the classroom. This had taken all morning, but now it was afternoon and the speaker had arrived.

The classroom was spotless. In fact, it positively gleamed. The speaker even commented on the condition of the place.

"What a lovely room!" commented the speaker. "What a wonderful bulletin board! What beautiful children you are! Honestly, I could just burst with pride and love!"

"Not here!" one youngster exclaimed, pointing with his thumb at the teacher, "or that old slave driver will make you clean it up!"

139. Cleanliness in the Classroom (III)

It was the end of the school year, and the children's excitement level was running high.

"One moment," said the teacher. "Before we leave for the summer, we have to make certain that everything is cleaned and put away."

So, the students worked: cleaning desks and putting books away, carrying things to the custodian to be discarded, taking down the bulletin board and seeing that all loose materials were stored in the closet, and the thousand and one other "little things" that have to be accomplished before school can shut down.

"Ma'am," said one busy student, "do we have to do this?"

"Certainly," explained the teacher. "We have to leave the room spotless."

"That makes no sense to me," the student continued half to himself. "We clean it up when there's gonna be nobody here to see it, and in two months a new class is gonna come in, and in less than a week, they'll probably have it dirtier than we ever did!"

140. The "Normal" Student

A teacher was passing by a room in school when she heard something and went to investigate. There was another teacher, seated at her desk, weeping. Naturally, the first teacher rushed to her aid.

"Jean," said the teacher, "whatever's wrong?"

"This," said the other. "I just got a report from the Child Study Team on that new student who transferred in."

"Is it bad?" asked the first teacher.

"According to this, the boy has a normal IQ; he's the right size and weight for his age; he's already adjusted well to the school; he's not dyslexic; he's not hyperactive; he has no discernable learning problems; he lives at home with both of his natural parents; and sometimes, he gets lazy and needs to be prodded to do his homework."

"But," said the first teacher, "that's a wonderful report! Whatever are you crying about?"

"I'm crying with joy!" exclaimed the second teacher. "Do you know how long it's been since I've had a *normal* student?"

141. The "Special" Student (I)

One of the students in our class was really active in gymnastics. She was very special, indeed, and had entered a number of competitions, placing well in several of them.

One day, I had planned to give an oral test, which I had discussed with my principal, who told me that he might drop in to see how it was going. My "special" student, however, had been in a competition the afternoon before, and she had won first place.

I figured the oral test could wait for a moment, and I asked the child to tell us all about what had happened. This she did with great enthusiasm, describing all the routines and activities that she had witnessed.

"Now," she concluded, "let me show you the special moves I did at the end of my routine!"

Before I could say anything, the girl did a handstand on my desk, pushed off, and did a summersault, landing perfectly on her feet.

Just as this was going on, the principal entered the room. He caught the final tumble and landing, and stood quietly while the class applauded.

"Well," he said, looking straight at me, "I don't know if that answer was right or wrong, but I'd certainly give her an *A* for effort!"

142. The "Special" Student (II)

As part of a mainstreaming effort, one of the children from the special education room was assigned to my class. The boy had some problems, without doubt, but I have seldom met a more willing student. I liked him instantly, and was all the more upset, therefore, when he began having trouble with some of the other students in the class.

There was a name-calling incident on the playground, and some instances of putting "kick me" signs on his back or distracting him and hiding his notebook. I was trying hard to keep on top of it, but I wasn't succeeding too well.

Then, one day, some students, including the "special" boy, were at the blackboard doing problems. The "special" boy did his entirely wrong.

"Dummy!" shouted a voice from the back of the room.

I whirled around with fire leaping from my eyes, but the "special" boy spoke first.

"Maybe I am a dummy," he said slowly, "but if I am, why don't you teach me what to do instead of just calling me names? You don't have trouble; I do. Don't you know that I'm here so you can have the chance to help?"

There was not one bit of trouble from that day on!

143. The Joy of Reading

The girl loved to read. Whenever you saw her, in fact, she had a book with her.

One spring day during her lunchtime, the girl was seated on the steps of the school when a truck passing the school lost control and smashed into the truck ahead of him. That truck was carrying a load of chickens and geese, which flew into the air upon impact and landed all over the lawn of the school, quacking and honking loudly as they were chased by many laughing students.

A passing driver, gawking at the commotion, ran over a fire hydrant which sent a magnificent spray of water into the sky. This rapidly formed a puddle in the front lawn, and several geese began to wade in.

The young lady put down her book and gazed towards the heavens.

"Reading is such a joy," she said to no one in particular. "What else can take you away from your boring and humdrum existence?"

144. Student Sent to the Principal

"I want you to talk to this boy," said the teacher to the principal.

"What has he done?" asked the principal.

"Every day," explained the teacher, "he goes back to the supply closet, takes a jar of paste, opens it, throws away the lid, and licks the paste. The paste jars are drying out without lids!"

Later that afternoon, the principal brought the boy to the classroom.

"He won't throw away the lid of the paste jar anymore," stated the principal.

"What did you do?" the teacher asked when the child had taken his seat.

"Simple," replied the principal, "I simply told him that the lid was the tastiest part!"

145. Student Sent to the Principal (II)

A student from the "gifted and talented" class had misbehaved and was sent to the principal.

The principal, who had had a hard morning and was looking at a harder afternoon, looked once at the girl and the referral slip.

"All right," the principal snapped, "sit down over there; keep your mouth shut, and don't you move an inch!"

With that, the principal returned to his office to attend to another pressing matter.

"Well!" huffed the G&T student. "I must say that if he maintains that attitude I will certainly not consider sending my children to this school!"

146. The Class Play

The young teacher had a rather difficult class, and she often sought advice from the more experienced veterans in the school. Therefore, when she decided to volunteer to put on a class play, she went to the other teachers to find out what they thought about it.

Sometime later, the principal of the school dropped by to talk to the teacher about the play. She had done many herself, and she wanted to make sure that the young teacher knew what she was getting into.

"Tell me," said the principal, "where will you get the makeup?"

"The parents will supply that," said the teacher.

"What about props like tables and chairs?"

"Again," said the teacher, "we'll raid the kid's garages and attics."

Then the principal thought about the old curtain that hung on the back wall of the stage in the gym.

"And what backdrop will you use?" the principal questioned. "You know, what will you produce it against?"

"That's easy," stated the young educator, "the advice of every other teacher in the school!"

147. The Class Picnic/Field Day

When the class picnic and field day was announced, there was great joy in the room. When it was announced that it would be held at a certain nearby park, there was even more rejoicing. The reason was that the park in question had a stream where many a local child liked to go to swim on a summer's day.

"However," announced the teacher, "there will be no swimming during the field day."

So, a plot began to brew among some of the children that they would sneak off during the festivities, meet at the river, and take a forbidden swim.

When the teacher heard of this, she called together all the parents and teachers who would be going and advised them to closely watch every exit from the assigned area.

"Watch those exits like hawks," she told them.

On the day of the picnic, the teacher was congratulating herself on her resourcefulness, when she noticed one boy with a dripping wet head. Then, she noticed another and another.

"All right," she said to one of the children, "I'm not mad, but please tell me how you got to the river? I know I had every exit blocked!"

"Yes, Ma'am, you did," answered the dripping boy. "You covered every exit from the field! But, you didn't think of covering the *entrance*, did you?"

148. Using the Blackboard

Mrs. Schell was a highly respected veteran teacher. Indeed, she had taught the parents of some of her current students. One day, Mr. Schell held a classroom presentation to which all the parents of the children were invited.

Before Mrs. Schell arrived, one of the parents who highly esteemed her wrote on the blackboard:

THIS SCHOOL
IS
MRS. SCHELL

When the teacher arrived, she was visibly touched by the tribute, and stood by the blackboard to address the assembled parents. When she turned to face her audience, her head and shoulder blocked part of the message. It blocked the letters *MRS. SC.*

The principal was passing by with the vice-principal, took a quick look through the glass in the classroom door, and turned to his companion.

"Hmmm!" he said. "It looks as if Mrs. Schell is regaling the parents with tales of her life in the classroom."

149. Children and Community Service

There is a church in our community that predates the Revolutionary War. It is considered a historic landmark, and the community is quite proud of it.

Understandably, it requires a great deal of maintenance. In fact, several years back, a civic group got together and offered to paint the structure. They didn't have much money, and the paint they used was of a poor quality, causing much streaking and discoloration within a relatively short time.

The Civics Club at the local high school was looking for a community project, and they considered sprucing up the historic site. It would be strictly volunteer work and would introduce the students to community service and pride.

"One thing," said the president of the club. "If we do this, let's do it right. Let's get really good paint, the kind you don't have to add paint thinner to, and the kind that will really cover over without streaking."

"Agreed," said another student, "and I know just the motto we should use to raise funds!"

"What's that?"

"Since it is a church," the student replied, "how about RE-PAINT AND THIN NO MORE!"

150. The Class and Summer Vacation

It was the last day of school, and the class parents had thrown a small party for the children. Now, the party was over, everything had been cleaned, all books and materials were put away for the summer, and the final bell had rung, dismissing the exuberant children.

The teacher came back from seeing her class off on the summer hiatus to discover four of the class mothers sitting in the room, their eyes filled with tears.

"Oh," said the teacher, "I understand completely. Over this year you have been privileged to witness the growth and development of your children. Therefore, this day is bound to be a letdown. I *do* understand."

"You *don't* understand," sniffed one mother. "School is over, all right, and that means we're gonna have them at home all day for the next two months!"

PRINCIPALS AND THEIR PRINCIPLES—A CLOSER LOOK AT SCHOOL ADMINISTRATION

The school administrator is in the forefront of education. Often, that means that he or she is the first person to meet head-on with the problems that beset the modern school. The hours are long and the work is hard, but, like every position in education, it has its rewards and its drawbacks.

In this section, we'll take a look at the principal of the school as others see him, as he sees himself, and as he goes through the vast interplay of contacts and decisions that are his alone. Sometimes, it is quite a trip!

151. The Difficulty of the Task (I)

The principal had worked at her desk all morning and most of the afternoon. Her back was stiff and her eyes refused to focus, so she thought it an excellent time to take a break from the heavy work load. She left the office and began to stroll the halls of the school.

As she walked down one hallway, she came face to face with a second-grader named Howard.

"I know who you are," affirmed the boy. "You're the principal!"

"Yes, I am. What are you doing in the halls?"

"I'm coming back from the boy's room," he answered. "What are you doing?"

"Well," smiled the principal, "I'm taking a relaxing walk down the hall."

"Shhh!" breathed Howard, "Not so loud!"

"What?"

"Don't you know yet?" the boy continued, looking furtively up and down the hallway, "If they find out you have nothing to do, they'll give you busy work!"

152. The Difficulty of the Task (II)

"What's it like being a principal?" someone asked.

"Let me tell you a story," replied the veteran administrator.

"I once visited a large city, and I took a cab from the airport, giving the driver the name and address of my hotel. It was the wildest ride of my life. That cabbie must have travelled sixty and seventy miles per hour over the city streets, barely missing cars and pedestrians along the way.

"After what seemed an eternity, we were still not at the hotel, and I thought I recognized a landmark on the opposite side of town from where I was staying.

" 'Driver,' I said, 'are you certain you know where my hotel is located?'

" 'Mister,' replied the cabbie, 'this is my first day driving a taxi. I don't know where the heck I'm going, but I'm going there as fast as I can!'

"Now there was a man who understood what it means to be a principal!"

153. The Principal and the Board of Education (Humorous)

The board of education in the small school district decided personally to do the interviewing for several jobs they had open. One job was that of assistant custodian and the other was for a secondary school principal. Somehow, the papers got mixed up, and when the candidate for the principalship appeared, the Board thought they were interviewing for the custodian's job.

"Have you had much experience washing and waxing floors?" asked the board president.

"Well, some . . . " answered the uneasy educator.

"Do you think you could do a good job cleaning desks?"

"I . . . I guess I could."

"Part of your job description is the cleaning of the student lavatories. Do you have any objection to that?" asked a board member.

"Look," said the frustrated candidate, "I want you to know that I'll do whatever it takes to get the job done, but I think you should know that this is a terrible waste of a Ph.D.!"

154. The Principal and the Board of Education (Serious)

For whatever reason, the president of the local board of education was not 100 percent certain about the new principal. One day the board president went to the principal's office.

"Look," said the president, "I have a proposition for you. You know those new textbooks that have been ordered for your building? What if you just said they arrived, and you and I split the money?"

"Really," said the principal, "and what if I told you to take a flying leap off the nearest bridge? What if I told you I quit!"

"What if I told you," said the president, "that all my doubts about you are gone? What if I apologized and told you I really want to work with you for this school?"

"Then," said the principal, "maybe we'd better stop asking so many questions and start looking for some answers!"

The two men have worked together in harmony for the past twenty years.

155. How the Job is Overwhelming

The principal came into his office one morning to find a stack of paperwork on his desk easily two feet high. He set about attacking it, but there were so many people to see and telephone calls to take, that by noon, hardly an inch of the stack had disappeared. To get more room on his desk, he removed the stack and placed it on the floor near his chair.

Just as he had finished that chore, the door to his office opened and his secretary entered, carrying a two and one-half foot stack of papers.

"Good, you finished the morning's work."

"These," she said, depositing the stack in the freshly cleared space, "have to be finished by the end of the day!"

156. How the Job is Time-Consuming

The newlywed bride was talking to her friend.

"Every day," she said, "I prepare a lovely dinner; something very tasty and unique. Then I set the table with a fresh tablecloth, cloth napkins, the best china and silverware, and candles in crystal holders.

"At precisely six o'clock, I light the candles, put the food on the table and turn on some soft and romantic music."

"How wonderful!" exclaimed the friend. "Then your husband sits down at the table and the two of you enjoy a relaxed and romantic dinner for two!"

"Don't be ridiculous," said the new bride. "My husband's the principal of the high school; he hasn't been home before nine in the past two weeks . . ."

"Then, what . . ."

"It's like my husband often tells me," smiled the principal's wife, "it's the principle of the thing that counts!"

157. The Principal in the Classroom (I)

The principal had been invited to the classroom to speak as part of a "Career Awareness Day" in the third grade. A police officer, a fire fighter, a scientist, and the like had all given their talks, and now it was the principal's turn.

On the level of third-grade understanding, the principal described his job and even told the children the salaries they might expect should they enter professional education as a career. Finally, the principal went through the educational background necessary for the position, detailing college and graduate school as part of the academic preparation.

"Now," concluded the principal, "are there any questions?"

"I'm never gonna be a principal," volunteered one child. "I could never stay in school all that time just to get a job."

"But, you need your education to get a job," continued the principal.

"Not me," said the child. "I got it all figured out, and the minute I learn enough to get a job that pays me $250,000 a year, I'm gonna kiss this place goodbye!"

158. The Principal in the Classroom (II)

The sixth-grade class was in the middle of a social studies class. The teacher was explaining the concepts of private property and the rights of the individual.

"So the owner of the property," explained the teacher, "has the right to say who does or does not come on his property. If someone comes on the property and the owner wants him to leave, that person must go, or the owner can call the police and have the person taken off. Possibly, that person might even be arrested for trespassing."

At that point, the principal of the school came in and took a seat in the back of the room.

One sixth-grader reached over to another who was about to sail a paper airplane across the room.

"Cool it, Bruce!" said the boy, pointing a thumb at the principal. "That's the guy who owns the school!"

159. Administering Discipline (I)

Two boys were brought to the principal's office for fighting on the playground. The principal seated them in her office on opposite sides of the room.

"Don't you realize," she began, "that when you fight, you place a black mark on this school. When you fight, you are telling this neighborhood that this is a bad place to be. When you fight, you are taking the fine reputation of this school and dragging it through the mud."

The children's eyes were beginning to fill, and the principal knew she was on the right track.

"Have you no pride in your school?" she continued. "Have you no respect for your school? Have you no loyalty for your school? Have you no love for your school?"

"Please stop!" said one of the offenders. "We have loyalty; we have pride; we love this school!"

"Yes!" chimed in the second student. "It's just that as much as we love the school, we really hate each other!"

160. Administering Discipline (II)

The student was referred to the office for disciplinary reasons, and before the principal saw the boy, he looked up his record and spoke with the teacher involved and the guidance counselor. Finally, the student was called into the office.

"Sit down," ordered the principal. "Your name is Bob Smith; you are in seventh grade; this is the seventh time this year that you have been sent to the office. You were sent here because the teacher asked you a question in class, and you said, 'Who the hell cares!', tossed your textbook in the air, kicked over your desk and sat there with your arms folded, refusing to speak."

"How did you know all that?" said the startled young man, his eyes wide.

"Bob," said the principal as he leaned in to the boy, "I know everything . . ."

"Then will you please tell me when Peter the Great became Czar of Russia?" asked the boy. "That's the dumb question that got me in trouble in the first place!"

161. Administering Discipline (III)

Two second-graders decided to play hookey one bright spring day. They were "picked up" and returned to school less than an hour later, and they now sat in the principal's office awaiting judgement.

"You two don't realize what a privilege it is to be able to attend school," the principal began. "Throughout our history, brave men and women have fought and died to give you the right to an education.

"And, think of the people from history who went through hardship to attend school. Think of Daniel Boone, who had to walk a great distance to get to school and had to carry a rifle to fight off bears and other wild animals. Now, you two just think of that for a while!"

Then the principal left the office, allowing the two offenders some time to think over what they had just been told.

There was silence for a moment, and then one second-grader leaned over to the other.

"You know," he said, "I don't think I'd mind coming to school if I could go hunting on the way!"

162. Setting the Tone of the School

The principal of the building wore a fresh white shirt every day, never a blue or a tan or a stripe. He also wore black ties almost exclusively. Indeed, it was rumored that he had a tie rack at home that held twenty-four ties, all black. He had also, over the years, managed to put on fifty extra pounds that gave him a distinctive appearance.

One day, he got up on stage and addressed the junior class.

"As principal," he told them, "it is my job to lead the way. I will not ask you to do anything that I would not do myself, but I do ask you to follow me in setting a tone for our school; a tone which encourages each of us to do his or her best.

"I will work hard for you, and I expect you to work equally as hard in return. I ask you to follow me as I set an example for you."

Sure enough, the next day the entire junior class came to school wearing white shirts, black ties, and with a pillow stuffed into their pants!

163. Dealing with the Faculty (I)

The teacher was on the phone with his wife.

"Yes," he said, "I know I promised to take the kids for new shoes after school today, but I had forgotten that there was going to be a faculty meeting!

"No, I can't just skip it; the principal is going to be speaking.

"No, I don't know when it's going to be over; it'll end when the principal finishes speaking."

Just then, the teacher saw the principal coming down the hallway toward him.

"Just a minute," the teacher said into the phone, "I'll ask him.

"Excuse me, Mr. Jones," the teacher shouted to the principal, "my wife would like to know if you're going to be interesting, informative, or just over-long?"

164. Dealing with the Faculty (II)

Every school has its "prophet of doom," the one person on the faculty or staff who *never* has a cheerful or positive word to say about anything.

So it was one morning that just such a person was holding forth in the faculty lounge.

"This school is a mess!" he proclaimed. "It is lacking true discipline; we have no leadership; the curriculum is pitiful; the organization barely exists; we are headed for an educational downfall that will destroy us all!"

At just that point, the teacher turned around and came face to face with the principal who had slipped in for a cup of coffee and caught most of the tirade.

The teacher paused for less than half a second before continuing.

"And, that," he announced in his strongest voice, "is exactly what *this* school would be like were it not for the sterling leadership of our current administration!"

165. Dealing with the Faculty (III)

It had been a particularly trying year for the new principal. Not only were there several notable academic and behavioral problems in the school, but the budget had been defeated and several groups of citizens were concerned about their special interests. To top it off, there had also been a number of contract disputes concerning the faculty and a number of grievances had been filed.

Everyone had lived through it, however, and it was the end of the school year. With a sigh, the principal watched everyone go.

One morning during the summer, he took some time and went for his annual physical checkup. When he returned, he found the assistant superintendent of schools waiting for him in his office.

"Well," said the superintendent, "Your first year is over, and I know you had a rough time of it, particularly with those union grievances, but I'd like to know if you got anything out of it. Can you say anything positive about it?"

"Why, certainly," stated the principal, "I just got back from the doctor's, and the positive news is that over the past year, I only lost *half* my hair and I only have *two* new ulcers!"

166. The Principal at the Faculty Meeting

As any professional educator knows, faculty meetings can be deadly. Sometimes, material is gone over in such a dry manner that eyes begin to close.

It was quite unique, therefore, that every faculty meeting held in our school was filled with highly attentive faculty members who virtually hung on every word. No one half-dozed or corrected papers or did anything except listen to the principal as she expounded on the problems of our school and their possible solutions.

I asked her one day, how she accounted for her success at these faculty meetings and how she managed to have everyone so attentive.

"What I do," she told me, "is to figure out what we have to cover during the meeting. Then I go to each teacher and ask him or her what they think needs to be done about it. At that point I thank them for their input and tell them to be certain to listen at the next faculty meeting, for I am certain they will hear their views voiced by me! Believe me, they have never failed to pay attention!"

167. Dealing with the Custodial Staff

The young principal was assigned to the school he would serve, and he went for a visit a week before he was scheduled to take over. It was during the summer hiatus, and desks and file cabinets littered the hallways as rooms were in the process of being painted and thoroughly cleaned.

As he entered the building, he noticed a pile of books, tied with a string, that were lying on the floor, directly in front of the main entrance.

Thinking this might be a hazard, the young principal picked up the books and moved them to a nearby table.

"Hey!" came a voice from down the hall, "Stop that!"

The voice belonged to a large man who wore the work clothes of the custodial staff.

"What are you doing?" he roared.

"I was moving these books," answered the young principal.

"Well, I'm the head custodian," proclaimed the man, "and it is definitely *my* job to move things. That's the trouble with you young teachers, you don't know the rules. You come in, and the first thing you know, you start doing my job!

"I tell you, kid, you're lucky the new principal isn't here yet, or I'd have him yell at you for trying to bust the Union!"

168. Interplay with the Student Body (I)

The principal had some bad news for the student council. Due to inflationary pressures, the board of education had cut the budget, and there would be no funds available for several student functions.

When the principal announced this, there was a great deal of disappointment, and several students asked for a further explanation, which the principal gave.

"It is inflation," the principal concluded, "pure and simple. Everything is rising; everything is going up, up, up!"

"Excuse me," said the student council president, "I know of one thing that will *not* be going up."

"Oh, what's that?"

"The students' opinion of the board of education!" she answered.

169. *Interplay with the Student Body (II)*

The principal, an ardent outdoorsman, had volunteered to take charge of a band of students who, as part of a project, were going to a nearby nature area.

After hiking for half a day, the principal ordered the camp to be pitched for the night.

"Now," he told the class, "I have a surprise for you. I did not bring any food for this evening. Instead, we are going to learn to live off the land. We'll fish; we'll hunt; we'll pick berries. We'll eat only those things we take for ourselves with our own hands. Could anything be better?"

"Sir," volunteered one child, "I think it would be better to just call one of those pizza places—they deliver!"

170. *An Unusual Student Remembered*

There was a student in the school who had become noted for his honesty as well as his intelligence. He had served as student council treasurer and president, and everyone in the school, both teachers and students, trusted this boy implicitly.

One day, the young man was in the library reading a book on law when I chanced by. I remarked upon his choice of reading matter and asked about his future plans.

"I intend to go into business," he told me, "but first I'm going to get a degree in corporate law."

"Very commendable," I remarked, "but why corporate law?"

"Sir," answered the young man, holding up the book he had been reading, "you would be surprised at all the sneaky stuff you can do in business and still stay legally honest. I don't want to miss one of them!"

171. *Encouraging Parental Participation*

The principal spoke to a group of school parents about their participation in the educational process of their children.

"You have a great responsibility," the principal proclaimed. "You must add to the future of this school; you must see to it that this school will continue to provide quality education; it is your duty to leave this school prepared for tomorrow!"

When his speech was finally over, there was tremendous applause, and the mothers flocked around the principal, congratulating him on his fine speech.

Finally, one mother took him aside.

"That was a wonderful speech," she said. "Yes, it is our duty to do something for this school. Oh, you've really inspired me, and I know just what I'm going to do to add to this school!"

"And what is that?" the principal asked.

"I'm rushing home right now," said the mother, "and getting pregnant again!"

172. The Principal and the Bond Issue

When the bond issue hit the town, the first thing it did was to polarize the community. As many people were for it as were against it, and both sides had solid reasons for their beliefs.

The principal of the high school had been asked to speak at several groups, but he did not desire to alienate any members of the community. Therefore, he prepared two speeches, one for the bond issue and one against the bond issue, which he gave before the appropriate group.

One evening, he went out to speak before a civic group, stood up and gave his speech roundly condemning the bond issue and giving the reasons against its passage. He was all but through when the president of the group slipped him a folded sheet of paper. It read, 'We are in favor of the Bond Issue!'

"Now," continued the principal without missing a beat, "I have just told you everything our opponents would say in their behalf, so let's look at the bond issue realistically, and I'll give you the truth of the matter!"

173. The Principal and School Athletics

The principal had promised to attend the big basketball game that was going to be held that afternoon in the gym. Pressing matters, however, tied him up in his office until well after the game had started, so he was late arriving.

He rushed in and sat down just as one of the school's athletes made a basket which put the school ahead by two points.

"Yes!" shouted the principal, "Tremendous! Great!"

The crowd around him stayed absolutely quiet.

Again, the school's team went ahead, and again the principal shouted, "That's the way! Go, guys, go!!!"

Again, the crowd around him made not a sound.

"What is the matter with you people?" the principal finally exploded. "Have you no school spirit? Have you no pride? Why aren't you cheering?"

Just then, one of the spectators reached over and tapped the principal on the shoulder.

"Sir," said a person the principal had never seen before, "we have a great deal of pride, but if you'll look around you, I think you'll find that you're sitting in the visitor's section!"

174. The Principal and School Expansion

There were plans to expand the school, since there was a perceptible need for more room. A bond issue had been proposed, and argument ensued everywhere.

One day, a group of "concerned citizens" came into the office and asked for a tour of the school.

The principal took them around personally and showed them the crowded conditions, but the group seemed unimpressed.

"This doesn't look *that* crowded," said one on the way back to the office.

"You can always squeeze in an extra chair," said another.

When the group got to the office, the principal asked them to step into his office to get their coats.

When all of them were inside, the principal opened the door to the narrow coat closet in his office and stuck his head inside.

"Excuse me for interrupting the gym class," he shouted into the closet, "but might I have our visitors' coats?"

175. Dealing with Parents

It had been a particularly harrowing day, with one phone call after another from either angry parents or parents concerned about their child's progress. Nonetheless, the phone had simply never stopped ringing.

Now, in late afternoon, the principal was exhausted.

"Well," said the school secretary as she prepared to leave for the day, "it's been quite a time. Is there anything I can do before I leave?"

"Yes," said the principal, "find out the names and locations of every orphanage in the area."

"Orphanages?"

"Yes," continued the principal. "Call them and tell them I'll work there for half my salary, just to be in a place where I don't have to deal with parents!"

176. The Principal and the PTA (I)

The principal's friend was about to become a father for the first time. As chance would have it, the man was visiting with the principal in the school when an urgent call came through that the man's wife had gone into labor and was being taken to the local hospital.

"You're in no condition to drive," said the principal. "I'll take you!"

With a stern determination, the principal wove expertly through heavy traffic, taking shortcuts over bumpy roads and arriving at the hospital just in time for the gentleman to join his wife in the delivery room.

Later, as the principal stood with his friend admiring his daughter, the man turned to the principal.

"I really appreciate your getting me here in time," said the man. "How can I ever thank you?"

"It's enough thanks to see that lovely, healthy baby," answered the principal.

Then, with a smile and a wink of the eye, the principal added, "Not to mention the fact that I now have a volunteer to head the PTA fundraiser, don't I?"

177. The Principal and the PTA (II)

In a drive to get more fathers to join the PTA, the principal sent home a "special" invitation to a "Dads Only" night. He also asked all the teachers to push the affair with their children and get out those fathers.

The evening turned out to be a huge success with a large attendance of fathers. The principal made a concerted effort to get these men to volunteer to join the PTA.

"I want this school to be a place where you, the fathers of our students, can feel at home," said the principal in conclusion. "If you come to a PTA meeting and you feel like taking off your shoes, you just go right ahead!"

"Can we also bring a TV set and watch the football game?" smiled one father.

"Certainly," answered the principal, "and to make you feel even more at home, I'll arrange for a group of our teachers to circulate among you and scream at you to shut the blasted things off!"

178. The Principal and the Union

The union representatives on the faculty had complained that they couldn't get a straight answer out of the principal. Naturally, that was denied by the principal. Finally, it was decided to have a meeting between the union representatives and the principal.

"Our problem," stated one of the representatives, "is that we never know with any certainty where you stand on an issue. We feel that you are often evasive with your answers."

"That is completely untrue!" affirmed the principal. "I think all of my answers are straightforward and to the point. I do not think that I equivocate."

"We think you do," said the representative.

"I tell you what," said the principal, "you ask me a probing and provocative question, and I'll give you a firm and decisive answer."

"All right," said the representative. "Do you believe that educators should have unions?"

Said the principal, "Yes and no."

179. When the School is Honored

The school had received a marvelous evaluation, and on top of that, the IOWA scores had returned showing the school to have the highest test results in the township and the county. Naturally, the newspapers picked this up, and there were several articles about the school and its principal in the local press.

The principal was in her office the day after the articles appeared and she received a call from her old friend, the principal of a school in another county. The secretary informed the principal that the caller said it was urgent business.

"Jane?" said the caller. "Is that you? Are you all right?"

"Certainly," said the principal, "I'm fine."

"You're alive, then, and in good health?"

"Of course I'm alive, Frank," said the principal. "Come on, what is this?"

"Well," said the friend, "I was just reading about you in the newspaper, and I figured that the only time anyone would say things that nice about you would be if you were dead, so I just called to see if you had kicked the bucket!"

180. Principals and Politics

Two local politicians were invited to attend a meeting of the local board of education. One of the items on the agenda was the confirmation of a new principal in the township. When the time came for that, the board president asked the principal candidate if he wanted to say anything before the board voted.

"Ladies and gentlemen," began the prospective principal, "ever since the days when our forefathers fought for liberty on this soil, America has stood for progress in education . . ."

The man went on like that for the next fifteen minutes, quoting the Declaration of Independence, the Bible, and several plays of Shakespeare.

"With hope and trust in the greatness of our nation," he concluded, "we will face tomorrow united and confident of victory!"

The crowd applauded wildly and jumped to their feet. As the applause died down, one politician leaned over to the other.

"If he doesn't get to be principal," said the local politico, "let's ask him to run for mayor—he's a natural born politician!"

181. The Principal and the School (I)

The principal was entertaining a group of citizens who were in the process of demanding major changes to the school without ever indicating where the funds for these changes would be coming from.

"I will have to admit," said the principal, "that some of your suggestions are very sound. I don't know of a school anywhere that couldn't use extra classroom space. Certainly, a new library would be a very welcome addition. This item, however, has me somewhat puzzled. You know, the suggestion about the swimming pool."

"What's so odd about that?" asked one citizen. "Lots of schools have swimming pools!"

"True," said the principal, "but not in every room!"

182. The Principal and the School (II)

"You will find," the older principal told the younger, "that it is not the great and grand problems that will make your life miserable; it is the tiny day-to-day annoyances that will drive you up a wall."

"Why do you suppose that is?" asked the younger.

"Let me ask you a question first," stated the older principal. "What is the difference between a log and a splinter?"

"Well, they're both wood, so that isn't it. I suppose it's that one is large and the other is small?"

"Not quite," smiled the other. "They are like the problems you will face. They're both made out of the same thing, but—you can sit comfortably on a log!"

183. The Principal and a Winning Team

The school team had just won the championship game, and on his way to the locker room, the principal was bragging to the reporters who surrounded him.

"Not only does our team possess superior physical ability," commented the principal, "but each one of our players is an honor student with outstanding academic abilities!"

When they got to the locker room, there was great joy everywhere. The principal stood on a bench and addressed the jubilant team. He told them how proud he was of them and what a fine job they had done. Finally, with reporters' cameras flashing, he lowered his eyes and assumed a serious tone.

"I just want you to know that today, each one of you played with sagacity and fervor!"

One student athlete raised his arm.

"Sir," the boy said, "could you point out those two kids? They must be new to the team!"

184. The Administrator and the Secretary

A new intercom system was installed between the secretary's desk and the principal's office. Now, instead of shouting, all the administrator had to do was push a button and the intercom on the secretary's desk would buzz.

At first, it was a novelty; then it became a convenience; finally, the secretary came to dread its buzzing as the principal was constantly calling her in for every little matter.

One afternoon, just as the secretary was preparing to leave for the day, the principal went to close a drawer in his desk and closed it directly on his index finger. He let out a yelp of pain and proceeded to dance around his office, holding the throbbing digit.

Attracted by the noise, the secretary opened the door to the principal's office, stood in the door frame, and took in the situation.

"Well," she said without sympathy, "if all I did all day was sit in here and push that buzzer, I'm sure *my* finger would cramp up, too!"

185. *Administrator as Viewed by Secretary*

As the secretary was about to leave for the day, she stopped by the principal's office. There was the principal hard at work on a stack of paperwork that would take her several more hours to finish.

"When I see you working so long and so hard," the secretary commented, "I am cut to the heart!"

"Thank you," said the principal. "Do you think you could manage to stay an extra hour and help me with this mess?"

"Did I say, 'cut'?" remarked the secretary as she glanced at her watch. "Perhaps 'pin-pricked' would be a somewhat better description!"

186. *Administrator as Viewed by Students (I)*

The principal had a reputation for always keeping a positive attitude. Whenever he was seen, whether by a student or a teacher, he was always smiling.

One day, two students were walking down the hallway when they chanced upon the principal.

"Hello, boys," smiled the principal. "Lovely day, isn't it?"

When the principal had passed, one boy turned to the other.

"What a great guy!" he said. "He's always happy and smiling!"

"He can afford to," said the other as he glanced over his report card, "he doesn't have to take gym and civics!"

187. *Administrator as Viewed by Students (II)*

During the "Career Day" assembly, the principal had spoken eloquently of the rewards of a career in education. He had not only extolled teaching, but he exhorted those who were interested to seriously think about setting their goals toward becoming a school administrator.

Following the activity, one student sought out the principal.

"I want you to know," said the student, "that your speech really got to me and set me thinking."

"I'm very pleased," said the administrator.

"In fact," continued the student, "I have made up my mind to work toward becoming a principal."

"Wonderful!" exclaimed the educator. "So, you want to help future generations of students to learn and achieve and have a hand in developing the future of our nation!"

"Heck, no!" said the student. "I want to become a principal so I can tell these blasted teachers where to get off!"

188. *Administrator as Viewed by the Coach*

The principal faced a hard decision. The star athlete on the basketball team had failed to meet the academic requirements for being on the team. To make matters worse, the big game was to be played in three days, and the coach had based the entire team strategy on that one player.

Yet the principal realized that education and not athletics was the primary task of the school, so he had no choice but to bar the failing student from play. Now, he faced the unhappy task of informing the coach.

"Coach," said the principal when the coach was seated in his office, "Johnson has failed all subjects; I'm removing him from the team as of now."

The coach's jaw dropped, his hands started to shake, he began to breathe heavily, and sweat stood out on his brow. The principal thought the man was having a heart attack, but after a drink of water and some deep breathing, the coach regained his composure.

"I'm so sorry," said the principal. "Are you all right now?"

"Yeah," sighed the coach, "but the next time you have news like that to give me, could you try to break it to me easy? You know, like . . . first tell me that my wife has left me!"

189. *Administrator as Viewed by the Public*

When the new principal was hired, the school board prepared a flyer detailing the distinguished career of the educator and sent it out to all the homes in the school district.

"Hey, Martha," said one citizen to his wife. "Look at this. It tells about the lady who's going to be the new principal. It says here that she was a teacher and department head in two school districts, chief guidance counselor in another district, served as a vice-principal in another school system, and now she's coming here as principal of the high school."

"What do you think of that, George?" said the man's wife.

"Well," the man said as he scratched his head, "that sure makes me wonder what's wrong with this lady that she can't hold down a steady job!"

190. Administrator as Viewed by Teachers

It was the beginning of the school year, and the principal was addressing the faculty. After welcoming them back from the summer hiatus, he launched into an impassioned speech about the values of education and this particular school.

"We shall accomplish these goals," he concluded, "even if we have to stay long hours after the students have left; even if we have to come back night after night for long hours of toil; even if we have to come back on Saturday mornings and afternoons!"

"Excuse me!" shouted one teacher from the audience. "Have you hired a second faculty we don't know about?"

191. Keeping a Positive Attitude in Negative Situations

The principal was in the school library, chatting with the librarian. Unbeknown to him, a heavy truck passing the school suddenly went out of control, jumped the curb, and came hurtling full power toward the school, headed directly for a wall, behind which lay the school's library.

The truck smashed into the wall, and bricks flew everywhere. When the dust settled, there was a gaping hole in the wall, and the principal, the only "casualty," was lying half-covered by brick and other assorted debris.

"You're going to be just fine," the paramedics told the principal when they arrived, "but your leg is broken. You're going to have to stay in the hospital for several days."

"At last!" exclaimed the principal, "a legitimate excuse for missing the PTA meeting tonight!"

192. Seeking Answers

Before we go about trying to find answers to the problems that beset us, let's consider the story of the man who really wanted to know the "true meaning of life." No answer he could find had satisfied him, and then he heard of an Eastern guru who supposedly knew the "true meaning of life." This guru was located on a mountaintop in Tibet, so the man sold all his possessions and took off for that country.

He had to travel the last hundred miles on the back of a mule and then had to scale the face of a mountain.

Finally, battered and exhausted, he arrived at a monastery on top of the mountain and was ushered into the presence of the guru.

"What," he panted, "is the true meaning of life?"

"The true meaning of life," said the mystic, "is this: Birds do not sing in the morning sun."

"But," said the man, "birds *do* sing in the morning sun."

Said the guru, "They do?"

Therefore, as we seek answers tonight, let's make every effort to make certain that we have all facts straight.

193. The Superintendent of Schools

The superintendent of schools was retiring after a long career in education, and the search was on for her replacement. Finally, the board announced their choice. The principal of the local high school was to take over the job.

At the high school, there was general rejoicing, and many good wishes were sent to the principal along with regret that he would no longer be at the school. After school, a senior member of the faculty paid a visit to the principal.

"I'm very happy for you," said the teacher, "but I can't help feeling a touch of sadness as well."

"Thank you so much," said the principal. "I really appreciate your good wishes, and I know what you mean. I, too, regret that I shall no longer be here to guide this school."

"That's not why I'm sad," said the teacher. "Now that you're the superintendent, not only will you honor this school by expecting us to do twice the work of other schools, but now that you have a new audience, we're going to have to listen to your jokes all over again!"

194. Elementary Versus Secondary Principal

A principal of an elementary school and a principal of a secondary school were comparing notes on their schools and the differences in the two levels.

"On the secondary level," said that principal, "we expect our students to have gained a degree of maturity; we expect them to be able to care for themselves. Even so, it doesn't always work out that way. You would be surprised, but sometimes we practically have to wipe their noses for them."

"You think that's bad," said the elementary principal. "In our school we have kindergarten and first grade, and you would be very surprised at what we *do* have to wipe!"

195. The Vice-Principal

It was going to be a long flight, and the two people seated next to each other began by introducing themselves.

"And, what do you do?" asked one passenger.

"I'm in education," answered the other.

"A teacher," said the first. "How nice."

"Well, not exactly a teacher. I'm a school administrator. I'm employed as the *vice*-principal of our local high school."

"You mean they have a principal just in charge of *that?*" said the first passenger with wide eyes. "That school must be in a very rough neighborhood!"

196. The Administrator and Money (I)

"Help! Help!" cried the woman on the busy street corner. Several people ran to her assistance.

"What is it?" they asked.

"It's my little boy!" she shouted. "He was playing with a quarter, and I think he swallowed it. He can't breathe! He's choking!"

Without a word, a man stepped forward and grabbed the child. Spinning the lad around, the man placed his arms around the child, made a fist, and pushed that fist into a place just below the boy's sternum.

There was a brief burst of air, and the quarter flew out of the child's mouth and spun to rest on the pavement.

As the crowd applauded, the boy's mother threw her arms around the man.

"Thank you, thank you!" she cried. "Are you a doctor?"

"No, Madam," replied the hero of the hour, "I am the principal of the high school, and I can assure you that this was nothing at all compared to trying to get funds out of the board of education!"

197. The Administrator and Money (II)

The school system had just installed a computer system in the schools. Not only was the system designed to handle attendance and student records, but, supposedly, this computer could also analyze situations and give educational advice.

Soon after its installation, the budget for the next school year was due, and the principal had worked long and hard and was still facing difficulty. Try as she might, the principal could not stay within the budgetary guidelines the board had imposed.

Finally, she decided to ask the computer for advice.

"Computer," she typed, "in today's modern school system, how can I provide a quality education for each child in the school and still stay within budgetary guidelines?"

The computer buzzed and whirred and something began to print out on the screen.

"ANSWER: Get rid of people who ask questions that don't have answers!"

198. Preparing the Budget

As he went about preparing the budget, the principal was shocked to find that the request submitted by the science department was several thousand dollars over budget.

Always one for direct action, the principal immediately went to see the department head in question.

"Look," said the principal, "this is impossible. Here is the figure you were allotted, and here is the figure you submitted."

"OK," said the department head, "so I spent five thousand dollars too much, but can you name *one* other extravagance?"

199. The Administrator and Public Relations (Humorous)

The principal was invited to make a speech on a local TV station. When he got there, he was so flustered by the lights and makeup and general confusion, that he completely forgot what he was going to say and was reduced to reading his speech, which came across the airwaves in a dull and monotonous manner.

In a local home, the father switched off the set at the conclusion of the principal's speech and stared at his son.

"Dad," said the boy, "why did you make me watch that?"

"Son," replied the father, "if you act up in school, the teacher will send you to that man's office, and he will talk to you like that for hours and hours. I just wanted you to keep that in mind if you ever felt like misbehaving!"

200. The Administrator and Public Relations (Serious)

A principal we know was scheduled to take over from a long-time administrator who was retiring. The new principal paid a visit to the retiring administrator and asked if he had any advice to give.

"Son," said the veteran, "I know you're going to do a fine job educationally, so the best advice I can give you is to start out with good public relations.

"You see, when you take over here, the first thing the parents and teachers and students will want to know about is not your plans for this school. What they'll want to know about is you—are you married? divorced? any scandals? problems?

"Therefore, the first thing I'd suggest is for you to prepare a one-page biography and get it out to every corner of the school and to the homes in the community.

"Once they find out that there's nothing to gossip about, they'll lose interest in you, and you can start working for the good of education!"

GROWING PERFECT WITH PRACTICE—THE WORLD OF PARENTS AND TEACHERS

Parents and teachers have many things in common, not the least of which is that both improve with experience. The path to that experience, however, is often rocky, seldom straightforward, and frequently detoured into various side roads. Sometimes the trip is nerve-wracking, and sometimes it is a light and joyous romp. It is never dull.

In this section, we'll take a look into the parallel worlds of parent and teacher as each works for the good of the child—the single object that both parties have always held paramount.

201. How Each Plays His Part

"I've tried everything with Bobby," wept Mrs. Jones at the parent conference, "and nothing seems to work! I don't know what to do with him!"

"There, there, Mrs. Jones," said the teacher, Mrs. Greene, as she handed the distraught parent a box of tissues. "There are many techniques we can use with children that will put them on the right path. Of course we often get tired and discouraged along the way, but I promise you that we'll get through this together. We won't give up on Bobby until he's at the head of the class."

Mrs. Jones dried her eyes and said, "Thank you so much! You've made me feel ever so much better!"

"Thank you, Mrs. Jones," said Mrs. Greene, "but you'll have to excuse me now. You see, my own child, Jimmy, goes to school here, and I always go to *that* teacher's conference about him."

Mrs. Jones understood and left. When she had gone, Mrs. Greene cleared her desk, took a folder with her son, Jimmy's, papers, and she walked out of the classroom, around a corner, and down the hall to the door of another teacher's room, the room where her own son attended second grade. The teacher beckoned her in, and Mrs. Greene sat down next to the teacher's desk.

"I've tried everything with Jimmy," Mrs. Greene broke down and sobbed, "and nothing seems to work! I don't know what to do with him!"

202. Parent-Teacher Associations (Humorous)

It was a PTA get-together for faculty and parents. The two women had been eyeing each other for some time. Finally, one of them spoke.

"Excuse me, but I think I know you; I mean long ago, when we were kids?"

They exchanged names and found that they had, indeed, gone to high school together, although they were only acquaintances and had quickly lost track of each other after graduation.

"You know," said one, "I remember you now. You never studied, never had your homework in on time, and never seemed to pay the least amount of attention in class. Now, here you are, teaching in this school. Who'd have ever thought *you* would become a teacher?"

"And, I remember you," said the other. "I remember that you never wore any makeup, never had time for boys, and never went to any of the dances. Gosh, who would have thought that *you* would be a mother?"

203. *Parent-Teacher Associations (Serious)*

I remember one PTA president, a marvelous woman who had done immeasurable good for the school, who was talking to another PTA volunteer at one of those PTA get-togethers filled with conversation, tea, and cookies.

She was talking to a woman who had been a PTA volunteer for less than a year. That woman had been greatly impressed by both the school and the highly organized activities of the PTA. The woman gave one glowing compliment after another.

"You know," she told the PTA president finally, "I really feel that I would gladly die for the children of this school!"

"I appreciate that feeling," said the PTA president, "but I assure you that that is not enough."

"What? I . . ."

"I think that many good people have the capacity to die for something in which they truly believe," the PTA president continued. "It is far more difficult, however, to get people to commit their lives to the doing of something and the giving of themselves on a daily basis for the advancement of a common goal. I appreciate the fact that you would die for these children, but it would be much better if you would commit yourself to living and working for them."

204. *Teaching at the Turn of the Century*

"What will it be like," mused one educator, "teaching at the turn of the twenty-first century? It's not that far off."

"Just think," added another, "at the turn of the twentieth century, they had blackboards, chalk, pencils, and pens with steel nibs that they dipped in a bottle of ink! In the twenty-first century, we'll have computers and monitors and overhead projectors and word processors!"

"What a difference! Blackboards and chalk versus computers and software!"

"Put those two turn-of-the-century classrooms together," mused the second educator, "and they have nothing in common—absolutely nothing!"

"I think you're wrong," added a third fellow. "I think they would have a great deal in common."

"Oh, and what might that be?"

"In both cases," he said, "there will be children filling the room, and, whatever the learning equipment might be, it will go unused unless there is a teacher there to lead the way."

205. The Parent and the Teacher Disagree (Humorous)

"I think you'd better come right away," a teacher told the principal, and led him to a room where the teacher, Mr. Howard, was engaged in a conference with the father of one of his students. From half way down the hall, you could hear the uproar.

When they got to the door, the principal looked in and there were Mr. Howard and the student's father, leaning across the desk at each other, their noses less than two inches apart, and screaming at each other!

"There must be a better way!" shouted the father.

"Of course there is—my way!" shouted the teacher.

"Gentlemen! Gentlemen!" exclaimed the principal as he rushed in and tried to part the near-combatants. "Whatever it is, I am certain that we can settle it in a civilized manner. If it's homework or grades or behavior in class—whatever the problem—we can discuss it calmly and seek a solution. Now, what is it that is causing such a turmoil between you two?"

"This nincompoop," said the father pointing at the teacher, "insists that to make a spare in bowling, you have to use a hook shot!"

"And this idiot," said the teacher, "actually believes that a straight-on shot is best!"

206. The Parent and the Teacher Disagree (Serious)

Of course there will be disagreements between parents and teachers. Since the first teacher sent home the first report card, there undoubtedly have been points of contention between the two. That, in and of itself, is not necessarily bad.

Allow me to illustrate with a story of a young man who was hired to do some work around a marina. The boss and the boss's wife took the young man to a section of the marina where several boats were docked.

"I want you to work on this boat," said the boss.

"No," said his wife, "first clean up the dock!"

"The boat first!"

"The dock!"

The boss and his wife stood arguing for a good five minutes. Finally, the boy stepped in.

"Excuse me," he said, "but when you two get finished deciding how I should spend my time, I'll be over here—fishing!"

So, let's make certain that we never forget the object of our disagreements and make every effort to get the problem settled fast!

207. *The Parent and the Teacher During an Election*

The parent and the teacher not only met during parent conferences, but they reaffirmed their relationship when both met at a political rally. Indeed, both shared the same political views as well as the same child, and they became friends.

One Saturday afternoon during election time, the two women decided to go door to door passing out literature for their candidate. They could not place the pamphlets in the mailbox, as this would be a violation of federal law, so they tucked them either into door handles or under one corner of the doormat.

They spent the entire afternoon in this pursuit, and both women were worn out. Finally, they came to rest on a bench at a bus stop.

"We must have passed out a thousand!" said one.

"Ten thousand!" sighed the other.

Just then, Brenda, the one's daughter and the other's student, came strolling up pulling a wagon containing a large cardboard box.

"What are you doing here?" the women asked in unison.

"I've had a terrible day," said the child. "I followed you this morning, and I saw you two littering, and both of you have told me that littering is wrong!"

"But, Honey," one stated, "we weren't littering . . ."

"It's all right," Brenda continued. "I didn't want you to get into trouble, so I went home and got my wagon, and I picked up every one you dropped!"

208. *What Children Tell Parents About School (Humorous, I)*

It was Back-to-School Night, in which children bring their parents to school to meet their teachers.

The army captain with his wife and son entered the room. They stood for a while as the line grew shorter, and finally it was their turn to meet the teacher.

As they approached the desk, the captain looked at the teacher. She stood about five feet six inches and was about twenty-five years old. She was dressed in an attractive suit, had lovely red hair, blue eyes, and a genuine smile on her lips.

"You're Ms. Kellog?" the captain asked. "Billy's teacher?"

"Yes," she smiled, "I am."

The captain wheeled upon his boy.

"Son," said the captain, "this is the person you described as some old crank who was as mean as a drill-sergeant?

"Boy, we are going to the post hospital tomorrow, and you're getting your eyes examined. If you can't tell the difference between this lady and a First Sergeant, you are never going to get into West Point!"

209. *What Children Tell Parents About School (Humorous, II)*

The teacher received a phone call after school one day from the mother of one of her students.

"I'd like to ask you a couple of questions," said the mother.

"Go right ahead."

"Did you go to a recognized college?"

"Yes."

"Did you take courses in education that were recognized as valid by the state?"

"Why, of course!"

"And, you've been teaching for a while?"

"Twelve years. Now, may I ask what the purpose of this is?"

"Well," said the mother, "I was talking to my son last night about the fact that he seemed to have nothing to do, and . . . well, let me put it this way: I don't suppose you went to a special teacher's college where they taught you not to give kids homework because it rots their brains?"

210. *What Children Tell Parents About School (Serious)*

It's not that children lie about what goes on in school, but they very frequently exaggerate and often misinterpret what they see. If we act on this without finding out the facts, the result can be devastating.

I remember a call from a parent bringing to my attention the "fact" that one of our teachers was a heavy drinker and had gotten so drunk *during the school day* that she had fallen down in class, before the children.

The teacher named was one of our finest educators, and I went to examine this immediately.

Would you like to know what happened? The teacher had her class seated for a story hour. She, herself, was seated on a low bench. The children were finishing their drinks, and the teacher tossed her head back in fun to drain her glass. The action was too much, and she fell off the low bench. She laughed; the class laughed; they went on with the activity.

Later that day, one of the children in that class told her mother, "The teacher was drinking in class, and she drank so much, she fell down!" You can easily imagine the rest. Had the rumor not been stopped, there could have been disastrous consequences.

Let's all vow to listen to our children, but let's also make certain that we check our facts!

211. A Child's Perception of Teachers (I)

"What's school like?" asked little Janie of her six-year-old brother who had just returned from his first day of first grade.

"It's OK," he answered, "and I almost got the whole thing figured out."

"Yeah?"

"Yeah," he continued. "It's just the teachers I can't figure out. I know that they live in the school, and that's how come they're always there in the morning when we come and in the afternoon when we leave. I figured out that they eat in the cafeteria, go to the AVA room to watch TV, and used the boy's and girl's rooms after we leave. The only thing I can't figure out is where they put the beds at night."

212. A Child's Perception of Teachers (II)

It was the end of the school day for the kindergarten teacher. During the course of the day, she had removed twenty-five pairs of boots, hung up coats, lifted books and toys, organized teams, taken the class outside, broken up two fights, patched a scraped knee, supervised cookies and milk, given a story hour, gotten attendance taken and in to the office, comforted several weeping children, put back the toys and games, held an art lesson, held a music lesson, gotten twenty-five coats and pairs of boots back on, seen the children to the bus stop, and finally returned to the room.

With a deep sigh, she sat at her desk and closed her eyes in the blessed quiet.

One of the kindergarten children had returned with her mother to pick up a doll that the child had left in the room. When they approached the door of the room, they saw the teacher, eyes closed, all but slumped in her chair.

"What's the matter with teacher?" asked the little girl.

"I think," said the perceptive mother, "that your teacher is very tired."

"What's she got to be tired about?" asked the child. "All she does all day is play with us—she doesn't work!"

213. A Child's Perception of Parents (I)

"You're always yelling at me!" said Jane to her parents. "It's always, 'Did you do your homework? Are you sure you have everything done? Do you have your composition for English class?' I tell you, Mom and Dad, it's driving me crazy. I am a responsible teenager, and I should be trusted to do what is necessary without having to be yelled at!"

The parents talked it over and decided to let Jane have her way for a month. No checking up; no yelling.

Three weeks into the process, Jane spoke up at the dinner table.

"I'm falling behind in math and social studies. In my other subjects, the teachers are getting concerned because I sometimes forget to do my homework. I also have a major composition due tomorrow, and I haven't even started it."

Father took a deep breath, "Does this mean that you now want us to go back to pushing you?"

"Well," said the daughter, "I still don't want you to push me—but I sure could use a little nudge every once and a while!"

214. A Child's Perception of Parents (II)

"Now, children," stated the teacher, "we are going to be filling in some forms that the school needs. Does everyone have a pencil and a form?"

Slowly, the teacher led the class through the information required on the paper. This included name, address, telephone number, and the like.

They came to a section titled "Parent's Occupation," and the teacher explained that "occupation" meant job, what work a person does for a living.

As the teacher circulated, she noticed that Francine had left the area blank next to "Mother's Occupation." The teacher stopped and bent down to Francine.

"Francine," the teacher whispered, "you left that space blank. What work does your mother do?"

"That's why I left it blank," replied the child. "All my Mom does is to take care of me, my two brothers, my sister and my Dad. That's not a job, is it?"

215. The Parent-Teacher Conference (I)

The two boys met in the hallway of the school.

"Well," said the one, "I really messed up this time!"

"Aw, it ain't that bad!" said the other.

"Oh, yeah? It is," replied the first. "You remember how the teacher held a conference with my mother yesterday afternoon?"

"Yeah."

"Well, when I got to the room, they were both crying, and now I'm going to military school at the end of the quarter!"

216. The Parent-Teacher Conference (II)

Mother and the teacher had worked out a strategy when they called little Harry into the parent-teacher conference. It seems that Harry had been threatening to "run away" from school, unless the teacher gave him good grades. Now, the teacher and the mother had figured on a way to cure Harry of this threat.

"Harry," said the teacher when the child had appeared, "I cannot give you good grades; you have to work for them. Therefore, if you have to run away, you'll just have to do it."

Harry's eyes grew wide, and he looked at his mother.

"That's right," said Mom. "See that big factory right across the way. You can run away over there, and they'll give you a job shovelling coal and cleaning the bathrooms. Go ahead, run away."

"Go ahead," chimed in the teacher, "the factory's just over there!"

"You guys are something!" stated Harry. "You can't even tell when a guy is joking; that's bad enough, but now you want me to run away when I'm not even allowed to cross the street by myself!"

217. The Teacher Calls Home (I)

"I think Rosie Sanders is the worst behaved child in my class," stated one teacher.

"It goes further than that," said another teacher. "Rosie Sanders is the worst behaved child in the school!"

"I think the problem is even bigger than that," added a third. "Let me prove it to you."

With that, the third teacher led the other two to the office where they found Rosie Sanders' home phone number and dialed it.

On the second ring, an answering machine picked up.

"You have reached the Sanders residence," a voice stated. "If you are calling about my daughter, leave a number where our lawyer can contact you. However, if you've never met Rosie, stay on the line and I'll be glad to chat for a while."

218. The Teacher Calls Home (II)

One teacher we know tried to call home one afternoon after school. After a few rings the phone was picked up and a young voice answered.

"I would like to speak to Mrs. Bender, please," said the teacher.

"Who is this?" asked the voice.

"This is Miss Gershom," the teacher said.

"From school!"

"Yes, from school. May I please speak with Mrs. Bender?"

"Er . . . " hesitated the voice, "she's not here; she moved!"

"Tommy!" said the teacher. "I know it's you. Now let me speak to your mother!"

"Honest, Miss Gershom," sputtered the boy, "she moved and I don't know where she is, and I can't ask her because I moved with her, and I don't even know where I am. Would you believe that?"

"I would not."

"In that case," sighed the boy, "I'll have her call you back *after* I've had dinner."

219. The Parent Calls the School

The call came into the school slightly after dismissal, and a teacher who happened to be in the main office took it.

"This is Mrs. Smith, mother of Albert Smith of the first grade of your school," said the caller. "I wish to speak to the fortunate teacher who has my darling boy in her class."

"I'm sorry," quipped the teacher who had answered, "but that teacher is out having a nervous breakdown at the moment. Might I do?"

220. Communications Between Home and School

When the student was out for three days, the teacher became slightly concerned and called home. There was no answer. She tried again the next day, and now she received a message that the phone had been disconnected.

Now the teacher was genuinely concerned, and she reported what she knew to the school officials.

Ten days passed, and one morning she received a letter in her mailbox. Even before she opened it, she recognized the handwriting of the student who had been the center of her concern.

The letter gave an address in another town as well as a phone number and stated that he missed her, but he was doing well in his new school.

The teacher called the number and got the mother.

"Why didn't you inform the school that you were moving?" she asked.

"Well," said the mother, "we know how good a student Tommy is, and we know how much you must adore him, so we didn't want you to get all upset and weepy with the fact that we were leaving!"

221. *Consequences of Poor Communications (Humorous)*

Certainly, we must all strive to achieve good communications between home and school, because the results of poor or improper communication can have a very bad effect.

I remember a story about a florist who received two telephone orders. One was to a small business that had decided to expand and open up a branch store. The other was from a woman who wished to send a spray of flowers for her uncle's funeral.

The flowers were beautiful, but somehow the instructions were poorly communicated to the delivery man.

So it was that in the middle of opening day festivities, the new store owners received a floral tribute with a card that read "With Deepest Sympathy . . . All Things Must Pass Away" while over at the funeral home, mourners wondered at the flowers with the card that stated "Best Wishes in Your New Location!"

222. *Consequences of Poor Communication (Serious)*

"I never interfere with my neighbors," said one farmer. "Once, I saw this melon patch going to seed, but I figured that since it wasn't *my* melon patch, I had no right to say a thing to my neighbor."

"Yep," said a second farmer, "I saw that melon patch, but I knew it wasn't mine, so when it got all seedy, I just shut my mouth and didn't say a word to my neighbor."

"Whose patch was it?" asked an observer.

"Don't know to this day," answered one, "but it doesn't matter. What matters is that we kept out of each other's way. That did a lot of good for both of us!"

"Perhaps," said the observer, "but it didn't do a heck of a lot for those melons!"

223. Parent's Influence on Children (I)

"Son," said father, "I want to tell you about a man who had a great deal of influence on me—your grandfather.

"Your grandfather was an immigrant who left his native soil as a young man and made a long and hazardous journey to America, where he knew he could be free. He arrived in this country with just the clothes on his back and a small cardboard suitcase. Even so, within ten years, he had built a large and successful business which sustains us today. Now, isn't that something to inspire you?"

"Wow!" said the son, "and all he had when he came here was the clothes on his back and an old cardboard suitcase?"

"Yes, that's right."

"And what was in the suitcase?"

"One million dollars in negotiable securities."

224. Parent's Influence on Children (II)

"Do you want to kiss me?" asked six-year-old Tara.

"Yep," said little Gary.

"OK," said Tara as she puckered up, "you can!"

"Just a minute!" protested the little boy. "We gotta do something first."

The boy took out a sheet of paper and began to scribble on it, since he was just a bit in front of the mystery of writing.

"Here," he said, shoving it toward Tara, "sign this first."

"What is it?"

"It's a paper that says you ain't gonna sue me."

"I'm not Sue," said the child. "I'm Tara!"

"I know," said Gary, "and I don't understand it myself, but my Daddy says this is what I gotta do, and he knows all about it; he's been divorced twice!"

225. Doing Homework (Humorous)

"I want to ask you a question, Betsy, and I want a straight answer," said the teacher. "Did one of your parents write your social studies composition?"

"I'm sorry, Ma'am," said Betsy, "but you're right! How did you figure it out?"

"It wasn't too difficult," the teacher answered.

"But, what should I tell them?"

"Tell them," said the teacher, "that most of my students, when they are assigned a composition on the Internal Revenue Service, do not refer to them as 'those blood-suckers in Washington,' nor would they end the composition with, 'and if you don't believe me, just ask our accountant!' "

226. Doing Homework (Serious)

I knew he was a former student of mine as soon as I saw him. He was older, of course, and had some facial hair, but I still recognized the kid who sat in one corner of my room through a school year some time ago.

"You know," he said to me, "I liked you as a teacher, but I got you, didn't I? You could never get me to do homework, could you?"

"No," I admitted, "that I could not do."

"I never did a thing, and that used to get you mad. Do you remember?"

"Yes, I remember."

"You used to talk to me until you were turning blue," he continued, "about doing my homework and studying and doing what I was supposed to do, right?"

"Right," I answered.

"Well," he laughed, "I sure showed you, didn't I?"

"You sure showed me," I said softly.

Then, we shook hands.

After that, I signaled, and a guard came to lead me out of the visiting room, while another guard came to lead my former student back to his prison cell.

227. Gifts to the Teacher (Humorous)

One day, as part of a discussion on the seashore, the teacher remarked that she loved seashells and that she, indeed, had a rather sizeable collection of them which she would one day bring in.

The next morning, there was a package on her desk wrapped in brown paper, with her name printed on it.

She opened it, and inside was a small, fairly common, but rather colorful seashell with grains of sand still sticking to it.

There was also a note included from one of her students.

"Dear Mrs. Harris," the note stated, "Here is a seashell for your collection. I intend to give you one every week. Please remember that if my marks go up, the shells can get bigger!"

228. Gifts to the Teacher (Serious)

It is a standing rule with all teachers we know that you accept any gift a child gives you *except* money. No teacher wishes to hurt a child's feeling by rejecting a gift offered in love, especially at certain times of the year, but no teacher will accept a card, let us say, with a five-dollar bill in it. That is returned gently and with thanks, but *it is returned.*

One Christmas, a number of children had brought me small gifts, and I was in the process of opening them when I opened an envelope and discovered a card with a dollar bill tucked inside. I went on with the festivities, but I later sought out the student giver in private.

"Bobby," I said, "I thank you for the gift, but I'm going to ask you to take it back. I'm very happy that you would want to give me this dollar, but I can't accept money from my students. Can you understand that?"

"Sir," said the boy, "you know how I was having trouble in math, and you kept me after school and worked with me until I could do it? Because I can do math now, I got a job at a grocery store. This is the first buck I ever earned. I couldn't have done it without you, and I wanted you to have it."

Then and there, I broke a standing rule of the profession, and I have that dollar bill to this day.

229. The Teacher Comes to Dinner (I)

The teacher was invited to come for dinner and accepted with thanks. Even little Herbert, whom the teacher had in class, was a model of good table manners.

The meal went pleasantly enough, and after dinner, they all retired to the living room, where a proud mother and father announced that their son would now entertain them with a musical interlude.

Picking up a violin, the little boy proceeded to saw away at the instrument for the next fifteen minutes, making the most nerve-shattering noise the teacher had ever experienced. She knew the lad must be playing *something,* but listen as hard as she might, she simply could not identify the tune.

When the "concert" was over, the teacher decided that it would be best to be honest.

"I'm sorry, Herbert," she said, "but what was that you were playing?"

"Gosh, Ma'am," said the boy, "don't you teachers know anything? That was a violin!"

230. The Teacher Comes to Dinner (II)

The teacher had come to dinner with the family of one of her students. The teacher had even learned some humorous stories to tell at the dinner table.

She told one of the stories, and everyone laughed. Then, she topped it with another and the table laughed again. Finally, she told a third story, and everyone jumped in their seats, squirming with laughter.

Everyone laughed, that is, except for the teacher's student who sat there with virtually no expression on her face.

"Come on, Jackie," said the teacher, "that had to be funny, or why would they be laughing so hard?"

"Because I warned them," she said in complete and total honesty, "that if they didn't laugh at your jokes, you'd probably just repeat them again until they did!"

231. Teacher's View of Parents and Home

My "inside" view of what home life must be like for some families came at a PTA meeting shortly after I started teaching. Several of us were meeting in the cafeteria of the school, and one of the parents present was Mrs. Johnson who was well known around the school, since she had eight children.

As the meeting droned on, Mrs. Johnson put her head down on one of the cafeteria tables and fell into a gentle sleep.

The speaker that night was extolling the virtues of motherhood. As he went on and on, he became louder and more enthusiastic.

"I will tell you," he voiced, "that there is no sweeter word in our tongue than this: mom, Mom, MOM!"

That last "MOM" made the light fixtures shake, and Mrs. Johnson's head came up from the cafeteria table with a start.

"I'm coming!" she shouted, still half asleep. "Just don't step in it until I get there!"

232. Parent's View of Teachers and School

It was a Parent Visitation Night, and Mr. and Mrs. Woods had just been introduced to their daughter's teacher.

"How fortunate you are to work with children," said Mrs. Woods. "It keeps you looking so young."

"Thank you," said the teacher.

"I will tell you honestly," continued the mother, "you don't look a day over forty."

"My wife is absolutely right," Mr. Woods joined in, "not a day over forty!"

"Thank you."

"If you don't mind my asking," Mrs. Woods continued, "how old are you?"

"Not at all," said the teacher, "I'm twenty-eight."

233. Role of Parents in the Learning Process

Mary did nothing but sit around the house watching TV. Finally, Mom and Dad decided that it was time to get some life into their child, so they sent her to camp.

Mary did not want to go, and she fought like a wildcat to stay home, but the parents prevailed and she was off.

Every day for two weeks, the parents received a postcard with the same four words on it: "This place is miserable!"

Finally, it was time for Mary to come home, and the parents steeled themselves for the onslaught of the "How could you do this to me?" that was bound to come.

Instead, when Mary got home, she embraced her parents and asked them to sit down with her.

"Mom and Dad," she said, "I want to thank you for sending me to camp."

"What?" said her father. "You wrote every day to tell us how miserable it was there."

"That's right," said Mary. "It was miserable, but then I realized something."

"What's that?"

"I realized," said Mary, "that if you hadn't pushed me out of here, I would never have known how much I missed it!"

234. The Student Athlete and Grades

The great majority of student athletes have little or no trouble keeping their grades up, but every now and then, there is one who may need some extra help along the way.

Thus it was that the coach and the star football player were called into the principal's office one day, where the athlete was informed that his grades had been slipping, and that while he was not in danger yet, he had better get some help before the grades dropped to the point where he would have to be removed from the team.

The next afternoon, the principal was passing by the gym, when he heard some noise coming from inside.

He stopped and peeked in, and there was the coach with the star player's math book and the player seated before him.

"You got five footballs," the coach was saying, "and you shove one down the fullback's throat. How many you got left? Think, man, think!"

235. The Parent and the Report Card (I)

"Dad," said the son, "do you believe a person should just blindly accept everything he reads?"

"Of course not, son," said the father, instantly becoming serious. "In fact, a person has a duty to question what is put before him. Just because you read something in the newspaper or in a book, that doesn't mean that it is true. You owe it to yourself to use your mind and question what you are told. If it is true and good, it will hold up under your questioning. Now, does that help you?"

"It sure does, Dad," said the boy as he handed his father a folded sheet of heavy paper.

"What's this?"

"It's my report card," said the lad, "and I would appreciate it if you kept in mind everything you just said as you read it!"

236. The Parent and the Report Card (II)

The teacher went with his friend to visit his friend's brother and his family. As they walked into the living room, the teacher looked at the couple.

"I beg your pardon," he said, "but do you have a child who is in a gifted and talented program in the local school?"

"Why, yes, we do," said the father.

"However did you guess?" asked the mother.

"It's really nothing," said the teacher. "It's just that I couldn't help noticing that you had had his report card bronzed, and it's hanging dead center on the mirror in the hallway!"

237. *Parents and Teachers as Partners (Humorous)*

The word got around the school that one set of parents and a particular teacher really got on well together. This "partnership" manifested itself in a student whose grades soared along with his self-esteem and ability to relate to others. So it was that on one PTA night, several parents and teachers cornered them and asked why they had such a very good relationship.

"We didn't start out that way," said the teacher.

"No," stated the parent. "We started out by arguing over the child, and it got so bad that we decided to take it to the principal."

"Right," said the teacher. "We went into his office, and he talked to both of us for over an hour, giving us his philosophy of education."

"When we came out," the parent continued, "I turned to him, and he turned to me."

"I said, 'Did you understand what he just said?' "

"And I said, 'Not a word!' "

"So, we decided that the only way we were going to get anything done was to work together. We've been friends ever since!"

238. *Parents and Teachers as Parents (Serious)*

"Why so glum, Fred?" asked the teacher.

"It's my homework," said the student, "here it is!"

"But, Fred," said the teacher, "this should make you feel great. It's perfect."

"I know," sulked the boy. "I don't have any choice. If I don't do it at home, Mom will get me, and if I don't hand it in here, you'll get me. I have no choice but to be smart! I don't know which are worse, parents or teachers!"

239. *Notes Between Parents and Teachers (I)*

The teacher sent home a note requesting that Mrs. Miller send in a copy of Nancy's birth certificate for the school records. The next day, Nancy did not have the document, nor did she have a note from her parents, so the teacher wrote another note and sent it home on the second day. Again, there was nothing forthcoming on the following morning. Therefore, the teacher sat down over lunch and typed a letter on school stationery, which she sent home with the child on the third day.

The next morning, Nancy arrived with the required paper and a note from home.

"Thank Goodness you sent me that typed letter," ran the note from home. "I couldn't read your handwriting, and I didn't want to insult you by calling and asking what you wanted, but I was getting so curious!"

240. *Notes Between Parents and Teachers (II)*

The science teacher had assigned several science projects to various members of the class, and one student had received a project that required several large aquariums, each filled with water. This the family had provided, and the experiment was currently being kept in the family room of the home.

One day, the science teacher received a hastily written note.

"All aquariums broken," the note stated. "Family room flooded. What do we do now?"

"What an opportunity," wrote back the scientist. "Teach your family to rise above it!"

241. *Planning for College*

The father and the teacher were talking about college.

"I believe," said the father, "that these brochures my son has received would indicate that one of the Ivy League colleges—perhaps Yale or Harvard—would be the best choice."

"I must disagree," said the teacher. "While these are certainly fine universities, I believe that your son's proclivity for math and science would seem to indicate a preference for a place of technical knowledge, such as M.I.T."

"Perhaps," commented the father. "Do you think his test scores and grades would gain him immediate entrance?"

"Hey," came the voice of the son from a corner of the room, "will you guys cool it? I'm only eight years old!"

242. *The Child Like the Parents*

Often, particularly in the lower grades, you get a fantastic insight into students' home life, as you watch them repeat phrases and actions that they have seen or heard repeated thousands of times at home.

A case in point is that of the first-grade teacher who was collecting funds for a class party. Each child was to bring in a dollar to help defray expenses. All the children had, except for Alice.

It was not a case of hardship, as Alice's records testified. Nonetheless, it was now several days past due, and the dollar had still not appeared.

The teacher reminded her about it one morning and decided to keep reminding her through the day in hopes that the message would finally get through.

"Don't forget your dollar tomorrow morning," she told the child with a smile, and at various times throughout the day would comment, "Alice, don't forget that dollar!"

That afternoon, the teacher once again reminded Alice of the funds due. This time, however, the child seemingly had had enough. She grabbed her doll, strode to the door of the classroom, and glared at the teacher.

"Really," she said in a very firm tone, "if you don't stop badgering me about money, my dear, I'm taking my dolly and going home to Mother!"

243. The Parents Like the Child

I once had a student whom I'll call Ridley. He was a likeable young fellow, and he did fairly well in class, managing $B+$s and a couple As. What singled him out was what I'd call his total gawkiness.

He carried a bookbag when none of the other students would be seen dead with one. The bookbag was constantly hitting him in the shins or getting in the way of him, other students, and often me. Moreover, he seemed almost continually disoriented. If I asked him to move to his right, he'd go left. He would walk across the room and bump into twelve students before he got to his desk. He would trip over his own feet—constantly; and I had to bring him back to what we were doing time and again.

It was an evening activity at which we were to meet the parents, and I stood at the door to my room. Down the hall came a man carrying a briefcase which knocked into several parents as he approached. He looked at a wrinkled piece of paper taken from his pocket, and looked at my room number. Finally, he asked if this was room 204.

"Yes," I said. "Right here! Come on in!"

He nodded his head, put the paper away, hefted his briefcase, and started off in the opposite direction.

"Mr. Ridley?" I shouted.

"Yes," he said, turning swiftly and almost falling in the process. "How did you know?"

244. A Student Recalls Parents and Teachers

"I remember that my parents and teachers were always fighting," she told me. "All through grammar school and high school, my teachers would want to do one thing with me, and my parents would object, or my parents would want something done, and my teachers would refuse. They were always fighting.

"It got so that I could use that to my advantage. I'd tell my teachers that my parents were giving me a hard time, and they'd let me go without homework for a while. I'd tell my parents that the teacher had it in for me because of them, and they'd yell at the school, and I'd get to stay home for a couple of days. I had them at each other's throats. Man, I had it made.

"Then I got out of school and into the world. I didn't have it so easy anymore. Suddenly, I needed skills that I just didn't have. There were no bosses fighting over me that I could pit against each other.

"It took me six years of going nights to get where I should have been when I started out.

"I wish someone had slapped me down when I tried that fighting game, but my parents and teachers were so busy fighting each other, I guess they didn't have time to see *me*. I sure wish they had."

245. Working Together on a Serious Problem (I)

The child had a learning problem. It was far from devastating, but it was serious enough to get the parents and teachers together to work out a plan for success. This they did, and they presented it to the child one afternoon after school.

They explained to the child how she needed some extra help and how, working together, they had set up a schedule for both extra help, homework, and time at home for reinforcing the skill taught each day.

"We know this seems like a lot of work," said the teacher, "but we're doing this because we love you."

"That's right," said her mother. "Your father and I love you, and your teacher loves you, too."

"Gosh," said the child as she looked over the schedule, "I'm sure glad you don't love me any more than you do now, or I'd have no time left to have fun at all!"

246. *Working Together on a Serious Problem (II)*

Patrick had muscular dystrophy, and he was dying. There would be no recovery; no return to school. Chronologically, he was in seventh grade.

There were decisions to be made. The best prognosis claimed that he would not outlive his fourteenth year. The temptation, a very real temptation, was to let him stay home, do whatever made him the most comfortable, and forget about school and homework and structured learning of any kind. Indeed, that option was seriously considered.

Yet, within the slowly wasting body, there was a mind his teachers had categorized as sharp and quick. We all recognized the truth of that statement, and we knew what had to be done.

The home and the school worked together. A system of home tutoring was established, with the parents working with him before and after the teacher's visits.

He graduated with his eighth grade class. He was in a wheelchair, pushed by his tutor, because he had no strength to operate it himself, and he received a spontaneous standing ovation from his classmates.

He was sixteen when he died on a Friday night in mid-July. Until just shortly before he lapsed into a coma, his mind was bright and sharp and clean.

The people who touched him and those he touched know that his life was not in vain. Each came away from him with something very precious and personal that they would always cherish.

Each of us had grown . . . and learned.

247. *Having Faith in Each Other*

If a liaison between parents and teachers is to work for the benefit of the student, we must learn to have faith in each other.

Consider, for a moment, the father who took his child to the zoo. They spent a fine day together and ended up at the lion cages, studying the snarling "King of Beasts."

"Daddy," mused the little girl, "if one of those lions got out of his cage and started to eat me, would you fight him off?"

"Jennie," said the father, "I would attack that lion with my bare hands. If he attacked you, I would jump on him and punch him and kick him until he let you go, even if it meant that he got me."

"Wow!" said the girl.

"Jennie," smiled the father, "what if that lion got out and attacked me, would you fight him off for me?"

"Sure I would," said the girl. "Dad?"

"Yes?"

"Just in case," she continued, "could you write down the number of the local ASPCA?"

248. Looking Back at it All

The child stood and looked about him. His room was in a shamble, with dirty clothes and toys and books and half-eaten sandwiches everywhere. Outside, he could hear his mother on the phone with his teacher. His mother was screaming; he figured that the teacher was screaming back. His homework was not done and would remain so. His sister was crying loudly in the living room. He remembered those candy bars he had stuffed into the pockets of his jeans and wondered what they would look like when the washing machine was through with them.

Just then, the boy's dog trotted into the room. The boy bent down and hugged the animal. The boy made a sweeping gesture with his hand which seemed to take in everyone and everything.

"Doesn't it give you a sense of accomplishment," he said to the dog, "to see a job well done?"

249. A Parent's Prayer

On the night his daughter was born, a friend of ours stood, looking at the infant, and his mind and heart turned toward heaven.

"Oh, God," he prayed, "that's my daughter. She's so little and so weak and so much lies before her. Protect her, Lord, and be with her every step of the way. And, be with me, also, for I will need guidance just as much as she. Make me mindful, Lord, that not only must I love and cherish and provide for her, but I must train her as well. Lord, I know she'll have lots of teachers along the way, but I also know that her mother and I will be her first teachers, her last teachers, and an intimate part of all her other teachers as she grows. So, guide me, Lord, as I guide her; teach me, Lord, as I teach her; grant me the strength and wisdom to get through each day, as each day I do my best for my family. Help us all to grow straight and true, and if we waver, guide us back with a gentle hand.

"Lord, you've allowed me to be a parent. That's so wonderful and so fearsome, that I know that I need something beyond me to take me through. Be that guide for me . . . and for my family.

"God help me, I'm a parent!"

250. A Teacher's Prayer

I was up at four in the morning on the first day that I taught, and in school before the custodian. I sat in my classroom and waited for the children to arrive. Finally, I heard them before I saw them. I prayed.

"God," I said, "help! They're going to be here any minute now. They're going to come in here and expect me to take control; they're going to expect me to teach them something; they're going to expect me to organize and direct. Lord, I think I've forgotten everything I ever learned!

"Please, Lord, don't stand there laughing, but help me! God, let my mind remember the knowledge I have and how deeply I want to give it to them. God, let my ears hear not only what is said, but what each child means, and let these ears hear the tears even when they are not to be seen. God, let my eyes see each one as an individual and never as a nameless mass, but as a child who needs help and guidance. God, let my hands do what they can to lift burdens and share work and give what needs to be given.

"God, please make me a teacher!

"And, God, if you could do all that really fast, I'd appreciate it; they're going to be here in less than thirty seconds!"

NOTES ON THE GREAT ADVENTURE—INVESTIGATING FAMILY LIVING

Slaying dragons, rescuing princesses from castle towers, and fighting evil on a galactic scale all pale before the greatest adventure most of us will ever know—raising a family. Ask anyone who knows, and they will tell you that family life is not for the faint of heart. It is a great adventure where battles are fought on a sometimes daily basis and progress is often measured in millimeters; yet it is also a place where rewards abound, even if there are no medals to cover up the battle scars. Let's take a look at this great and epic adventure as we investigate the trials and the triumphs of the family.

251. *Family Embarrassed by Child's Manners*

Guests were going to be coming to dinner, and mother took some time rehearsing little Joey in the proper table manners he was to use.

"Now, above all," said Mother, "I want you to remember not to feed the dog during dinnner. I know I sometimes let you feed Skipper, but I don't want you to do it tonight. Say this after me: 'It is not polite to feed the dog from the table.'"

"It is not polite to feed the dog from the table," Joey intoned seriously.

The dinner that evening was going fine, until the guest noticed Skipper sitting to one side of the dining room with a very forlorn look.

"Oh, how cute!" said the guest. "The doggie wants a treat. Here you are, Sweetie."

With that, the guest took a small slice of the roast from her plate and held it out as Skipper rapidly snapped it up.

"Hey!" shouted Joey. "Don't you know it ain't polite to feed the dog from the table?"

Whereupon, Joey grabbed Skipper, pried the meat from the dog's jaws, and ate it himself!

252. *Children and Manners (I)*

"We should have plenty of everything," mother told her teenaged son, "but if it should happen that there is only one of something—the last slice of roast, perhaps—make certain that it goes to our guest!"

The dinner progressed nicely, and there was, indeed, an abundance of everything. Then it was time for dessert, and the cake that Mother had made went over extremely well—so well, in fact, that there was soon only one slice left. The teenager was reaching for that very slice, when Mother intervened.

"Bobby!" she said with an undertone of menace creeping in, "Were you about to offer that cake to our guest?"

"Oh, yeah, I guess . . ."

"I don't know," giggled the guest. "I should be watching my weight you know."

"I'll tell you what," said the teenager, as he took the serving plate and placed it on the floor, "I'll put it down here. You stand up, and if you can see it over that bulging waistline of yours, then you take it, OK?"

253. Children and Manners (II)

Father had brought his son, Harry, to an evening affair for fathers and sons sponsored by father's employer. They met many people, and finally it was time for father to introduce his son to the president of the company.

"How are you, Harry?" said the president.

"I'm OK," replied Harry who then proceeded to do an imitation of the Sphinx.

"Son," said his father, giving the boy a slight nudge, "this is Mr. Blandings, the president of our company. Aren't you going to ask him how he is?"

"No," said Harry with complete candor. "That's your boss, and if he's as stupid as you tell Mom and me, then I don't want to know how he is!"

254. The Son Comes of Age

It was all but a ritual. The dinner dishes would be cleared, and my father would look at me and smile. "Want to arm wrestle?" he'd ask, and I would bound from my seat to have my child's hand bound up and lost in his, waiting for the "contest" to begin, a contest he would always win, even though he feigned that I might somehow be pushing back that massive arm only to have it come rising back to pin my own and then enfold me in its loving grasp.

I close my eyes, and the years roll by. The child within me flexes and grows; the roller skates get tossed into a closet; the comic books turn into magazines; I outgrow more and more clothes, and my father and I have not played the game in years and years.

One night he turns to me at the dinner table and intones the ancient rite, "Want to arm wrestle?" I have places to go now and schedules to be kept, but there is something . . . something . . . "Sure," I say, and we join our equal hands.

It is no easy thing; the strength still flows, but all at once, I know that I am winning. My father is struggling, really struggling, and I give an extra push and his arm goes back an inch. I know that I can pin him, and I smile . . . and fix his eyes.

And, there is something in those eyes—fear or wonder or regret or vanished pride—something that tells me that he knows what is happening as well as I. I look and understand.

I relax just a bit, and his arm crushes mine to the table. My mother jokes about the "old man" still having "it," and my father locks my eyes with his.

We have never spoken so eloquently before.

255. The Son Joins the School Team

Ted wanted to join the school football team and spoke to his mother and father about it.

"I want to try out for the football team," the boy said. "I know you might be worried about my getting hurt, but I want you to remember what you told me. Great Grandpa played football; Grandpa was on the football team; and you, Dad, played football for your high school. I really want to carry on the proud tradition of the men in our family."

So Ted tried out for the football team, and at the very first scrimmage, with Dad looking on from the sidelines, he was handed the ball, took two steps, and was assaulted by seven defensive players, all of whom threw themselves into a huge pile, with Ted on the bottom.

Dad ran out on to the field and got there just as the last defensive player was being peeled off the boy who now made a permanent indentation in the field.

"Are you all right?" his father asked as he knelt beside the boy.

"Dad," said Ted, gulping in great quantities of air, "I hear the Stamp and Coin Club is looking for new members. Don't you think it's time our family put a stop to all this macho tradition junk?"

256. The Daughter Comes of Age

It was necessary for Mother to be away for a few days, and Mom and Dad thought this an excellent opportunity to teach their teenaged daughter about responsibility.

"While I'm gone," Mother told her daughter, "I want you to take charge the way I do. I want you to plan nutritious meals for the three days, assign household tasks to your brother and sister and yourself, supervise the TV programs they watch, see to it that they clean up after themselves and do their homework, and take charge of washing and dressing them for school and enforcing those bedtimes. Think you can handle that?"

"Sure, Mom. Nothing to it!"

Three days later, Mother returned, and later that evening, the daughter pulled her into a private room.

"I'm so glad you're home!" the daughter said.

"So am I," said Mother, "and I want to thank you for being such a great help. Did you learn anything?"

"I'll say!" she responded. "I learned three things. I learned never to give an open-faced jelly sandwich to a six-year-old; I learned that when there's nobody else around, you got to take out the garbage by yourself; and I learned one other thing . . ."

"What's that?"

"Well, I learned why you get so grouchy sometimes. All this responsibility must be driving you nuts!"

257. The Daughter Becomes a Cheerleader

Sally was trying out for the school cheerleading squad, and there was stiff competition that year. They would select only twenty girls, and almost sixty had tried out. One night, mother walked past Sally's room and heard weeping. She went in and sat on Sally's bed.

"What's wrong?" asked Mother.

"It's the cheerleading," Sally sniffled. "Those other girls are really good. I . . . I don't think I'm going to make the squad."

"Sally," said Mother, "I think it is very commendable that you tried out and have a firm desire to serve your school. That's what counts. And, even if you don't make the cheerleaders, there are many other fine school organizations that will allow you to channel your energies into serving your fellow students and your school . . ."

"Serving?" sobbed Sally. "Who cares about serving? How am I ever going to date the football players if I'm not a cheerleader?"

258. Children and Relatives

Uncle Ted came for a visit, and he was no sooner in the door when little Scott came running into the room and flung himself into his uncle's arms.

"Just a minute," smiled his uncle, giving the boy a big hug. "I'm glad to see you, too, but how come the big greeting?"

"Are you OK?" asked the boy with obvious tears in his eyes.

"Yes, Scott, I'm fine," said Uncle Ted. "Really, I'm OK. Why, did you think something was wrong with me?"

"Yes, Uncle Ted. I heard Mommy and Daddy talking about you this afternoon . . ."

"Yes?"

"Well," continued Scott, "I hear what they usually say about you, but this afternoon, they were saying such nice things—I thought you were dead!"

259. *Children and Standardized Test Scores*

"I have a problem," said the teacher to Mother. "The standardized test results just came back, and they indicated that Billy is a full three years behind grade level in practically everything. The only problem is, as you well know, Billy is a bright boy who consistently gets Bs and As. Something is not right here."

Mother agreed, and the teacher and Mother called Billy into the conference. They explained the results and asked Billy if he could explain it.

Billy went scarlet, and he hung his head.

"Come on, Billy," said the teacher, "it's truth time."

"Tell us, Son," said Mother.

"Well," answered Billy, still deeply embarrassed, "on the day of the test, I wasn't paying attention; I was looking out the window. When the test began, I didn't know what to do, and I was too ashamed to admit that I'd been daydreaming, so . . . so . . ."

"Yes, Billy."

"So, I filled in everything and connected all the dots!"

260. *Children and Honesty*

One of the neighbors had dropped in and stayed for two hours. During that time, little Debbie had been a terror, interrupting and knocking things over and generally making a nuisance of herself. Once or twice, Mother had glared vehemently in her direction.

Finally, the neighbor stood up and said, "Well, I think it's time for me to be going."

"Oh, no," said Debbie. "Don't go. Stay and talk some more."

"Why, thank you, Debbie," said the neighbor. "I'm so pleased that you want me to stay. Do you like hearing me talk to your mother?"

"Naw!" said Debbie. "I think you're a big bore, but I want you to stay, because the way Mom looks, if you leave, I'm gonna get my bottom spanked!"

261. *Children and Embarrassing Honesty*

Several couples were over for the evening, and seven-year-old Helen was invited to join them instead of playing in her room. For the most part, everything went smoothly, and Helen played quietly in a corner of the room.

In a jovial vein, the conversation got around to the hair color of women relative to disposition.

"I think blondes have the nicest personality," said one.

"No," said another, "I think redheads are by far the more congenial."

"Brunettes," said a third, "are certainly the friendliest."

"What about you, Helen?" someone asked the child. "What do you think?"

"I think you should ask Mommy," said the little girl. "She's been all three, so she should know!"

262. Children and Horribly Embarrassing Honesty

The family had been invited to dinner at a neighbor's, and mother did her best to rehearse Billy in all the proper manners. At the end of the dinner, for instance, Billy was to place his napkin next to his plate and say, "Thank you very much; that was a delicious dinner." Billy and his mother practiced until everything was perfect.

The trouble was that the neighbor served a meal that would have been rejected by the Foreign Legion. Everything was burnt or overly salted. It was a disaster.

Billy, however, acquitted himself wonderfully—he used the proper knives and forks; he kept his elbows off the table; and he used his napkin to perfection. The meal ended, and there was only one hurdle left.

"Billy," urged Mother, "isn't there something you would like to tell Mrs. Jones?"

"Oh, yeah," said Billy. "Thank you very much, Mrs. Jones; that was a delicious dinner."

And, as Mr. and Mrs. Jones smiled sweetly and Mother and Father beamed with pride, Billy leaned over to his mother and, in a whisper that could have been heard on a football field, said, "Now what do I do with this napkin where I spit all that crud she served us?"

263. Sibling Rivalry (I)

Mary and Bobby were fighting—again. The reason had been lost long ago, but that did not deter the brother and sister from their epic battle of words.

"You're stupid and you stink!" cried Mary.

"You're an ugly dog!" Bobby countered. "Mom and Dad should buy you a flea collar!"

At that point, Father entered the room in time to hear Bobby's last remark.

"That's enough, young man!" he stated strongly. "You will not call your sister a dog! Now, apologize to her at once!"

"But, Dad . . ."

"I don't want to hear it! Apologize!"

"Mary," Bobby said, as he turned to his sister, "I'm sorry I called you a dog. I apologize for saying that you should wear a flea collar."

"There," said Father, "isn't that better?"

"Yeah," said Billy, "and to prove how sorry I am, I'm gonna do something for you."

"What?" asked Mary.

"When I go to the store tomorrow," Bobby said with a sugary-sweet smile, "I'll buy you a rawhide chew bone!"

264. Sibling Rivalry (II)

Mom and Dad went out for the evening, leaving Sis in charge of her younger brother. This was not done without misgivings on the part of both parents, but Sis assured them that all would be all right, even though she and her brother were continuously locked in sibling battle.

The minds of Mom and Dad were really on the children that evening, and they got home much earlier than even they expected. The house was perfectly quiet, with Sis asleep on the living room couch.

There was a sheet of paper on the coffee table upon which Sis had apparantly been writing, and Mother glanced at it. It read: "Replace adhesive tape and gauze bandages."

"What!" shouted Mother and wakening Sis. "Adhesive tape? Gauze bandages? Mary, what happened here tonight? Is your brother all right?"

"Relax, Mom," said Sis. "He isn't hurt. Those were just my baby-sitting supplies."

"Baby-sitting supplies?"

"Yeah," Sis replied. "I used the adhesive tape to gag him and the gauze bandages to tie him to his bed, and we didn't fight once all evening!"

265. The Child and School Sports

I remember a boy we'll call Jason. He was in a "special" class in our school, and it was obvious from the moment you met him that he did, indeed, have some very special problems.

Jason loved football, and more than anything else, he wanted to be a member of the school's football team. In perfect honesty, given Jason's mental and physical problems, there was absolutely no chance of that happening.

Yet Jason kept at it. He would try to get to see the coach at least ten times a day, and he saw me even more frequently. "I want to be on the team," he would tell us. "I can do it! I can!"

There were tryouts and the team was selected without Jason, and still the boy persisted. Finally, with the blessings of all concerned, Jason was asked if he wanted to become the "water boy" for the team. With unhidden joy, he accepted. Jason was overjoyed that he had become part of the team.

At the end of the season, an awards banquet was held. Jason won two awards that evening, both awards voted on by the players. He was given an award as the team's most loyal fan, and he was presented with a certificate for serving the best water in the division. When he rose to accept them, the entire team and coaching staff gave him a standing ovation.

I am reminded of Jason from time to time, when I hear people tell me how they would like to help out, but there is really nothing they can do. It's then I remember standing for the brave and wonderful boy who always served the best water in the entire division.

266. *The Facts of Life (I)*

Mother was pregnant for the second time, and she decided that this was a good opportunity to introduce her first child to some of the facts of life.

"Jill," said Mother, "do you know about where babies come from? I mean, do you know how you're going to get a new brother or sister?"

"Yes, Mama, I do," said Jill. "The baby is inside you, Mama. It's growing in there, and when it gets big enough to live outside, it will come out, and that's what people call being born."

"Jill, that's excellent!" said Mother. "That's exactly what happens. Now, Honey, do you have any questions about that?"

"Just one," stated Jill. "The only thing I can't figure out is how the stork got you to swallow a whole baby so it could get inside you in the first place."

267. *The Facts of Life (II)*

Dad was walking down the hallway, when he chanced to hear seven-year-old Kevin talking to his five-year-old brother.

"So remember," Kevin was saying, "when a Mommy and Daddy want a baby, they call up the stork, and the stork brings the baby and drops it down the chimney . . ."

At that point, Father interrupted the conversation and called Kevin out in the hall for a moment.

"Son," said Father, "when you asked me where babies came from, didn't we sit down together, and didn't I explain the whole thing to you?"

"Yes."

"Then why are you telling your brother all this about storks and chimneys?"

"Come on, Dad," said Kevin. "You told me all about little swimming things with long tails and eggs that grow inside people. That's so wild, nobody could believe it. I'm gonna make sure my brother gets the facts!"

268. A Note from School (I)

"Mike is to be congratulated," read the note from school, "because he handed in an absolutely perfect homework paper this afternoon." It was signed by the teacher.

"How wonderful!" exclaimed Mother. "You know Mike, I was worried for a while, because you were doing such poor homework. That's why a note like this means so much."

She began to read again, ". . . a perfect homework paper this afternoon . . . perfect paper this afternoon."

"Come on," she smiled, "let's go show your father."

"In a minute, Mom," said Mike. "First I got to go out to the back yard and give this dollar to Billy Crammer."

"Billy can wait, come with me, now."

"Really, Mom, I gotta do it now. If I don't pay him on time he says he won't sell me any more of his homework papers!"

269. A Note from School (II)

"Timmy," yelled Father, "get in here!"

When Timmy had arrived, Father and Mother were glaring down at him.

"Young man," said Father, "this is a note from your teacher. It's about the poor quality of your homework. You need to put more effort into doing homework!"

"More effort!" said Timmy, his eyes wide with amazement. "Mom and Dad, I spend half my time calling kids on the phone to get the answers or copying from their papers in school. Good Grief! How much more time can I put in?"

270. *The Report Card (Humorous)*

"I'm worried about my father," one student told another. "He went to the doctor yesterday, and the doc told him that he has low blood pressure."

"Don't worry about it," said her companion. "Just give him this."

He handed the girl a folded piece of paper.

"What's this? Is it some new medicine?"

"Better than that," said her friend. "It's my report card. When I showed it to my father last night, he got red in the face, and his blood pressure got so high, we had to give him pills to bring it down!"

271. *The Report Card (Serious)*

There are no schools we know of that do not issue some type or form of report card. Indeed, whether they are called "report cards" or "progress reports" or whatever else, they are indicators to parents of the progress or lack of it that is being made by the child in school.

It was suggested once in a tongue-in-cheek manner that the schools and the parents should receive a "report card" as well. If that were to become an actuality, what might it indicate?

Would school receive an *A* for each child who reached the honor roll, and a *D* or *F* for each child who failed?

Would parents get an *A* for helping with homework and an *F* for doing it for the child?

Would the school receive an *A* for the number of noses wiped, boots put on, hands held, and tears dried?

Would parents get an *A* for each hour of worry and concern over the future of their child?

Would schools get *A*s for each bully that had been faced down, each underachiever who had been cajoled or threatened or guided back to productivity, and each child who suddenly saw the light under some teacher's guidance?

Would the home receive an *A* in the unspoken and unreckoned hours of tenderness and love toward a child that often had to manifest itself in the form of strong discipline?

And, finally, would both the school and the home be awarded an *A* + in the sorrows of the human heart?

272. Children and Cooking

The principal and her husband were having dinner at the home of the PTA president and her husband. The meal had been fine, and when dessert had been brought to the table, Mother made an announcement.

"I'd like you to know that Karen helped with the meal this evening. She made these muffins."

Everyone beamed at the little girl, especially the principal who was busy on her second muffin.

"These are great!" she said through a mouthful of dessert. "What a great flavor!"

"Yes," said the principal's husband, "these are delicious! Did you use a special recipe, Karen?"

"Nope," said the child. "It's just a recipe out of one of our cook books."

"Come on," urged the principal reaching for her third, "you must have done something special."

"No, honest!" said Karen. "I did it just as the recipe said." Then she paused.

"Of course," she added, "the recipe did call for raisins, and we didn't have any, but that shouldn't make any difference. I used a box of cat treats, and they look just the same as raisins!"

273. The Family and the School Play

Sammy had a part in the school play, and he was overjoyed about it. The fact that the part consisted of one line of spoken dialog didn't deter him or cool his spirits a bit. In fact, he rehearsed that one line so often that everyone in the house knew it by heart.

The only trouble was that Sammy had trouble with the line. Perhaps it was a mental block, but no matter how often he practiced the single line, he always got one or two words out of place or reversed or left out.

Finally, it was the night of the performance, and Dad took Sammy aside.

"Sammy," he said, "we're all going to be out in that audience. When you say that line, we'll be saying it in our minds with you. We love you no matter what; just go up there and do your best."

So it happened that Sammy, in costume and makeup, stood on stage and said, "Sire, I will venture forth and slay the dragon!" He did it perfectly, for the first time ever. Then, he broke from the stage, ran down to the footlights and screamed, "Hey, Dad! Did you hear? We got it right!"

274. A Guest Comes to Dinner

"Remember," Father told Sally, "the guest always comes first. So, if there is only one of something left, like the last chop or the last serving of potatoes, make certain our guest gets it."

Actually, there was plenty of everything, and all went fine until the dessert came along. It was a particularly fine cake which Mother had personally baked, and everyone loved it. In fact, they loved it so much that everyone had seconds, and it soon came down to one slice of cake left on the plate.

"Go ahead, Sally," said the guest. "Take that piece."

"No," said Sally, "you take it!"

"I admit it's tempting, but I couldn't."

"You'd better!" snarled Sally.

"What do you mean?"

"If you don't take it soon," said Sally, "I will, and you have no idea of the amount of guilt Mom and Dad can lay on me!"

275. Children and Pets

Ruffy, the family dog, had slept with Billy since the dog was a puppy. However, Mom and Dad had listened to some relatives expound about how unsanitary it was for an animal to share a bed with the boy. Consequently, one evening, Mom and Dad announced that Ruffy would not be permitted to sleep on Billy's bed any longer.

"But, Mom! Dad!" protested Billy.

"No," said Father, "we've made up our minds. Ruffy does not sleep with you any longer. That's final!"

And, in spite of vociferous arguments to the contrary, they stuck to the order of no Ruffy on Billy's bed.

The following morning, Mother passed Billy's room and peeked in. Billy was gone. His bed had been turned down, but the boy was no where to be found. Calling her husband, they began a search of the house.

"Here," said Father, finally, as he led Mother to the door of the kitchen. "He did not disobey us."

Mother looked, and there was Billy, one arm around Ruffy, sound asleep—in the dog's bed!

276. The Family on Vacation (I)

On vacation, the family went to the Pennsylvania town of Gettysburg, site of the great Civil War battle. In that town, there are retired National Park Rangers who, for a nominal fee, will go with you in your car and take you on a personally guided tour of the battlefield and environs. It is a fantastic experience.

For the entire two and one-half hours of the tour, Bobby sat enthralled as the guide pointed out the various areas of the locality and made history come alive. Bobby's eyes were shining as he relived the battle through the guide's words.

Finally, the tour was over, and the guide leaned down to Bobby.

"Now," said the guide, "I'm going to give you the names of some books which will tell you even more about this place."

"Books!" said Bobby, and his eyes grew wide.

"This ain't fair!" he protested as he turned to his parents. "All this time the man was talking to us, he was TEACHING us! That's not fair; I'm supposed to be on vacation!"

277. The Family on Vacation (II)

"We are going on vacation," Mom told brother and sister. "I want to enjoy this vacation. I want this vacation to run smoothly. You two will not fight on this vacation! Do you hear me?"

"Yes, Mom!" they said in unison.

And, in all truthfulness, the vacation went wonderfully. The family spent a delightful two weeks in a rented cottage by the seashore. The days were warm and sunny; the nights were cool and filled with stars. Never was heard a discouraging word from either brother or sister, let alone a squabble of even the smallest variety. They got along better than the United Nations!

At the end of two weeks the family packed up and headed back home.

After they had unpacked, Mother flopped into a living room chair and sighed, "Well, we're home. Vacation's over."

"Is vacation really over?" asked brother.

"I'm afraid so," said Mother.

"Good," said the boy who turned and punched his sister in the arm.

"Thank goodness," echoed the sister as she kicked her brother in the shins, "I don't think I could have lasted another week!"

278. The Family Sits Down to Dinner (I)

"I tell you," Mother said, "your son could eat us out of house and home if we let him."

"All kids have good appetites," said Father.

"OK, just watch Jimmy at dinner tonight."

Mother seemed to have the situation pegged. At dinner that evening, Jimmy had double and triple helpings of everything! At dessert, however, he seemed to slow down and actually refused a third helping of cake.

"What's the matter?" smiled Father. "Did you finally run out of steam?"

"I guess so," said Jimmy.

Mother and Dad smiled at each other.

"Actually," Jimmy continued, "if I'd have known that you were going to offer me all the dessert I wanted, I never would have had that whole pizza and that quart of ice cream an hour before dinner!"

279. The Family Sits Down to Dinner (II)

The family had sat down to dinner and the meal had begun, when young George turned unexpectedly and knocked his plate from the table. The plate did not break, merely made noise, and George quickly retrieved it and placed it back in his place.

"No, Son," said Mother, "you don't eat from a plate that has fallen to the floor. Go get yourself a clean plate from the kitchen."

The boy returned with a new plate, and Mother dished some casserole upon it. As George was beginning to eat, however, Mother looked a bit closer at what appeared to be streaks along one edge of the plate.

"George," said Mother, "are you certain this was a clean plate you got?"

"Sure it is, Mom," replied George between bites. "I watched the dog lick it clean as a whistle when I fed him from it just a little while ago!"

280. The Family Sits Down to Dinner (III)

"Dinner time is the worst time of the day," the man told me. "We do nothing but fight. We fight over the food—it's too salty; it's too cold; it's too hot. We argue over who's going to get the drumstick. My son screams that his sister just stuck her tongue out at him. My daughter swears that her brother kicked her under the table. The baby takes the mashed potatoes and throws them directly at me. My wife and I argue about the bad behavior of the kids at the dinner table, and in the meantime, the kids are throwing food and making life miserable. Finally, dinner is over and the kids go off to their rooms or their friends, and I can get a little peace. I tell you, dinner with the family is driving me nuts!"

I'm no expert," I replied, "but if the dinner time is what's causing the trouble, why don't you try eating separately for a while?"

"I couldn't do that!" replied the gentleman, deeply shocked. "Why, dinner is the only opportunity we have for spending quality family time together!"

281. The Family at Thanksgiving

"Before we ask God's blessing on this food," said Grandfather as he presided over the Thanksgiving feast, "I'd like to go around the table and have each one of us tell the one thing we are most thankful for."

So the family began. Grandma told how she was thankful that all her children and grandchildren were healthy; Father told how he was grateful for Mother and the children; the eldest daughter, Sandy, expounded on how thankful she was that she was doing well in college, and so forth.

Finally, it came time for six-year-only Harry.

"Well, Harry," said Grandfather, "have you had time to figure out what you're thankful for?"

"I sure have," said Harry. "I been looking at your faces, and the thing I'm most thankful for right now is that I'm not this turkey!"

282. The Family and Christmas

On Christmas Day, the family had risen early and spent those first hours lost in torn wrapping paper beneath the shimmering tree. Later, they had attended church services and returned home to be joined by Grandma and Grandad for a sumptuous Christmas feast. They sat around admiring the gifts, and toward evening, a fire was kindled and the entire family sang Christmas carols.

When bedtime finally arrived, little Beth was tucked in and kissed, and before Mother and Father left the room, she called to them.

"Daddy," she said, "how come everybody feels so good today?"

"Well, honey," answered Father, "I think it's because this is a special day when we celebrate God's love for us."

"Does God only love us on this one day?" asked the child.

"Oh, no," Mother answered. "God loves us every day of the year. Why do you ask?"

"Well," she said, "if God loves us every day of the year the same as He does at Christmas, how come we don't act the way we do at Christmas on all the other days?"

That question was asked twenty years ago.

I still don't have an answer.

Do you?

283. The Family and Hanukkah

"Go get the matches from the kitchen," Father told little Scott. "It's time to light the first candle on the menorah."

"Daddy," said Scott as he returned, "is it true that Hanukkah is about a miracle?"

"That's right," said Father. "Hanukkah celebrates a miracle that happened when God kept the lamp burning in the Tabernacle for eight days without oil. That's why we light a candle each night—to remember the miracle."

"So, it was a miracle?" asked Scott.

"Yes, it was," answered Father, "but why do you keep asking about miracles?"

"Well," said Scott, "I think we're going to need another miracle, because while I was out in the kitchen, I dropped the matches into the sink!"

284. Helping with Homework (Humorous)

"Bonnie," said the teacher, "would you please come to my desk?"

Bonnie walked slowly to the teacher's desk and stood as if expecting calamity at any moment.

"Don't be so nervous, Bonnie," said the teacher. "I called you up to congratulate you. For a while there, the quality of your homework was headed downhill, but lately, it has been improving and getting quite good."

"Oh, thank you, Ma'am," said Bonnie.

"Just one more thing. Do you have any reason for this turnaround in your homework? Is their a particular reason why your homework has improved?"

"Yes, Ma'am," said Bonnie with a smile. "My father started taking a night course at college, and he can't help me with it any more!"

285. *Helping with Homework (Serious)*

"Son," said the older man as he opened the door. "Come on in, but where's Jenny and the kids?"

"I didn't bring them," said the younger of the two men. "I wanted to talk to you alone and tell you off."

"Tell me off? Son, what do you mean?"

"Do you remember when I was a kid, and you used to help me with my homework? You'd never give me the answer, and if I got something wrong, you'd make me do it over until I got it right."

"Yes," said the older man, "of course I remember."

"And do you remember how I used to blow up at you and tell you how you were a slave driver and how I would never, never put my children through that sort of thing?"

"I remember quite well."

"Well, Dad," said the younger man, "now I have children of my own, and last night I made my daughter do a math problem three times until she got it right, and she sobbed and told me that I didn't love her. Dad, I never realized until then how much love it takes to do what's right rather than what's easy. I just dropped by to say thanks and to tell you that I hope I can turn out to be half as good a slave driver as you were!"

286. *Brother and Sister Fight*

"Mom!" yelled Annie, "I'm going out and I can't find my mascara! I know Billy took it!"

"Billy," asked Mother, "did you take your sister's mascara?"

"I sure did," stated Billy.

"How many times have I told you not to take . . ."

"But, Mom," Billy said, "earlier today I made myself a peanut butter and jelly sandwich, and when I turned around it was gone, because Annie snitched it!"

"Well," said Mother, "I certainly don't condone her taking it from you, but perhaps she was hungry. What possible need could you have for her mascara?"

"Please, Mother," said Billy in a highly offended tone, "you don't have to fulfill a need when honor demands that you act upon the principle of the thing!"

287. Father and Son Fight

"That settles it!" roared Father. "You are going to your room and staying there!"

"But, Dad," said the Son, "I have that game tonight, and . . ."

"To your room!"

"Wait a minute!" said the Son. "Didn't you once tell me that when people are angry, they should wait twenty-four hours before acting to give themselves a chance to cool down?"

"Not exactly," said Dad. "That's what I used to tell *my* father when I wanted to get out of punishment from him. It didn't work then, either!"

288. Father and Daughter Fight

Father entered the room to find a boy with spiked hair, a dog collar around his neck, and four earrings in his left ear sitting in Dad's favorite chair, with his motorcycle-booted feet up on the coffee table.

"Who are you?" exclaimed Father.

Before the boy could answer, Daughter arrived with a book.

"Daddy," she said, "this is Dogmeat. He dropped by to get this book. He's going now."

When the boy had left, Father whirled on his daughter.

"Listen," he stated, "if you are even thinking of dating that, that . . ."

"Easy, Dad," said Daughter, "I don't think I'd feel right dating somebody named Dogmeat, do you? But, I did invite him to come over this afternoon."

"What? Why did you . . ."

"You see," continued Daughter, "I did meet this nice boy who's on the football team, and I invited him for dinner tonight.

"That's why I invited Dogmeat this afternoon—so you'd have a basis for a favorable comparison!"

289. Mother and Son Fight

Mother and her small son were having an argument, because Mother insisted that the lad clean his room immediately.

"All you ever do is yell at me!" stated the Son. "I'm tired of you yelling at me!"

"Clean up your room," said Mother, "and I won't have to yell."

"That's it!" said the boy, and he turned and walked away.

"Where are you going?"

"I'm leaving!" said the boy. "I'm running away! I'm going someplace where they treat you good. You'll be sorry. You'll never see me again!"

With that, the lad turned and stamped from the room, only to return less than five seconds later and march straight up to Mother.

"Before I go," he asked, scratching his toe on the floor, "could you make me some chocolate chip cookies to take with me?"

290. Mother and Daughter Fight

The teenage daughter was going out on a date with a boy whom mother had not met. Mother visited the girl in her room.

"This boy you're going out with tonight—what's he like?"

"Here," said the daughter, handing mother a photograph.

The picture showed a young man in a black leather jacket with a skull and crossbones on one sleeve. The boy had hair twisted into spikes, several earrings dangling from his left ear, and wore a sardonic and defiant grin showing two missing teeth. His left hand held a bicycle chain menacingly.

"This . . ." stammered mother, "this . . . is the boy . . . you're going out with?"

"No," said the daughter, "this is." She handed her mother a photo of a clean-shaven young man in a jacket and tie.

"But . . . I don't understand . . ."

"Well," said the daughter with a smile, "I showed you both photos, because I figured you just might be grateful enough to let me stay out until midnight?"

291. Brothers and Sisters Protecting Each Other

Bobby and his friend Alan were playing in the back yard when Bobby's younger sister came out and began to "hang around" her brother and his friend.

"Hey, Ugly!" said the friend. "You ain't wanted here! Get out!" And, he pushed her.

Bobby was up in a flash and on top of Alan even faster. Before he knew what was happening, Alan was pinned to the ground, and Bobby knelt on top of him with balled fists.

"Don't you ever push my sister!" roared Bobby. "And don't call her 'Ugly', either!"

"I . . . I'm sorry!"

"OK," said Bobby, helping up his friend. "You just remember; you **never** call her 'Ugly,' and you never hit her!"

Then, turning toward his admiring sister, he added, "That's my job!"

And, with complete disdain, Bobby placed a kick in his sister's britches and snapped, "Get out of here, Ugly!"

292. Keeping Peace in the Family

"Arnie," said Father to his son, "I'd like to tell you a secret in the strictest confidence. The other day, your sister came to me and told me how much she admires you. She said that she thought you were good looking and kind and intelligent, and she was proud to have you as a brother. So, Son, when I see you mocking your sister and fighting with her, it gives me a lot of pain. We won't mention this talk to your sister, because it would embarrass her, but do you think you can act a little better toward your sister from now on?"

With tears flowing down his cheeks, little Arnie gave protestations that he would evermore be "nice" to his sister.

Five minutes later, Father called his daughter into the room. When she was seated, he began a speech which started, "Ellen, I'd like to tell you a secret in the strictest confidence . . ." and ended, ". . . do you think you can act a little better toward your brother from now on?"

After Ellen, also in tears, had left with assurances similar to her brother's, Father sat back and turned his eyes toward heaven.

"Oh, Lord," he sighed, "the things I do to keep peace in this family!"

293. The Teacher Visits the Family

"Tommy and Rose," Mother called, "come here, please!"

The children ran into the room and stood before Mother.

"How are you doing in school, Tommy?" asked Mother. "Have you been paying attention and doing your homework and studying for your tests?"

"Yes, Mom."

"Rose, have you been doing the same good things as your brother?" asked Mother.

"Yes, Mama, I have."

"Neither of you have been acting up, have you?"

"No, Mama!" they answered in unison.

Just then the doorbell rang.

"Good," said Mother, "because as I was looking out the window a moment ago, I saw your teacher pulling up to the curb. That's her at the door, and you two had better have been telling me the truth, because there is no time left to pretend we're not home!"

294. Illness in the Family

When I was a child, my grandmother lived with us. She was prone to "headaches" as we called them, although with hindsight, they were most likely migraines.

When Grandma got one of her "spells," there was nothing to do for it but to let her lie down with a cool compress on her head and keep the house quiet. As a child, that was all but a sentence of doom, for a quiet house meant no running, no yelling, no radio (TV was several years away), and no games that involved shouting or even talking loudly. For a child, it took every ounce of will (my own and my parents) to keep those silent vigils.

It was during this time that I discovered books. In those quiet afternoons, I had no need of sitting and pouting for lack of activity, for while the entire house lay hushed and cool, I sailed the seas with Long John Silver, fought glorious battles beside Sir Lancelot, and braved the hazards of the Yukon with Jack London.

Grandma died when I was twelve, and by then, reading was so much a part of me, there was no way the habit could be broken.

I have not thought of those days for some time, but when I do turn my mind back to those summers of long ago, I wish I could tell my Grandmother how sorry I am that she suffered those headaches, but that I hope she never had any regrets about having to keep the house quiet.

I wonder, Grandma, if it weren't for your illness, would I have learned to love to read?

295. When Tragedy Strikes the Family

Kevin was a teenager. He had been assigned some tasks around the house, but they were seldom done without repeated injunctions, warnings, reminders, and even threats. Most obnoxious seemed to be the taking out of the garbage, a job he so often neglected that major battles had been fought over huge piles of refuse. Moreover, his relationship to his younger brother was relegated to punches and sharp, crackling words.

One night, Dad did not come home from work. The police arrived and reported the accident. He had not suffered; death was instantaneous.

The funeral was, as most blessedly are, a blur. Now the widow and the two sons were back in the house and the silence had followed them.

As Mother sat for a moment in the kitchen, she heard the soft sobs of her younger child and went toward their source in the living room. As she arrived, she saw that someone else had gotten there before her, and Kevin sat, his brother in his arms, gently smoothing the boy's hair and whispering softly into his ear. When the younger boy had calmed his breathing, Kevin left for the kitchen. A few moments later, he emerged carrying the garbage and heading for the back door. He looked up and his eyes met those of his mother.

At that moment, she told me many years later, she realized with crystal certainty that there had been a death, but there had also been a birth; something had ended, but something new had just begun.

296. The Family Pulls Together

How many families have I had personal experience with? Even I don't know, but certainly, over the years, it must have been hundreds. I have sat and listened to distraught parents tell me of battles fought between brothers and sisters, of children who refused to do any chores at all around the home, or glacial silences where parents didn't talk to children and children all but ignored the existence of parents, and of cases far worse and so confidentially traumatic, they may not be retold. I have heard and experienced it all.

Yet, rarely, and certainly never that I can remember of my own experience, have I dealt with a family that didn't pull together when something threatened the family unit. Perhaps it was the death of a family member, a financial crisis such as the loss of a job, a traumatic illness of one of the children or a parent—whatever the tragedy, rarely have I seen the family not pull together to solve the problem, so that they could get back to the security of fighting among themselves.

I knew of one boy who had hovered at the brink of failure and hung out with the worst kids in school. When his mother got sick and required extended care, he changed along with the situation. He was never an honor student, but his grades went up and the bad companions were left behind, because, as he told me, he couldn't "afford" them anymore, since he had serious things that needed doing.

We can fight among ourselves, but when the storm arrives, we will hold hands and draw close until the tempest passes.

297. The Family and God

The family had been talking just before dinner about the traveling they had done over the years. Mother, for instance, had been born and raised in various towns in New Jersey, while Father was brought up in Houston, Texas. Harry, the eldest child, saw the light of day in Portland, Oregon. Dolly, the next in line, had been born in Sheridan, Wyoming. Kenny had joined the family in Dothan, Alabama. Finally, Mary Beth, the youngest, had been born in Binghamton, New York. A map of the United States was produced and each location marked with a pin.

Dinner was served, and as the entire family sat down at the table, Father asked Mary Beth to say grace for the meal. As the rest of the family lowered their eyes, Mary Beth raised hers to the ceiling.

"Hey, God!" she prayed. "Thanks for the food, and bless us all, and grandma and grandpa, too . . . and God—I don't know how You ever got us together from all those different places, but I'm real glad You did! I love You, God! Thanks!"

298. The Rewards of Family Living (Humorous, I)

"You know, Honey," Mother said to Father as they lay in bed one night, "I was just thinking how wonderful it was that we met and married and had a family."

"You were?"

"Yes, I was thinking how happy I am to have you as a husband and our three lovely children. I was thinking how rewarding it is to get up each morning to be with you and to care for the kids and to see them through the day and school and all their little problems. How lucky and happy I am!"

"Darling!" said Father, as he turned to hold her.

"And, I was also thinking something else."

"What's that, my dearest?"

"Well," said Mother, "I was thinking that while we are both in this loving mood, maybe we could take a vacation, just you and I, and get away from this menagerie for a while!"

299. The Rewards of Family Living (Humorous, II)

Father was talking to his unmarried brother, telling him about the rewards of family life.

"It is beyond description," commented Father. "There you are, sitting in your favorite chair. You have just had a wonderful dinner, and now, your little son crawls up into your lap to be held before bedtime. You have the feeling that you know what life is all about; you have a great sense of peace; your heart overflows with joy . . ."

"And how long does that feeling last?" asked the brother.

"Let's see," said Father reflectively, "until your wife asks you to take out the garbage, the baby pulls the cat's tail, and brother and sister become locked in mortal combat—about 30 seconds!"

300. The Rewards of Family Living (Serious)

There have been families that have produced horse thieves and bank robbers while other families have produced doctors and clergymen and philosophers. There have been families that have done very well financially, while others have barely eeked out a living. There have been families that have breezed through life with a smile and a song, and other families that have met tragedy and pain at every turn.

Yet all of them have held one possession in common. Because they were a family, they have always had each other. Yes, fights and squabbles are a part of family life, but they are the storms that come and go upon the mountain while the mountain remains.

When we talk of the true rewards of family living, the first and foremost of all will always be the people who make up the family. These are the arms that hold and are held; the lips that sometimes scold and sometimes soothe; the eyes that watch a thousand stories of power and glory unfold; the ears that listen to daylight shouts and midnight whispers. These are the people who make up the family.

They are the greatest reward. They are family. They are mine.

WHEN THE RUBBER CHICKEN BOUNCES—STORIES FOR THE AFTER-DINNER SPEAKER

The "Rubber Chicken Route," so named because chicken is so often served at group luncheons and dinners, has existed for years. Rarely will a group of people organize a dinner or a dinner affair where it is not expected that there will be at least one and probably several speakers following the main meal. If you are to be one of these speakers, then once the "rubber chicken" has bounced around the room, you will be expected to rise and entertain, enliven, and inspire the gathering. It's enough to give anyone indigestion!

In this section, you will find stories specifically suited to after-dinner speeches and speakers, including many that will serve you well if you are to be the master/mistress-of-ceremonies for the evening. Always remember that if you have a good time and obviously enjoy yourself, your audience will enjoy you as well. *Bon appetit!*

301. The Untenable Position of the After-Dinner Speaker (I)

I tell you frankly that I feel rather like some relatives of mine who invited the boss (in a moment of weakness) to dinner. That boss was easily the most tiresome individual in the world, and all afternoon, Mom and Dad had argued about it as they went about preparing the meal.

That evening, as the crew sat down to eat, Father asked the "boss" if he'd like to say grace, but the guest deferred to the child of the household.

"But," said the seven-year-old, "I don't know what to say!"

"Nonsense," smiled Mother, "just say what you hear Mommy and Daddy say at the table."

"Oh," murmured the boy.

Then the child cleared his throat, folded his hands, and, looking heavenward, intoned, "Oh, God, what could have possessed me to invite that crashing bore to dinner?"

302. The Untenable Position of the After-Dinner Speaker (II)

One of the things you learn about as an after-dinner speaker is that there are many kinds of audiences. There are audiences that are for you and there are audiences that are against you, and with either audience, you stand a reasonable chance of success. The one type of audience that will give you fits, however, is the apathetic audience. To speak before a group that sits with a blank and uncaring expression is enough to make a boulder perspire.

I was very glad, therefore, to find out that you are not an apathetic audience. I must admit, I went straight to the source. I asked your president about you.

"Bob," I asked, "you should know best; is this group apathetic?"

And Bob looked me straight in the eye and with absolute candor told me, "I don't know, and I don't care!"

303. The Food Served at the Dinner (I)

Before I begin, I would like to make a comment about the food that we have just had.

What can I say? I have eaten at many restaurants and had many dinners such as this one. Rarely have I felt so much like a Greek god.

That's right, after that dinner, I feel just like a Greek god. I don't know when I've had a better burnt offering put before me!

304. The Food Served at the Dinner (II)

I simply must remark that the food was delicious. It was truly an outstanding meal. It was so good, in fact, that I could barely get down the fourth and fifth helpings.

In fact, I think this dinner really contributed to my overweight problem. Your president just now told me that I looked like a sharp dresser. I said, "How do you mean?" and he said, "Your middle drawer is hanging out!"

Even that wouldn't have been so bad, but I stepped out to the lobby, and they had one of those "talking scales." I got on, and do you know what it said? "One at a time, please!"

305. The Food Here Compared to Cafeteria Food

Actually, the food served tonight was wonderful compared to what I usually get from our cafeteria.

I'm not saying that our cafeteria food is bad, but our physical education department has been known to use the cafeteria's hotcakes as bases for softball games.

When I was just starting out in school, my supervisor came to observe me. Afterward it was lunchtime, so we went to the cafeteria.

"Well," I asked my observer, "how was I?"

"I think," she said, "that you were at least as good as this food."

I cried for three days!

306. *Getting Your Facts Straight*

If we are going to truly communicate, then it is vitally important that we get our facts straight.

I remember that I once entered an elevator, and there was only one other fellow besides myself. We stood in silence as the door closed, and I immediately noticed an overwhelming odor eminating from the general direction of my fellow passenger.

Finally, I could stand it no more.

"Pardon me, Sir," I said, "but I think your deodorant has failed."

The fellow sniffed the air.

"It must be yours," he answered, "I don't wear any deodorant!"

307. *What the Audience Wants to Hear*

It was a few weeks back that your president called me on the phone and asked if I would speak at this affair. I was overjoyed and honored, and I accepted at once.

The only thing that gave me trouble was selecting a topic for the evening, so I called your president back and asked her.

"Look," I told her, "I can talk about a lot of topics. I can talk about education, the school, memories of school, politics, the economy . . . take your pick."

"Anything you choose," she said, "will be fine."

"Let me rephrase," I said, getting a bit frustrated. "You know your people far better than I do. Put yourself in their position, and tell me exactly what they would like to hear me say."

"That's easy," she said without missing a beat. " 'Thank you, and good night!' "

308. *How the Audience Reacts (I)*

A rather famous speaker was once asked to address a group of farmers from a rather rural area. He accepted the challenge and gave the best speech of which he was capable, which was formidable.

The audience sat stoney-faced. As the speaker went on for thirty minutes, they sat as if encased in ice. Not a comment was made; not a laugh erupted; there was a complete lack of applause throughout the speech. In short, it wasn't that they reacted badly to the speech, but there was simply no reaction.

When the speaker finally finished, there was polite applause and the farmers filed out of the hall, still not uttering a word.

Totally frustrated by this lack of reaction, the speaker ran after and caught up with the last farmer to leave.

"Look," said the speaker, "I'm not angry, but was my speech that bad?"

"Your speech was fine," said the farmer. "It was thrilling."

"I don't understand. If my speech was so good, why didn't you laugh or applaud during it?"

"Because," answered the farmer, "you gave us a lot of ideas tonight. You might say that you were like a farmer, planting those ideas in our minds. You planted those seeds, and every farmer knows that you don't go around making a commotion and digging it up until the seed's had a chance to grow. What did you want? Clapping or learning?"

309. How the Audience Reacts (II)

Whenever someone asks me how I feel when an audience reacts or doesn't react to what I am saying, I tell them the story of Abraham Lincoln at Gettysburg. His invitation to be present was almost an afterthought. He was not to be the principal speaker, and he had jotted down his short speech on the back of an envelope during his train ride from Washington.

The main speaker gave a long and impassioned speech which was met by thunderous applause. Then Lincoln stood. It took him less than two minutes to say what he had written, and when he finished, there was not a sound, not one clap, not a cheer; the audience merely stood.

That simple speech was so powerful that it had touched the hearts and minds of all present. In the midst of a great and bloody Civil War, this speech had been an enduring tribute to all who had fallen in battle and a rededication of those living to the future. People stood with their hands at their sides; their mouths closed tightly; their eyes moist. There was no applause, because there could be none. The audience had been stirred to their very souls, and there was no room for anything else.

Take that to heart and know that I believe that the reaction of an audience to a speech is not what matters, whereas the reaction the speech has upon the audience is everything!

310. *Boring Speeches and Speakers (I)*

The speaker had droned on for hours, or so it seemed. The audience had grown restless, but the speaker didn't seem to notice.

"Remember," intoned the speaker, "my motto is: If it feels good, do it! If it feels good, do it! If it feels good, do it!"

Just then, one man in the audience pushed back his chair, stretched his arms and yawned loudly, and, with a sigh, he started out of the hall.

"Just one moment, Sir!" said the speaker. "Why are you leaving?"

"Because," said the gentleman, "I have finally taken your speech to heart. I'm getting out of here, because it feels good! It feels good! It feels good!!!"

311. *Boring Speeches and Speakers (II)*

I once knew a young man who wanted me to teach him to be a speaker. He had been asked to give a speech, and he wanted a "crash course" before the event.

I wasn't able to give him much, and when I learned that he was going to read a prepared speech, I gave him the standard stuff that you probably already know—you pause half a beat at commas and a full beat at periods.

With that information, he rose to read his speech.

Well, it was the most disjointed thing you have ever heard. He paused in the middle of a thought; he stopped in mid-sentence; nothing he did seemed to have any reason at all!

After the speech, I ran up to him. "What did you do?" I asked. "Why did you pause like that?"

"I was just doing what you told me; I was stopping at the periods and commas!"

I looked at his speech, looked closely at him, and said, "You idiot, those aren't periods! You forgot to clean your glasses!"

312. *Length of the Speech (I)*

Someone asked me how long a speech is supposed to be, and I told him that a good speech is like a woman's skirt—long enough to cover the subject but short enough to keep it interesting.

That didn't seem to satisfy him, so I told him the one secret that someone told me when I started to speak.

"Son," I said, "if you speak until you hear the first snore, you will know that you have gone too long. Keep your speech short enough that it never gets to that point."

313. *Length of the Speech (II)*

When I asked to speak tonight, I asked your president how long I should talk. He very graciously told me that I could take as long as I wanted.

"Yes," I said, "I appreciate that, but what if I wanted to talk until eleven-thirty?"

"You go right ahead and speak until eleven-thirty," your president told me. "Of course, the rest of us will be leaving at eleven, but you speak as long as you like."

314. *The Purpose of the Gathering*

A child was taken by his father to visit the workshop of a sculptor. As the child watched, the sculptor chipped away at a block of marble from which was emerging a beautiful statue of a Roman soldier.

"How do you do that?" asked the child.

"Simple," replied the sculptor, "I just take away all the marble that's not the sculpture."

"Gosh," said the boy pointing to the emerging statue, "and I'll bet he never knew he was in there!"

Let's believe that our gathering tonight will be rather like that boy's visit to the sculptor. Let us hope that we may chip away everything that is not essential for our endeavor, and let us hope that this evening, there is something of beauty just waiting to emerge.

315. *Administrator Suited to the Task*

Your president came to my school to ask if I would speak to you this evening, and after I had accepted, she said that she thought I was a good choice, because a school administrator always makes a good speaker.

"Oh?" I said. "Is that because of my experience in education?"

"No."

"Because of my experience speaking before different audiences?"

"No."

"Because I have had experience as a teacher?"

"Nope."

"Then why?"

"Because," she said, "you are one of the few people I know who has never allowed lack of knowledge on a subject to interfere with your opening your mouth and speaking out about it!"

316. How After-Dinner Speeches Got Started

Of course, no one knows for certain how after-dinner speeches got started, but I have my own theory.

I think there were a group of cavemen and cavewomen who had just finished a huge dinner of filet of Mammoth with Pterodactyl Sauce. They were all sitting around burping and feeling very relaxed, when someone suggested that they take a snooze to help the digestion.

I'm certain they all tried to sleep, but those were perilous times, and the thought of a wandering Saber-toothed tiger dropping in must have kept them watchful and alert.

At that point, I think that one of those fellows looked over at his fellow Neanderthal and said, "Hey, Ugg! This isn't working; we're wide awake. Why don't you tell us that boring story about the tar pit and the Wooly rhinoceros? Then we'll have no trouble falling asleep at all!"

I tend to think that that's the way these speeches got started, and it is nice to know that I stand before you this afternoon at the end of such a long and prestigious history!

317. A Benediction for the Gathering

I remember a minister who was invited to attend one of these affairs, and he was beseiged all afternoon by various members of the organization. The poor man hardly had time to eat.

When the meal was over, the president of the organization rose and proclaimed, "Since we have Reverend Jones with us this afternoon, I'm certain it will not be imposing if I ask him to come up here and give a short benediction for our gathering."

This took the Reverend completely by surprise, and as he made his way to the dais, he very audibly asked the president, "What would you have me say?"

"Whatever you are inspired to say," answered the president. "Perhaps there is some Bible verse that would sum up our meeting?"

"That I can do," said the reverend, and he turned and looked directly at the audience.

"Ladies and Gentlemen," he said. "Luke 23:34—'Father, forgive them, for they know not what they do!' "

And he sat down!

318. Humorous "Roast" of the Honored Guest (I)

Our guest this evening has had a long relationship with education, and I remember one incident that occurred in school that truly bespeaks her character.

She was coming out of the school one afternoon, when she saw a bunch of children standing around a cardboard box, from which peeked the head of a kitten.

"Kids," she said, "what are you doing here?"

"Well, Ma'am," said one child, "I got this kitten to give away, and everybody wants it, so we're holding a contest. The kid who can tell the biggest lie gets to take the cat home."

"Children!" said our guest, "that's terrible. You shouldn't make lying the basis for winning a contest. You should tell the truth, as I do. I have never told a lie in my life, and I never will. I have always been steadfast and upright!"

"OK," said one boy as he handed our friend the box, "you won. Just remember to give it lots of milk!"

319. Humorous "Roast" of the Honored Guest (II)

When he was a young man, our guest and his brother were in the trucking business. They used to make short hauls and earn some extra money that way.

One day, they got a notice that a panel on trucking safety wanted to speak to them and ask them some questions about trucking, just for their own information.

"Let's just imagine," the head of the panel asked our guest, "that you are driving the rig alone. Your brother is behind the seat, sleeping. You're headed down a grade, when all at once, your brakes fail. You try your emergency brake, and that fails, too! You look up and you are headed for a railroad crossing where a locomotive has just started to cross.

"Now, what do you do?"

"Easy," said our guest. "I wake up my brother, because this is going to be one heck of an accident, and he's going to want to see it, first hand!"

320. Humorous "Roast" of the Honored Guest (III)

You know, several of us wanted to get something very special for our honored guest this evening; something out of the ordinary. We had many suggestions, and we rejected them all.

Finally, someone suggested that we might want to do something for his home; something like convert one of the rooms into a den.

We thought that this was a dandy idea, and we went to see his wife.

"We'd like to take one of your rooms and turn it into a den for your husband," we told her. "Which room do you suggest?"

"That's simple," she said. "Choose any one you like; he roars in all of them!"

321. Humorous "Roast" of the Honored Guest (IV)

Our honored guest, George Smith, insisted on taking me out to dinner last night, and at the end of the meal (which were some of the best hamburgers I've ever had in that particular fast-food chain), he took out some cash to pay the check.

"Don't you usually use a credit card?" I asked. "I seem to remember that you use the plastic to keep a record of what you spend."

"Normally I do," George replied, "but my credit card was stolen about ten months ago."

"That's terrible," I said, "but do you mean they haven't cancelled the old one and given you a new card by now?"

"I guess they would have," George said, "but I never reported it stolen."

"Never reported it! Why not?"

"Well," he told me, "whoever took that credit card is spending about two hundred dollars a month less than my wife, and I don't want to spoil a good deal!"

322. Humorous "Roast" of the Honored Guest (V)

Most of you know that our honored guest this evening is something of a health and fitness nut, but many of you don't realize that it wasn't always that way. In fact, at one time he was so run down that he went to his doctor for a complete physical examination.

His doctor told him that he was in fair health but could use some exercise.

"What do you think I should do?" he asked the doctor.

"Here's what I want," said the doctor. "I want you to walk ten miles a day, and call me in a week."

So, our guest took that advice to heart and started to walk. One week later, he called the doctor.

"Look," said the doctor, "I'm really busy right now, but I do want to talk to you. Where can I reach you this afternoon?"

"I have no idea," said our guest. "I'm seventy miles from home, and I don't know where the heck I am!"

323. Comments on Fellow Educators Present

When I see so many educators together for a meeting like this, I think of a story about a man who was taking his absolutely first airplane flight.

As the Captain was making his way back through the passengers, he noticed that this gentleman was extremely agitated.

"Don't worry, Sir," assured the Captain. "You'll notice that we're travelling over water, but I want you to know that even if the plane went down, we have plenty of flotation devices and life rafts."

"That doesn't help me," said the gentleman. "You see, I can swim a little, but I can't fly a bit!"

I tell that, because the educators present here are people who have taken the earthbound and the fearful and taught them how to soar with eagles.

What a privilege it is to have them here this evening.

324. Comments on a Former Student

And right over there is John Pierson. As many of you know, John is a former student of mine. Now, if I have to be honest, I never much liked John as a student. He was a pain in the opposite side of my lap. In class, whatever I said, John had his hand in the air, asking a question. Whatever statement I made,

John would challenge it. If I said that this or that was so, John would be right there asking, "How come?"

After a while, it got so that every time I saw him, I just knew he would challenge me or be asking some question.

Then, the school year ended, John went on, and the next class came. Peace and quiet returned and nobody challenged or even asked questions.

It was at that point that my entire opinion of John changed, and I missed his presence in class as much as I have ever missed any outstanding student.

You see, it suddenly occurred to me—John was the only one paying attention!

325. Remembering the Honored Guest Fondly

I remember our guest tonight as a woman of great faith and conviction, a person who holds firm beliefs that both guide and comfort her life.

In fact, recently we were talking about the laws regarding separation of church and state and particularly the ban on prayer in school.

"You know," she told me, "they never should have taken prayer out of the schools."

"Why not?" I asked, expecting some discussion of constitutional law.

"Good grief," she said, "are you too old to remember that prayer was the only way a lot of us got through? Look, as long as teachers continue to give unit tests and pop quizzes, there will be prayer in school!"

326. Memories of Former Speeches

People have asked me how I learned to do public speaking. I tell them that I had a rather unique start in the game. You see, I always wanted to talk before large groups, but I had enough sense to realize that I needed practice.

Then, one summer I got a job as a night guard at a mortuary. Now, that was not as bad as it may sound. No one ever bothered me, and no one ever complained. Also, it gave me a chance to practice my public speaking. Every night, when all the others had gone, I used to practice by delivering speeches to the mortuary's "guests."

The only drawback was that my audience never reacted—I never got a giggle, a laugh, or any applause. And, that has been a tremendous help to me in all the public speaking I've done since.

You see, now when I speak before a group, when I pause—if I can hear the audience breathing, I figure I'm ahead!

327. The Sports Award Dinner

I suppose it is inevitable on occasions such as this sports award dinner that the attention of the group falls upon the coach. Well, tonight is no exception.

Now, we are all aware that our coach has a reputation for being—now how shall I put this—rather determined in his outlook. How was that? I didn't use the words "stubborn" or "pig-headed" once, did I?

Actually, one of the alumni once asked our coach if he was a dictator. Well, the coach took great exception to that and replied that he was no dictator—he considered himself an orchestra conductor.

"An orchestra conductor?" said the alumnus. "How do you figure?"

"It's like this," said the coach. "I figure that every game we play is like a musical composition, and my job is that of conductor—to make sure the thing is performed properly."

"I see," the alumnus reflected.

"Of course," continued the coach, "Lord help the player who does a solo in the middle of my symphony!"

328. In Memoriam (I)

In Cumberland, England there is an old graveyard. Etched on an old store are these words:

> The wonder of the world,
> the beauty and the Power,
> the shape of things,
> their colors, lights and shades;
> these I saw.
> Look ye also while life lasts.

The person we honor this evening might well have written that epitaph, for he was one who walked among the wonders of this world and added to its beauty.

329. In Memoriam (II)

To say that she never had a detractor would not be true, for there were people who disagreed with her on a number of issues. To say that even those who opposed her had only the deepest respect and admiration for her would, however, be accurate. I asked her about that once.

"How do you account for the fact that no one has anything bad to say about you?" I asked, half joking.

"Because," she answered, "I have nothing bad to say about them."

"Come on," I said, "Don't you ever want to 'get even' with someone who's opposed you?"

She looked at me and sighed.

"Yes," she told me, "there are times when I get angry, but I simply never felt that I could ever withhold from another the forgiveness which I am in such need of myself."

330. Offering Congratulations (I)

Whenever we have a situation such as the one this evening where we are gathered to congratulate and honor our guest, it is always a bit of a problem. Along with the great accomplishments of great people, invariably there comes a great humility as well. It is far easier, to some people, to deal with the obstacles that need to be overcome than to deal with the praises of one's colleagues.

The accomplishments of our guest speak for themselves and do so quite eloquently. The warmth of personality and the gentleness of spirit that we all have come to respect and love are also part and parcel of our guest.

What he must feel this evening was best summed up, I feel, by that great actor of another era, John Barrymore.

Mr. Barrymore once wrote that praise is "a sort of hippopotamus that, having pushed one's front door open with his nose, squats with a dripping smile in a pool on one's hearth rug. Its impulse is charming, but one doesn't quite know what the devil to do with him!"

331. Offering Congratulations (II)

I want our guest this evening to understand that the congratulations we offer her come directly from our hearts. I would also remind her of what the Roman philosopher Plautus said: "I much prefer a compliment, insincere or not, to sincere criticism."

Yet, there will be no insincerity tonight, for we are unanimous in our praise and the congratulations we offer.

Indeed, it is our sincere hope that by the end of the evening you won't feel like the person in the story told by Mark Twain. That individual had been tarred and feathered by an angry crowd and was in the process of being ridden out of town on a rail.

When asked what he thought about the situation, the man replied, "If it weren't for the honor of the occasion, I'd just as soon miss it!"

332. Commentary for a Retirement Dinner (Humorous)

Over a long and illustrious career, our guest this evening has seen many changes, and I am positive that being a witness to those changes has inspired his decision to finally retire and take the enjoyment he so richly deserves.

I asked him about that, and he, in turn, asked me if I could remember any cliché about doing things right now rather than waiting.

"Of course," I said. "Don't put off until tomorrow what you can do today."

"Yes," he said, "but do you know why that's true?"

"No."

"The chief reason," he told me, "not to put things off until tomorrow is that—tomorrow there will probably be a law against it!"

333. Commentary for a Retirement Dinner (Serious)

According to a release by the Associated Press, the perennial holiday favorite, "Jingle Bells," was written in the 1850s. It was written by a James Pierpont who lived in Massachusetts. At that time in the state, sleighs were a common means of transportation during those cold New England winter months. The sleigh bells were thought of as traffic horns are today—they were a signal and a warning that the vehicle was approaching. Sleigh owners were fined by the police if they didn't have their bells on.

Now, I tell you this story not because I think that our guest was there to help Mr. Pierpont write the song, but because it is appropriate for someone who was always there with bells on—whenever he was needed!

334. *Presenting an Award (I)*

A man walked into a psychiatrist's office.

"Doctor," the man said, "please tell me: Do I have an inferiority complex?"

"Of course not," said the doctor. "You don't have an inferiority complex; you're just no good!"

If you'll excuse my twisting of the words a bit, that is precisely why we are presenting this award to our recipient tonight—not because she has asked for it or desired it, but because she is *just soooo good!*"

335. *Presenting an Award (II)*

Would you like to know why our guest this evening is deserving of the award we are about to give her? I'll tell you.

When I was a kid, I rushed home from school one autumn day to find that my mother and father had bought me a ten-speed bicycle for my birthday. I took exceptional care of it, and it grew to be the pride of my young life.

Now, of all the time I rode it from that day until adult concerns robbed my time, I don't think I ever used more than four or five of those gears. Oh, I knew they were there, and I probably went through them once, but most of my riding never required more than those familiar four or five gears, and the others went unused.

So it seems to me that for each of us, there may be speeds and modes of operation that most of us will never use as we ride along the pathway of life.

Therefore, when we meet an individual who uses all the gears, who pulls out all the stops, who uses twelve speeds on a ten-speed bike, it is only fitting and proper that we should gather to honor her in some way.

That's why we're here this evening.

336. Accepting an Award

I want to thank everyone here for this wonderful award. I want you to know that I will cherish it, and it will have a permanent place in my office. After all, I want everyone to see it!

It was many, many years ago that I stood as a child and listened as the pastor of our church told me, "Son, it is possible to give without loving, but it is never possible to love without giving."

I don't even remember what occasioned his remark, but the remark itself has stayed with me over the years and over confirmation upon confirmation of its truth.

Therefore, I thank you for being people who are very easy to love and, consequently, who make giving such an enjoyable task.

337. Commenting on Your Retirement

Now that I'm retiring, I don't know whether I've left too early or stayed too late!

Actually, with all the comments that have been made this evening about my age, and all the stories about all those days gone by, I feel rather like the time the preacher told his congregation that that day he would be giving a sermon on physical sexual relations.

"Before we begin," the preacher said, "Deacon Jones will lead us in a hymn."

Deacon Jones, who was ninety-three, tottered to his feet and announced, "We will now sing Number 72, Precious Memories!"

338. The Length of the Other Speeches

One very hot Fourth of July, I went to a patriotic affair sponsored by our school system. A number of local politicians and civic leaders had been invited to speak, and in spite of the soaring mercury, all speeches met with applause throughout.

That is, most of the audience applauded. I was sitting there when I noticed one man who was seated with his legs stretched out before him, his arms folded, and a dreamy expression in his eyes. As I watched, I noticed that he did not applaud once. It wasn't that he applauded for some and not for others—he didn't applaud at all.

During a break, I went over to him and asked him about it.

"Won't you applaud for anything?" I asked.

"Certainly," he answered. "The moment the MC states that the last speaker has spoken and we are dismissed, I shall applaud for all I'm worth. Then I'll have a reason to celebrate!"

339. School Administrator as the Honored Guest

Our honored guest this evening is a man who has spent his life as a school administrator. Let me tell you what that means.

I had bought something at a local department store, and when I got it home, I found out that it was broken. Therefore, I trudged back to the store and up to the complaint department.

I stood in line for a while until I got to the desk, and I had a chance to observe human nature first hand. That clerk was yelled at, threatened, had his ancestry doubted, and, in general, was misused all the time I watched. Angry people yelled and shouted and pounded the desk.

Through it all, the clerk remained calm and peaceful, with a smile on his lips and a cheerful voice and word for everyone.

When I had finished my business, I sought out the store manager and complimented the complaint department clerk.

"Yes," said the manager, "it's working out very well."

"What do you mean?"

"You see," the manager continued, "we just instituted a new policy. For the Complaint Department we hire only retired school administrators. They're so used to being abused that by the time we get them, they hardly notice!"

340. Teacher as the Honored Guest

Our honored guest this evening is a man who has spent his life as a teacher. Let me tell you what that means.

An elderly lady was walking through the park when a group of young toughs jumped out of the bushes and began snatching her jewelry and pushing her around.

All at once, a man who had been walking by stopped and waded into the gang. He grabbed one by the neck and tossed him aside as if he weighed nothing. A second one he tripped and shoved to the ground. The third youth he grabbed by the ear, pushed to the ground and sat on him as they waited for the police, whose whistles and sirens were audible in the distance.

"Bravo!" shouted the elderly woman to her rescuer. "Are you a police undercover agent or perhaps someone from the secret service?"

"Not at all," said the man. "I'm a teacher, and compared to my third-period class, these guys were a piece of cake!"

341. Community Leader as the Honored Guest

Our honored guest this evening is a woman who has spent her life as a community leader. Let me tell you what that means.

There was a young office-holder who was fantastically impressed by the mayor of the town. This man gave speeches on an average of three a week. Yet, whenever he spoke, his voice was clear, his tones dulcet, and his spirit indomitable. The young man asked the mayor how he learned to speak so well and be such a dynamic community leader.

"In my youth," said the mayor, "I took lessons from an extremely talented teacher. He had me go get a sack of marbles. Then he asked me to put all the marbles in my mouth and deliver a speech. Each day, I was to remove one marble and give my speech with the remaining marbles intact and in place."

"What was the purpose of that?"

"That's just what I asked," answered the Mayor, "and he told me—when I have finally lost my marbles, then I'll be ready to be a speaker and community leader!"

Now, that's a secret our guest knows only too well!

342. School Board Member as the Honored Guest

Our honored guest this evening is a person who has spent much of her life as a member of our school board. Let me tell you what that means.

As a member of our school board, she has always been on the lookout for sources of revenue for our schools and community. Once, the situation got really bad, and she went to church to pray about it. As she prayed, she felt a special closeness to God, and she felt as if the Almighty were speaking directly to her.

"Lord," she prayed, "what is a million years to You?"

God answered, "To Me, a million years is as a single minute."

"Oh, God," continued our guest, "in your Glory, what is a million dollars to you?"

In her heart, she heard God answer, "To Me, a million dollars is as one penny."

"Well, then, God," prayed our guest with a sly smile, "do You think you could give me just one penny?"

At which, a voice from Heaven intoned, "Sure, but you'll have to wait one minute!"

343. Politician as the Honored Guest

Our honored guest this evening is a person who has spent his life in service as a political figure. Let me tell you what that means.

At the turn of the last century, the population of our country, when analyzed by age levels, looked somewhat like a pyramid. At the top were very few older people, and most of our population were youth or children who made up the broad base.

By mid-century, that had changed, and the majority of our population was in the middle; a graph of it would look like a barrel with its sides bulging out.

Now, nearing the end of the century, that picture has shifted again. A visual representation might look something like one of those hot-air balloons we sometimes see, with older people making up the largest bulge at the top.

Which is why we are honored to have with us a political figure who is well acquainted with youth, age, and, of course, hot air!

344. The Importance of Words

It is through words that we communicate; it is through words that we get to know each other; and it is through words that we often bring about difficulties.

You see, sometimes the words we use simply make no sense at all. I mean, if the plural of 'mouse' is 'mice,' then how come the plural of 'house' is 'houses' and not 'hice?'

Can anyone tell me why we park in a "driveway" and drive on a "parkway?"

Have you noticed that feet smell while noses run?

And, of course, one question that has never been answered to my satisfaction is this: If "vegetarians" eat vegetables, what do "humanitarians" eat?

345. *When You Are the First Speaker*

Ladies and gentlemen, I am delighted to be the first speaker of the evening. I want you to know that I really enjoy meeting and speaking to people like you. I only hope that when my speech is finished, you'll like me as well.

I may be the first speaker of the evening, but this is not my first speech. My first speech was given years ago, and at the end of that evening, I was walking to my car when I was acosted by a man with a gun who demanded my money.

"Don't shoot," I said, "I'm only a poor public speaker!"

"I know," said the crook, "I've heard you, but you could practice!"

And, that's what I've been doing ever since.

346. *When You Are the Last Speaker*

Well, here I am, the last speaker of the evening.

You know, psychologists tell us that in affairs of this type, the audience is more apt to remember the words of the last speaker than any other.

Now, that may be because by the time the last speaker gets up the audience is awakening from their snooze and getting ready to go home. But, whatever the reason, it places a tremendous responsibility upon me.

You see, I'm going to have to make certain that my words are seasoned well, because I never do know which ones I might have to eat tomorrow.

347. *Dismissing the Audience*

I remember that at the start of my first teaching assignment I had one particularly difficult class. At best, they were extremely frustrating to me as a young teacher who was, I assure you, learning very quickly.

One day, when the bell rang for the end of the period, I was so glad that the class was finally over, that I threw up my hands in near despair and shouted, "Get out; go home! I don't care how you do it; just get out of my sight!"

I remember even after all these years that they took me at my word, and in a flash, students were pouring out of the windows of my classroom (which, fortunately, was on the ground floor) and into the mid-September sunshine.

I ran after them, shouting for them to come back, and just as I stuck my head and half my body out one of those windows, I came almost nose to nose with the principal who had been enjoying a stroll around the campus.

"You know," he said, "in all my years as an educator, I have never seen that particular method of dismissal used with such joyful abandon. Could we get together and talk about it?"

Since that time, I have learned to properly dismiss any group which I stand before.

You, ladies and gentlemen, far from being frustrating, have been most fulfilling, but it is time to go home now, and I would appreciate it if you would please use the proper doors and exits!

348. *Leaving a Positive Memory (I)*

It was the end of the school year with all the hectic activity that goes with it. I was busy with a hundred and one details that had to be taken care of "right away," when one of my students came up to my desk and stood before me.

"Look!" he proclaimed. "Look at me!"

I did, and the boy proceeded to smile and lift up five peeled bananas for me to see. Before I could say a word, he had opened wide and one by one shoved them in until he stood before me with five bananas crammed into his mouth, looking like some insane chipmunk who had just spent a night of abandon in a nut factory.

He was already chewing and swallowing when I got to him, and he was breathing hard but steadily. So I waited until the last banana scrap had fallen into the bottomless pit.

"What has gotten into you besides bananas?" I stammered. "Why would you do something like that?"

"Well," he said, "it's the last day of school; we're going to be moving over the summer, and I probably won't ever see you again. I . . . I just wanted to make sure that you didn't ever forget me."

The incident happened around a quarter past ten on a Wednesday morning in June some twenty-eight years ago. The boy's name was Sean. I have never forgotten.

See how well it worked!

349. *Leaving a Positive Memory (II)*

When I was in college, I took a course in public speaking. One day, our professor came in carrying a white paper bag which, he explained, contained some cream puffs he was bringing home for dessert. He placed the bag on top of a vacant desk.

His lesson that day was about leaving a positive memory with your audience when you spoke. As he continued, he really got into his subject, and he was proceeding eloquently. It was his habit often to perch on top of a spare desk as he spoke, and this, in the heat of his speaking, he did with his usual abandon—right on top of the bag of tasty, gooey cream puffs!

The bag literally exploded. Whipped cream flew everywhere: on the walls, the ceiling, his dark blue trousers.

The class sat in a stunned silence, as the professor slowly stood up, looked at the squashed cream puffs and the attendant mess, and then turned to us.

"That, ladies and gentlemen," he said with great dignity, "is the most important thought I would give you today: Before you can leave a positive memory of yourself with others, make certain that you know how to get to the bottom of your own problems."

I don't know whether I will leave any positive memories of myself with you this evening, but I do know that through programs such as the one tonight, we are all attempting to deal with those issues that lie at the bottom of our difficulties.

That is a memory of you that I shall gladly carry!

350. The Final Word

I once dealt with a boy in school who was a fairly nice kid, except that he had this virtually neurotic compulsion to always have the last word. This was driving his teachers, his fellow students, the cafeteria workers, the custodians, and the boy's own parents to distraction. You would speak to this boy, say something you really felt was meaningful, send him on his way, and he'd mumble something under his breath. So the confrontation would continue, only to have it end with another mumbling assertion of the final word.

One day, I stopped the lad in the hallway for running and ended my lecture by sending him to class. He left without a word—in fact, he hadn't said anything through the whole incident. I was so amazed that I called his older sister to my office and asked her if perhaps her brother had turned over a new leaf.

"No chance," she answered. "He did it with me, just last night. That's why he didn't say anything to you today."

"Oh, you mean he got it all out of his system last night?"

"No!" she replied, smiling broadly. "I got so mad at him that I slugged him and knocked out a front tooth. Now he's too embarrassed to open his mouth to say anything!"

I hope I'm not like that boy, but if I had to have the final word this evening, it would be the word, "you," as in the expression, "It has been wonderful, because of you," and in the simple phrase which I repeat from my heart, "Thank you, thank you, thank you!"

ANYTHING THAT CAN GO WRONG—TAKING A LOOK AT TROUBLESOME TOPICS

The infamous "Murphy's Law" which states that "anything that can go wrong, will go wrong" must have been written with the school in mind. We are only too aware of the tensions, the trouble, and the trauma that are part and parcel of school life. In this section, we'll take a look at several of the more troublesome aspects of the modern school, with the understanding that problems are universal and exist in all schools, just as all schools work tirelessly and constantly to effectively deal with them.

351. Preparing for a Crisis

Our cafeteria is noted for its oatmeal cookies. Of course I'm prejudiced, but a finger-licking faculty and student body will back up my assertion that our oatmeal cookies, baked on the premises by Mrs. Granger, the head of our cafeteria, are the best in the state if not the nation. The demand for them is so great that they are a standard menu item, baked every day.

One afternoon, we had a surprise locker clean-out, with huge trash barrels in the halls for the waste that generally accumulates in student lockers. I was busy supervising when I was pulled aside by one of our teachers with the admonition, "You have to see this!"

I was taken to the locker of one of our students who was ordered to open the door.

I stepped back in amazement, for the locker was crammed from floor to top with oatmeal cookies—there must have been several thousand of them. There was not an inch of locker space that did not contain a whole or fragmented oatmeal cookie.

"Son," I began, "this is impossible . . ."

"But, Sir," the boy implored, "what if Mrs. Granger got sick or had a baby and couldn't make them any more?"

"You don't understand," I started to explain. "This is a health hazard, against the rules, and requires punishment."

"Sir," intoned the boy with great indignation, "how do you expect your students to learn good citizenship if a person is reprimanded merely for preparing for a crisis?"

352. Introducing a Crisis Plan

I was walking to school one morning during the driest fall in the history of our local weather bureau, when I spotted a man on a street corner hawking umbrellas.

"Buy an umbrella?" he asked. "They're guaranteed to keep you dry during the strongest rain."

"Pal," I said, "it hasn't as much as sprinkled in five weeks. Why do I need an umbrella?"

"Because you're dry now, but you won't always be. When it's pouring on your head and you're watching your shoes fill up with water, that is not the time to come looking for me to sell you an umbrella to keep you dry."

"You convinced me," I said, digging into my pocket, "give me that one. By the way, I work at (name) School; you can call me (your name)."

"Thanks," he answered, extending his hand. "This is just a sideline for me. My regular job is in shipbuilding; my friends call me Noah!"

And, if there is a moral to that story that may apply to us, it is this: Don't wait until you're sopping wet to look for the umbrella salesman, and let's not wait for a crisis to strike before we hit on a plan for handling it!

353. After a Crisis

Well, the school budget has been passed, and that means that there will be no jobs lost from this building. It also means, quite frankly, that a number of cuts in supplies, trips, and programs will have to be made. While I rejoice for the former, I cannot help but view the latter with mixed feelings.

In one of the schools where I taught, there was a teacher who was bitterly complaining about the cost of her automobile insurance and the fact that she surely could not meet the premium and didn't know what to do.

That same day, one of the township trucks came to pick up the trash, backed into her car, and sent it scooting down the parking lot, over the edge of the grass, and down an embankment of the stream that ran past our school. There the vehicle settled in seven feet of muddy water.

The principal was the first to learn of the incident and went to see the teacher.

"Mrs. Jones," he said, "I know that this will all depend upon your point of view, but I think I have some wonderful news for you about not having to pay that insurance premium!"

Now that the crisis is over, I think that's almost how I feel this afternoon.

354. Dealing with Racial Tensions

In the class there were two thirteen-year-old girls who "palled-around" together much of the time. One girl was black and the other was white, but it seemed that neither girl took notice of this fact until one day when a loud argument broke out between them in the back of the class.

"Girls!" exclaimed the teacher, "what are you shouting about?"

"We're arguing about color," said one girl.

"Yeah," chimed in the other, "we want to know which color is best!"

The teacher's eyes grew wide, and immediately, she instructed the girls to stay after class and turned the class's attention to another matter.

At the end of class, when she had the two girls alone, the teacher began to gently enlighten the girls about the struggle for equal rights, equality under the law, the need for all people to disregard such factors as race, and the evils of racial prejudice.

"What prejudice?" said one girl. "We were arguing about color."

"Right," said the other. "She want us to wear yellow dresses to the dance, and I think green ones would be better. What do you think, Ms. Jones?"

355. The Aftermath of Violence

A teacher had just finished a unit on the 1920s and announced that he was going to show his class a movie dealing with gangsters and crime in Chicago during that period. A colleague was most displeased when he heard of the teacher's plans. "There's too much violence in that movie. It will have a bad effect upon the students. You shouldn't show it."

"Nonsense," the other replied, "there is no proof that watching a violent movie will affect a child!"

The battle was joined, and the two teachers debated loudly in the hallway as their students looked on.

The next afternoon, the first teacher met his colleague in the hallway once again and announced that he had shown the class the movie. Another loud argument ensued.

"Watching a violent movie has no effect upon students; everybody knows that!" was the teacher's parting shot.

"Gosh, Mr. Martin," said one of this teacher's students, "Mr. Jones sure made you angry."

"That's all right, Billy," the teacher answered. "We were just having a difference of opinion."

"Well," said Billy as he leaned closer to the teacher and began to whisper, "don't you worry about him. Some of us kids have chipped in, and we're gonna hire an eighth grader to break his kneecaps, just like in the movie!"

356. The Aftermath of a Natural Disaster

It is no secret that the storm which visited our community a few days ago left a grim legacy of destruction. One look at our school is enough to realize that there is a long road ahead filled with work before we are able to return to anything like "normal."

Yet, I can't help thinking of a man I know about who lost his leg in a horseback riding accident. The young man had been a laborer, but now, with a wooden leg instead of a real one, that job was out of the question. His entire future was questionable as well, especially when the girl to whom he was engaged broke off the alliance.

Broken-hearted, he moved away from the area and went to barber school, figuring that he could stand behind a barber's chair without moving too much. He got a job; he started to work; he met a girl who worked in a shop next to his.

Not to belabor the point, he ended up marrying the girl, having a family, and owning three barber shops of his own.

The question that keeps sticking in my mind is this: I wonder where I would be today if my grandfather hadn't lost his leg.

Yes, we are faced with the aftermath of disaster, but instead of concentrating on it, let us, rather, concentrate on the future and what we shall do to make certain that tomorrow never regrets what we do today.

357. A Loss to the School Community

One of our teachers died suddenly. He left school one afternoon and never returned. When it was learned that he had died, there was an outpouring of grief from all directions; he had been respected and loved by students and his colleagues. We all went through the attendant ceremonies; speeches were delivered and editorials published. Then it was over, and we returned, so we thought, to the routine that served us so well.

Three months passed; a season came and went.

I was walking in an upstairs hall one afternoon, when I spotted a child standing alone near the door to the stairwell. I approached, on the lookout for potential class-cutters, and as I drew near, I saw the tears that stained the young face.

He looked up at me as I approached. "You know," he said, his words thick and wet, "Mr. Jones used to sit here on hall duty. Sometimes, when I had to leave class, he'd be here, and he always smiled at me. He'd say, 'Hurry back to class before your teacher gets lonely!' "

Then I was holding him, and his tears were coming faster. I waited, and when the surge had ebbed and eyes had been dried, I looked at him and said, "Hurry back to class before your teacher gets lonely."

He smiled and went—but it was not the same.

It was not the same.

358. The Budget is Up for a Vote

Soon, this community will be voting on the budget. The passage or defeat of that budget will have tremendous implications for our school system and education in general.

A group of our students once ran a Saturday car wash in order to raise money for their activity. I was there when the first car pulled in and a dozen students descended on it with hoses and brushes. When the job was finished and the car drove away, I approached the student who was in charge.

"How much did you get?" I asked.

"Twenty-five cents," he said with a sullen face.

"That's ridiculous!" I said. "Why did he only give you twenty-five cents?"

"Well," answered the lad, "I think he would have given us more if we had remembered to roll up the windows before we turned on the hoses!"

Let's make certain that we roll up all the windows, cover all the bases in getting the word out to this community, before we risk the chance of being deluged in the polls.

359. When the Budget Has Been Voted Down

There is no one here who is not aware of the fact that the school budget has been rejected by the voters of this community. A while ago, someone asked me how I felt about that. I think I have an answer.

One morning, a wife was awakened by a loud noise. As she became aware of her surroundings, she realized that the noise came from her husband who had just knocked over a small table in their bedroom. The room was almost totally dark in the pre-dawn hour, and the husband was stumbling over objects, banging into walls, and muttering choice epithets under his voice.

"What's the matter?" asked the wife.

"I keep stubbing my toe and banging into things!" said her exasperated husband.

"Why didn't you just turn on the light?" asked the wife.

"Gosh, Honey," said her husband, "I didn't want to wake you up!"

Naturally, that wife and husband love each other, just as we still have the highest respect and concern for our community. But when the effects of the budget defeat begin to manifest themselves, and the community asks why we didn't just "turn on the light," we will most definitely have an answer.

360. *When a Bond Issue Has Lost*

There is a story told of a woman who was in a large department store when she was confronted by a very aggressive salesman who wanted to sell her a "state-of-the-art" microwave oven with all the latest features.

"Madam," said the salesman, "this will pay for itself in the money you'll save by not going out to restaurants and diners!"

"Let me tell you something," the woman replied. "Currently, I am paying off a car on the money I'm saving not having to take taxis. I'm paying for a house on the money I'm saving not paying apartment rent, and I'm making payments on a washer and dryer from the savings of not having to use a laundry service.

"Pal, if I manage to save any more money, I'm going to have to declare bankruptcy!"

When I heard of the defeat of the bond issue, believe me, I knew exactly how that woman felt!

361. *Conditions During Building Renovations*

When renovations occur during the time that school is in session, problems are going to happen.

I was teaching when the school roof, badly in need of repair for a long, long time, was being redone. Not only did the air almost constantly smell of tar, but great billows of dust would tumble in the open windows at the most unexpected times, and there was the constant noise of the men working on the roof. At times, that noise would grow to fever pitch and temporarily drown out the lesson.

The champion of all interruptions came, however, as I taught a lesson during which I quoted from an anonymous poem.

"O Wild West Wind," I quoted, "When wilt thou blow/That the small rain down can rain . . ."

At that point, there was a cracking in the ceiling, and a worker from the roof crashed through the ceiling and landed in a gigantic cloud of dirt and debris about two feet from my desk.

"Well," said one of my students dryly, "look what the wind blew in!"

I have had students visit me years later and tell me that while they certainly don't know who the fellow was who dropped in, they have never forgotten that poem!

362. *Effects of Budget Cuts and Layoffs*

So it is that we are faced with a number of budget cuts, and now they are considering the possibility of layoffs. Most certainly, these actions are going to have an effect upon our school. Even so, we've all heard the talk that now is the time to be tough, the time to get hard, the time to "take control" and slash away.

Well, I know of one ill-advised young man who told his young wife that he was taking charge.

"Me Tarzan!" he exclaimed. "You Jane!"

And, sure enough, in a little while, he was acting like Cheetah!

Of course, tough times require tough action, but that action must always be tempered by understanding and foresight. Where education is concerned, no one can afford to monkey around!

363. *Overcrowding in the Schools*

I once took a bus during a city's peak rush hour. There were no seats left when I got on, and the aisle was filled with the straphangers who stood and swayed with the motion of the bus as it made its way through heavy traffic.

I looked down at a woman who was standing beside me and said, "I beg your pardon, Madam, but do you have a strap to hang on to?"

"Yes," she answered, "I do."

"Wonderful," I said. "Then would you mind letting go of my tie? You're beginning to cut off my air supply!"

So it is with our schools as well. We had better do whatever we can to eliminate overcrowding before we begin to feel that tug at our ties—before we begin to feel the free air of education being slowly choked off!

364. *Poor Building Conditions and Education*

Of course learning can take place anywhere, but it is obvious and well known that structured learning is best facilitated in an environment conducive to it. Put in simpler terms, students learn better in a room where they do not have to constantly worry about the possibility of the ceiling falling in on them.

There is a story told of a school building that had been neglected for years and was in terrible condition. The local board, rife with politics, did nothing to help the situation but had decided nonetheless to prepare a brochure of the schools in the district. Consequently, they sent a photographer to take pictures of that school for the proposed publication.

When the photos were developed, the photographer submitted them to the board. They showed horrendous conditions of a school that had been fearfully neglected.

"Really," said the president of the board, "I don't think these photos do us justice."

"I've been in that school," replied the photographer, "and believe me, you don't need justice—you need mercy!"

365. The School is Reprimanded

It is inevitable, I suppose, that people will find fault with whatever is done. Indeed, it often seems that all the good that is done on a daily basis is ignored or swept away in favor of concentrating on those elements that are of concern to those who look in that direction.

Let me tell you how I feel about this current criticism.

I was in church one Sunday morning, and the minister was preaching a terrific sermon. He was really into his subject, and the congregation was there with him. His subject was the sin of pride, and as he warmed to the subject, he looked out over the flock.

"If there is anyone here today who is perfect, I want him or her to stand up!" the preacher shouted.

With that, one man rose to his feet.

"Sir," said the minister, "are you trying to tell this congregation that you are perfect in every way?"

"Heavens, no, Preacher," said the man. "I'm standing up in proxy for my wife's first husband!"

366. After a Scandal

Throughout history, there have always been scandals. Inevitably, people make mistakes, and when they do, the onus of those mistakes is often visited upon others. It is no different with a school. Anything that happens reflects upon the school and the educational community as a whole. There is no denying that fact.

There is also no denying the fact that the sooner we put the trouble behind us and begin again to work toward the future, the sooner we will be carrying out our primary mission of educating the youth of our community.

Sometimes, I feel like the old woman whose car stalled at a busy intersection. She was trying to restart her car when the vehicle behind her began to sound its horn. The elderly woman tried and tried as the horn-blower behind her kept up a steady pressure on his instrument.

Finally, the old woman got out of her car and walked to the automobile behind her.

"Mister," she said, "I'll tell you what. You go up there and start my car, and I promise I'll keep blowing your horn!"

367. Teenagers and Alcohol

A priest was visiting the local jail when he was introduced to an elderly prisoner named Joshua.

Recalling the Bible story of Joshua who commanded the sun to stand still, the priest smiled and asked the man, "What are you in here for, making the sun stop?"

"No, Father," replied the prisoner, "for making the moonshine!"

Of course, we can smile at that anecdote, but as we do, let's remember that for thousands of teenaged drinkers, the moon will no longer shine; their sun has already set. Let's remember that alcohol, for them, was the end of their lives. Let's see what we can do, working together, to effectively deal with this dangerous drug.

368. Teenagers and Smoking

The teenaged boy exploded into the house one afternoon and slammed down his books.

"What's the matter?" his mother asked.

"I got in trouble in school," he answered. "In fact, I got suspended."

"What?" exclaimed his mother. "Why?"

"I got suspended just for answering the teacher's question!" said the boy.

"You can't get suspended for answering a question in school," Mother said. "What did the teacher ask?"

Sighed the boy, " 'Whose cigarettes are these?' "

369. Before a Teacher Strike

We are all well aware of the possibility of what may be happening in a few days. In the meantime, I want you to know that we are all working feverishly to avoid that occurrence.

It's rather like the two ducks who were flying leisurely one afternoon when an air force jet fighter streaked by.

"Wow!" said one of the ducks, "Wouldn't you like to fly that fast?"

"I don't know," answered the other, "if my tail were on fire like that, you'd be surprised how fast I could move!"

It is the eleventh hour. We can smell the smoke, and we are all moving as fast as we can!

370. After a Teacher Strike

Our daughter was due home at eleven o'clock. We knew and trusted the boy she was with, but we also trusted in curfews.

Eleven o'clock came and went. She did not come home. Eleven-fifteen. No daughter. Eleven-thirty. Not a word.

By now, I was furious. I wore a groove into the floor and regaled my wife with tales of what I was going to do to "her" daughter when she finally decided to return home. At the very least, she would be grounded for so long, she'd be ready for Social Security by the time she had her next date.

Eleven-forty-five came and then midnight. The phone was ominously silent. I no longer ranted and raved, and my wife and I held each other close. What if something had happened to her? Fear, like a sharp-clawed cat, began to climb my spine. The silence became intolerable and filled with the worst of unspoken conjectures.

At twelve-fifteen, the front door opened and our daughter waltzed in. We ran to her and enfolded her in our arms.

"Jim's mom and dad ordered pizza, and it didn't get there until late," she explained.

"Why didn't you call?" her mother asked.

"I was going to, but it was already late by then, and I knew you'd be angry. So, I figured that if I just came home after it was finished, you'd be so glad to see me, you'd forget any trouble there was!"

The strike is over, ladies and gentlemen—welcome home!

371. The School During Negotiations

We all realize and appreciate that negotiations are often a delicate matter. Indeed, we will all live for many years with the outcome these talks produce.

It's rather like the hunter who went out to the woods one day to shoot a bear. After following the bear's tracks for some time, he came upon the animal in a clearing in the woods and raised his rifle to shoot.

Just then, the bear raised a massive paw and held it out toward the hunter.

"Wait a minute," said the bear, "let's sit down and see if we can come to some sort of understanding."

So, the bear and the hunter sat down on a log and began to talk.

"Look," said the bear, "all I want is a full stomach. Is that so much to ask?"

"Actually," said the hunter, "all I want is a warm fur coat to put around me. What's wrong with that?"

So, through negotiations, they settled the matter amicably.

The bear ate the hunter, and each had what he wanted!

372. Dealing with the Homeless Student

While images of those classified as "homeless" are very often relegated to scenes of adults in various stages of cleanliness huddled in cardboard boxes or encamped on benches in the local train station, that is far from the entire story.

There are children who are homeless, too. To categorize them as children of unfeeling and uncaring parents would be folly, since the reasons for those conditions are as varied as the people themselves. No one thing classifies everyone.

I dealt with a student once who was homeless. His mother and he lived in various shelters, some public and some church-related. In the school, we were able to help somewhat, but the boy's condition lasted for the better part of the school year.

Even so, he was always clean, always courteous, and always positive about everything.

If I had any doubts about his mother's treatment of him, they were dispelled one day when I had him alone in my office.

"Son," I said, "I am truly sorry that you have no home."

"But, we do have a home, my Mom and me," he said with a smile. "We just don't have a house to put it in."

373. Dealing with Censorship

There are all types of censorship, and the blatant, burn-that-book type is not the most insidious. At least there, you know what you are dealing with. Rather, the subtle changes in the truth that creep in on velvet slippers are often the most damning.

Take, for example the man who wanted to run for the board of education. He had checked his own family history and found, to his amazement, that a "long lost" uncle of his had been executed in the state's electric chair. What could he do with that fact?

When his campaign literature came out, mention was made of his uncle. The man, it claimed, was associated with a large Federal institution, attached to applied electronics. The man, it went on to say, had been tied to his work, and his departure from this world certainly came as a sudden shock.

374. Fostering Multicultural Awareness

One night, Mama Mouse and Baby Mouse went out for a stroll on the kitchen floor. All was going well, until they looked up and saw the cat heading directly for them, his teeth and claws gleaming.

When he was about five feet away, Mama Mouse whirled to face him.

"Woof!" she said as she began to wag her tail furiously and utter a low growl.

The cat stopped dead in his tracks, blinked his eyes, and turned and ran away as fast as he could.

"Now," said Mama Mouse to Baby Mouse, "perhaps you can finally realize the advantages of understanding a culture other than your own!"

375. The Neglected Child

Just because you supply food, clothing, and lodging to a child doesn't mean that you are caring for that child. I have known many, many children who came from homes where their physical needs were exceptionally well cared for, yet whom I would classify as neglected.

There was one father, for instance, who went so far as to tape record a story from a book in order that he would not have to "waste" time on that activity each evening.

One night, his young son came down to the living room with the book.

"Come on," said the father, "I recorded that story for you. Why don't you just turn on the recorder?"

"Because," said the lad, "I can't sit in the recorder's lap."

When giving your children the things that they need, don't neglect to give of yourself as well.

376. The School and the Transient Student

While it is encouraging to think of the progress that has been made in dealing with the transient student, the problem is far from over. The student who is here this week and gone by next week presents a real problem, and many serious attempts must be made to provide a continuum in that child's education.

That can never happen until we begin to see the child as a person who will be going through our schools, albeit a number of them, looking to complete an education rather than grab pieces of it along the way.

It's rather like the farmer who was sitting on a fence beside a road when a sports car drove up.

Said the driver, "There you are just sitting, while I'm on the go all the time."

"I don't think we're that much different," replied the farmer. "I sit on fences and watch cars go by, and you sit in your car and watch fences go by. It's really just a matter of point of view!"

377. Programs for English as a Second Language

I know a young man who has just graduated from college. He came to the United States when he was ten years old, speaking not one word of English. Naturally, the school got him an ESL specialist immediately, and between that and the marvelous way kids have of communicating, he was soon speaking highly colloquial English.

This young man recalls an experience he had in the program which, for him, typifies the troubles he faced with his new language.

He recalls that the ESL teacher learned that he went to church with his family every Sunday, and one day, she accompanied them.

"Teacher," said the boy, his English labored and heavily accented, "how come when song is over, people say 'a-men?' How come nobody say 'a-woman?' "

As the boy remembers, without missing a beat of the song, the ESL teacher leaned down to him and said, "Because they're *hymns!*"

378. The Busing of Students

The busing of students, particularly the busing of students outside of the district where they would normally attend school, has always been surrounded by controversy. In order to achieve racial balance and equality of educational opportunities, however, it has been a part of life for many a student over the years.

I had the chance to speak to someone who knew about busing from the inside—he had been one of the children who had been part of the parade that entered the yellow behemoth each morning for the long ride to a distant classroom.

The child, now a successful businessman, had ridden for nearly an hour to get to school and, of course, an equal time to return home. By the time his education was completed, he estimates that he had spent almost the equivalant of a year of school time just riding back and forth.

I asked him if the experience had any effect upon him.

"Oh, yes," he answered. "During those long drives, sometimes over bumpy roads and sometimes through endless traffic, I had many a chance to think about my situation. I distinctly remember that it was during one of those rides that I made three vows which I have kept to this day."

"Would you share them?" I asked.

"First," he replied, "I vowed that I would finish my education and try to amount to something; second, I vowed that I would never forget the civil rights issues that got me on that bus to begin with; and, finally, I vowed that for the rest of my life, I would never, ever . . . ride on a blasted bus again!"

379. Teenagers and Cars

The PTA of our school had arranged for several local businesses to be represented at a PTA function to explain the goods and services that were offered within the community served by the school. Such an exchange was always good both for parents as consumers and the local businesses as suppliers.

So it was that one evening the owner of a local car dealership was addressing a group of parents.

"It all depends," he was saying, "on what you want to get out of a car. You, sir . . . perhaps what you want out of a car is good styling, while you, madam, may want outstanding performance. You, sir, may want ease of operation or gas economy. You see, it all depends."

Turning to one parent, the owner continued, "You, sir—you look like an average parent here tonight. Think for a moment, and tell us honestly, what do you most want to get out of your car?"

"I don't have to think about it," said the parent. "What I want most to get out of my car . . . is my teenager!"

380. Parking Problems at the School

At one major high school, the parking problem got so severe that the school hired people to patrol the parking lot, issuing "parking tickets" to those cars that were parked illegally, without the proper school ID tags. This extra revenue went into the student welfare fund, and the school became quite adamant about collecting the fines. After a while, it did seem to ease the parking problem considerably.

The principal had a private parking spot right next to the school, of course, so he never got the "tags" required of the students. One day, however, heavy equipment from the repair of the school roof had been dumped directly across the principal's assigned space, and try as he might, he could not find a vacant space anywhere except in the student parking lot.

He pulled into the student lot, parked his car, and with a smile, he wrote and attached to his windshield a note to the security guard.

"I am the principal of the school," ran the note. "I have no place else to park. I don't want a ticket. Forgive us our trespasses!"

Upon his return, the principal found a ticket and another note. It read, "I am the giver of tickets. If I listened to you, I'd be out of a job. Principal or not, you have to pay your fine. Lead us not into temptation!"

381. The Over-Crowded Classroom

"Look," said the school board member to the principal, "our classes aren't that overcrowded. As long as education can continue and kids are learning, why should it matter if there are one or two more kids than usual in the class?"

"Yesterday," responded the principal, "I visited a third-grade classroom. There were all those kids, their eyes wide; ready to learn. The teacher asked a question and a whole bunch of hands went up."

"You see," said the board member, "education is taking place! There's no problem here!"

"Oh, but there was a problem."

"With all those kids raising their hands to answer, what could possibly be a problem?"

"Oh," said the principal, "just that it's sometimes difficult to know which of the four children shoved into the one desk to call on."

382. Dealing with Vandalism

A student in our school had been caught red-handed spray-painting his name on a wall. The student had been suspended, and upon his return, close tabs had been kept upon him.

A month passed, and this student, who had never been noted for his good conduct before, was rapidly becoming a model citizen.

I took him aside one day and asked him about it.

"Well," answered the boy, "when I got suspended for vandalism and the school sent me the bill for damages, my father took me to the garage and had a talk with me."

"Aha!" I exclaimed, "so your father made you see the light?"

"Sir," said the boy, "I couldn't sit down for a week! I don't know whether I saw the light, but I sure felt the heat!"

383. Gangs in the School and Community

Call him Bob. He was a student in the school, and he was also a member of a gang in the community.

Bob's teachers were unanimous in appraising the fact that he had ability and an excellent mind, but they were just as united in the knowledge that he refused to use that mind for schoolwork. Bob should have been an honor student, but he dragged by on the continual edge of failure despite all efforts to get him to achieve.

You see, the gang was the most important thing in his life. In the gang he had position, a grudging respect born of fear. He had a place where he was admired, a place where he was important, a place that was, to him, home.

What, in opposition to that, could the school offer him? The future was a phantom, something to be relegated to a forgotten corner of the mind as his gang fought for what today could bring. Achievement was only viewed in relationship to the adulation of his fellow gang members and the "respect" they granted him based on raw power. That was instant and obtainable. A report card filled with good grades would have gone unnoticed and unheralded by family and peers.

Bob even got a headline in the papers when he was killed in a gang fight. The members of the gang thought about him for a couple days, until the power struggle for gang leadership began.

And, the school stood ready to receive one more ghost of what might have been but had been lost forever.

384. Problems of Ability Grouping

Of course there are problems with ability grouping. There are arguments for heterogeneous and homogeneous grouping that could fill several bookshelves with the research alone. Whatever view we favor, however, the one thing we must never forget is that we are not dealing with IQs and Stanines and the results of achievement tests; we are dealing with children—individual children.

In another time and another era, a six-year-old child was sent to school for the first time. Early into that first year, the teacher wrote a note home to the child's parents. The teacher stated, firmly and authoritatively, that it was obvious that this child was too stupid to learn. She knew that not only would the child never learn anything, but at best he might, someday, hold a job as a common laborer. The teacher advised the parents to take the child out of school immediately and put him to work, possibly in some factory where he could at least earn some money.

The child of whom she wrote was Thomas Alva Edison, and we don't need to belabor the point.

If Thomas Edison were in school today, what ability grouping would you suggest for him?

385. The Hostile Parent

The vast majority of parents with whom I have dealt over the years have been concerned, rational, intelligent individuals, anxious about their children's education and more than willing to cooperate in that process. There have been a few, however, who stand out in my mind as examples of what not to be like.

There have been parents who have stormed in, shouted and railed, threatened lawsuits, and demanded that the entire school be fired. I have seen hostile parents throw chairs, break desks, scream and threaten, and I have watched their children watch them, learning how to follow in their footsteps.

Often, I have to hold back a desire to tell them the story of the little boy who refused to eat his brussels sprouts and was sent to his room to pray for forgiveness. As the boy entered his room, a violent thunderstorm erupted. The boy went to the window and watched for a moment as lightning split the sky and thunder cannonballed across the clouds. The boy blinked, looked upward, and said, "Gee, God! Such a big deal over a couple of lousy brussels sprouts!"

386. Dealing with the Class Bully

Richie was the class bully. In spite of punishment and untold hours of counseling from his teacher, the boy continued to intimidate, threaten, and generally make life miserable for his classmates.

One of Richie's "tricks" was to offer to shake hands with his intended victim. If the person offered a hand in friendship, Richie would grab it, hold on to it, and use his other hand to pummel the unsuspecting object of his fury.

A new student was transferred in and assigned to Richie's class. At recess that first day, Richie went up to the boy and extended his hand.

"Hi!" he said with a steel-like glint in his eye. "Let's be friends!"

The new kid took the extended hand, yanked Richie forward, and smashed him with a left hook that sent Richie sprawling.

"We had bullies in my old school," said the new boy, "and they tried that trick, too!"

At that point the rest of the class closed in upon the prostrate Richie, and it took two teachers to rescue him.

Later, in tears, Richie bemoaned the fact that you couldn't trust anyone anymore. But the class went for the rest of the year without a class bully.

387. The Abused Child

I had been teaching less than two years when I came across my first case of child abuse. Admittedly, I was young and inexperienced. When I noticed the discolorations on the sleeve of the child's shirt and then saw him wince when another child touched him, I took it on myself to investigate. At first, the boy resisted, but I pressed the matter, and the sleeve was rolled back.

The burns were methodical and precise: angry, round blotches more or less evenly spaced. It took no great insight; you would have to have been a brick in the wall not to know that those were burns from a cigarette.

"How did this happen?" I blurted. "Who did this to you?"

"Er . . . some kids . . . some boys . . . they took me behind a building and . . . some kids did it."

A horrible, twisted demon began to rise in the back of my mind, and I asked, "John, did your father do this?"

"No!" he all but screamed at me, backing away, his eyes liquid and shining. "My father loves me! He does! He didn't do this! He didn't!"

The machinery was not in place in those days, and the incident went uninvestigated. John passed out of my class, out of the school, and I never heard of him again. But, I still remember those well-spaced red points of fury on the boy's young flesh. I still see them.

By now, of course, the burns will have healed. I can make no such guarantee for the child.

388. The Underachieving Student

Certainly, we have all been faced with students whom we generally classify as "underachievers." They are perhaps the most frustrating of all children we meet on a daily basis.

Teachers have an inordinate amount of patience with the child who has difficulty learning, but it is extremely frustrating to deal with the child who has the ability but refuses to work up to his or her capacity.

A friend of mine once asked his class to name the nine greatest Americans of all time. One child, the classic underachiever in the class, took much longer than the others.

"What's taking you so much time?" asked the teacher.

"I'm having trouble," replied the boy. "I can't decide on who the first baseman should be."

Sometimes, it just ain't easy.

389. Dealing with the Drug Problem (I)

I noticed that one of the boys in my class had fallen asleep at his desk. I decided to pull a joke on him. I softly told the rest of the class to leave very quietly, and I stood at the door and hushed the incoming class. My idea was to have the new class surround the boy, then wake him up and watch his reaction as he slowly realized that he was in a totally different class.

I did just that, and when the new class had settled around him with giggles and titters, I went over to his desk, stood about a foot from him, and shouted his name.

There was no reaction.

Again, I shouted; again, there was no reaction.

I took him by the shoulder and shook. He flowed out of his desk and slumped to the floor. His lips were caked with dried saliva; his face reflected a bluish cast.

There were ambulances, the principal, police. He did not die that day, even though the drugs he had taken had all but squeezed him dry of life.

It was almost his death, and it was my introduction to the drug problem.

390. Dealing with the Drug Problem (II)

The story is told of the captain of an ocean liner who was busy socializing with a group of passengers when a steward came up and asked if he could speak privately with the captain about something the first mate wanted to tell him.

"Nonsense," said the captain with a broad smile to the passengers, "I have no secrets from our guests. Whatever you have to tell me, you can say in front of our friends."

"But, Sir . . . " protested the steward.

"Our clients are our friends," continued the captain, "and we have no secrets. Come now, what message did the first mate have for me?"

"OK," sighed the steward as he took a deep breath. "The first mate would like you to quit greasing up the passengers and get up to the bridge, because the ship is sinking!"

Come to think of it, if I had one thing to convey to our lawmakers about the drug problem in our schools, that wouldn't be such a bad message!

391. The Unexpected Problem

If there is one thing that you can absolutely expect, it is that unexpected problems will always show up. Certainly, we in education try to plan for every contingency, but life has a way of filling in the gaps that we leave.

When such problems occur, we have the choice of either allowing them to devastate us or viewing them as a temporary inconvenience that will leave us better off after we have worked together to find a solution. That attitude can work miracles in any school system.

It's rather like the father and son who were walking down the main street of town. As they approached the candy store, the little boy looked up at his parent.

"Dad," asked the child, "were you ever a little kid like me?"

"Certainly, Son," replied the father.

"Oh," smiled the child, "then I guess you know what it feels like to get a double-dip chocolate ice cream cone when you're not expecting it, huh?"

Working together, we can make that unexpected problem disappear as quickly as an ice cream cone!

392. *Dealing with the Media*

The candidate for the board of education who called the local press and arranged for a press conference greeted the reporters and announced that he would like to make a statement of his position on the state of local education.

The gentleman began a long, involved, rambling speech that lasted the better part of an hour. At its conclusion, he asked if there were any questions.

"Sir," said one reporter, "I must tell you that I have just listened to you for almost an hour and I have absolutely no understanding of how you stand on the issues."

"Thank goodness," replied the candidate. "It took me five hours to get it like that!"

"In that case," replied the reporter, "I'll merely report more than you told me."

393. *Sex Education (I)*

It was lunchtime, and the faculty lounge was filled with teachers having their noontime meal. Several were chatting as they ate, and one physical education and health teacher was busy correcting papers. One of those papers fell to the floor and was picked up by another teacher who chanced to glance at it.

That teacher's eyes grew wide as she stared at the paper which contained drawings of the male and female reproductive systems with blank lines next to each part which, obviously, the students had been required to fill in. The teacher remarked that she was somewhat taken aback by the paper. Here was something that would have been confiscated and had a student suspended back when she was in seventh grade, and now here it was as part of a middle school curriculum. Many of the other teachers agreed with her.

The health teacher smiled and handed out copies of the test to all the teachers present and asked if they would care to take it and label the parts of the reproductive systems. Of those who tried, more than half did not know the correct terms for all the body parts nor could they explain their functions. And many of these people were parents themselves.

"And that," commented the health teacher as she gathered up her papers, "is one of the best arguments for sex education that I've seen in a long time!"

394. Sex Education (II)

I firmly believe that sex education is the duty and province of the home. I have felt that way for many years, and I still do.

I remember, however, the first pregnant teenager I ever dealt with as a teacher. It was soon after I had started teaching, and she was fourteen years old. I was trying to earn some extra money, and I had taken the assignment of tutoring her.

They tell you not to get emotionally involved with your students, but you can't help but be touched by them. I soon grew to like and feel the deepest sympathy for this child who now faced a world of adult responsibilities along with ever-mounting pressures, some of them oppressively harsh, from family, "friends," and society at large.

I tutored her until the time of her delivery and for a month afterwards. She had given up the baby for adoption. She returned to school. She was scorned, mocked, laughed at, insulted. Her eyes grew hard, and she was never again the child I had tutored.

She was pregnant because her "boyfriend," a boy of seventeen, had assured her, with his superior knowledge, that the only time she could become pregnant was during her period. She tried to talk to her mother about that, and she tried to talk to her mother about the pressures the boy was putting on her. Her mother told her that she didn't like to talk about those subjects and perhaps she should go look it up in the library.

I still believe sex education is the duty of the home, but I know that it needs to be in our schools as well.

395. A Heart-Breaking Discovery

My first teaching assignment was in a school that did not have a cafeteria. It was also a place where most kids came by bus, so there was no possibility of going home for lunch. Lunch, therefore, was eaten in the classroom. At lunchtime, two students would go to the custodian's room and pick up a case of milk. Students would get lunches from lockers, and the classroom would become the lunchroom. Refuse, the tag ends of sandwiches and fruit, would be collected in a large cardboard carton, which would then be taken down to the custodian's room for disposal.

On the first day of school, a boy approached me and asked for the job of taking down the refuse. He told me that he had done it the year before, never made any mess, and would always remember without being told. I gave him the job, and he did it well.

It took a month for me to realize that he wasn't eating lunch with the other kids. I watched more closely, and he drank the milk which the school provided, but I never saw him eat. A thought rose up and lodged itself in the back of my mind, but I dismissed it.

Then, one day, I arranged for another teacher to cover my class, and I followed the boy. He and the box went to a remote corner of the school, where the boy proceeded to sift through the refuse and eat the thrown-out edges of sandwiches and the fruit that still clung to discarded cores.

So it was that I was introduced to poverty and the fact that there are children who go hungry, and my heart was broken for the first of many times.

396. *Introducing New Technology*

Can you conceive of a modern school without a computer? Yet, when these mechanical monsters were first introduced in the schools they often met with great resistance.

One teacher in our school, for instance, steadfastly refused to use any computer for any reason whatsoever. In spite of the fact that in-service training had been offered and that most of the faculty now used the computer lab for help in test-making, grading, attendance, and many other of the more tiresome jobs, this teacher remained adamant.

Therefore, the teacher in charge of the computer lab programmed a special disk that would print certain messages no matter what the input was. Then, the recalcitrant teacher was cajoled into sitting down at a computer "just to see" what happened. The teacher was told to type any message, which he did. The screen flashed to life.

"Gosh, Bob," read the screen, "I'm sorry you don't like me, because I like you. Really, Bob, I think we could work very well together. If you'll give me a try, I'll bet I'll become a favorite of yours in no time . . ."

"That's it!" exclaimed the teacher as he rose from the seat. "It was bad enough when all it did was to violate your mind, but now it's turned immoral. Did you see that? It tried to seduce me!"

397. A Call for Reform in the School

Whenever I hear a call in the media about the need for reform in our schools, I am reminded of a time when I was walking down the street and saw a small child with a huge dog.

The dog had a collar and a leash, and the child was holding the leash, but it was obvious that the dog was leading and the kid was being pulled along for the ride.

"Friend," I said, "where are you taking that dog?"

"Mister," replied the child, "I don't know, but I'll tell you this: When he makes up his mind where he's going, I'm gonna take him there!"

In education, we are holding that leash, and should the reformers ever figure out where we are headed, you can bet that we'll be the ones to get that animal to his destination.

398. Dealing with Negative Behavior (I)

Mother was busy in the kitchen when she heard a scream coming from the living room. She rushed in to find her two-year-old grinning happily, while the six-year-old sat rubbing his head and sobbing.

"What happened?" she asked.

"The baby pulled my hair!" exclaimed the six-year-old. "I hurt!"

"Now, now," said Mother. "She's just a baby. She doesn't know that she hurt you when she pulled your hair. She doesn't know that it hurts."

The youngster was kissed and tears were dried, and Mother returned to the kitchen.

Two minutes later, the six-year-old appeared at the kitchen door as a piercing howl emerged from the living room.

"Mom," said the child, "you know how you said that when the baby pulled my hair, she didn't know that it hurt? Well, now she knows!"

399. Dealing with Negative Behavior (II)

I'm going to tell you how to kill a mouse. Believe me, it works, so you'd better take notes.

First, you give Dad a very hard day at work and put him in a traffic jam as he drives home. When he gets there, the first thing he does is to ask if his favorite pants got back from the cleaners, and when he finds that they didn't, he yells at Mother and asks if she can't get anything right. Mother steams off and on the way encounters junior who is covered with paint from head to toe. She screams at him and orders him to wash and then go to his room and stay there for twenty years. The child pouts off to the bathroom where the dog comes up wagging his tail. Junior tosses water on the dog and the animal high-tails it out of there and runs into the cat at whom the dog barks and shows his teeth. The cat runs and hides, its tail like a fuzzy baseball bat, and spots a field mouse which has crept in through a half-opened door. In one great pounce, the mouse is dead. Killing a mouse is really an easy process.

Which is why, when dealing with negative behavior, you'd best not look only at the end result; it surely wouldn't hurt to trace it all the way back to the traffic jam on the way home.

400. The School, Business and the Community

A very successful entrepreneur was a graduate of a small college located in the community where her business was located. After some reflection, the entrepreneur decided that she wanted to make a sizeable donation to the school that had given her so much. She looked up one of her former teachers at the school and went to visit him.

After she had explained to the professor what she wanted to give to the school, she asked, "What do you think, sir? What do you think I might best do with this money I intend to give to the school? Build an infirmary, a new gymnasium, what? What studies did I most excel at? Perhaps I should endow a new business school?"

"I have a suggestion," stated the professor. "Why don't you think back and recall what you did the most of in my class, and that might give you an idea."

"That's it!" exclaimed the entrepreneur. "I'll build a dormitory where students can sleep!"

Section Nine

THE STORY AND THE GLORY—EXAMINING THE EDUCATIONAL PROCESS

Day after day in schools throughout our nation, the educational process grinds slowly along. It is an everchanging entity that is constantly being revised, replenished, and refurbished. It is a growing being that has, in turn, nurtured the youth of this nation since its inception. From teacher training to the future of American education, here are stories filled with the glory of today's educational process.

401. Teacher Preparation

Certainly, I was prepared to teach by my professors in college. I took all the required courses, learned the history of education, dabbled in tests and measurements, investigated the psychology of education, and even went through eight weeks of supervised "practice" teaching. I received passing grades from my professors and a certificate from the state that allowed me to enter the public schools and call myself "teacher."

I was more than half way through my first day of "real" teaching, and I was congratulating myself that everything was going well. I had organized and planned and actuated those plans, and I was, quite frankly, feeling pleased with myself.

Then a child came up to my desk and asked to go to the school nurse.

"Why?" I asked. "What's wrong?"

And the kid threw up—all over me!

The class began shrieking with disgust and delight. The boy was turning pale green and crying. I was standing there desperately trying not to join the young man in his previous activity as my neat little classroom world was collapsing around me.

I wondered what page in my college textbook had covered this situation. Perhaps I had been absent on that day?

402. The Substitute Teacher

It started as a joke. The substitute was in for a teacher who taught the odd combination of history and science. The teacher's history class, knowing there was a substitute, informed her of the "fact" that they were a science class, not a history class. The substitute looked at the schedule, but the class informed her that there was a mistake and assured her that she should be teaching science.

The substitute could find no plans, so she told them about a book she had been reading that spoke about Gregor Mendel, who had discovered the rules of heredity. She drew diagrams on the blackboard and spoke with enthusiasm about the wonder of heredity as it had unfolded to her. The class who thought that they had pulled off a fine joke, soon settled down and became fascinated by the obvious enthusiasm of this substitute teacher.

One of the boys in that class was so impressed, in fact, that he went to the library to look up more about the subject. His interest grew. The stories the substitute told never left him. He graduated and went on to college, graduating there with a degree in biology. He teaches college and does research in genetics. It all started as a joke on the substitute teacher.

As Henry Adams wrote, "A teacher affects eternity; he can never tell where his influence stops."

403. Using Proper Motivational Techniques

Someone once told me the story of a farmer who was trying to get a stubborn mule to move. The mule wasn't having any of it, refused to budge, and the farmer was berating the mule in very strong terms.

Just then a neighbor chanced by and reproached the farmer. "That's no way to treat that mule," said the neighbor. "If you want him to move, you have to use kindness and understanding."

"Oh, yeah?" said the farmer. "Let's see you handle him."

"OK," replied the neighbor who proceeded to walk over and stand before the mule. He paused a moment, and then he hauled off and threw a round-house right that smacked the mule in the jaw so hard, the mule sat down on his haunches.

"What did you do that for?" exclaimed the farmer. "I thought you said that you had to treat him with kindness and understanding?"

"You do," replied the neighbor, "but first you have to get his attention!"

404. Dealing with the Science Fair

One of the highlights of the science fair was to be the eruption of a volcano. Not a real volcano, of course, but a student-constructed affair was to erupt on cue with smoke and ash and lava flowing down its scale-model flanks.

All this was to take place in the center of the gymnasium, and at the appointed time, there was a huge gathering of parents and students who stood watching as the science teacher and several students went through the procedures to set it off.

To this day, no one knows what really happened, but instead of a roar, there was a faint "pop!" and billows of smoke began to issue from the scaled-down volcano crater. It wasn't just smoke, it was SMOKE! Billowy gray clouds shot into the air, curled around the ceiling, and descended on the parents. Within minutes, the entire room was filled with smoke, and coughing people groped their ways to the exits whose red signs glowed through the gathering fog.

Outside, on the front lawn of the school, the science teacher stood with several of the students involved. When he had stopped coughing and his eyes were no longer watering, he looked at them.

"Well, guys," he said, "this is a great lesson for you. Many times in life you will be offered a deal that looks like it is going to explode with fireworks, but when it gets to the point where there is nothing but smoke and it's starting to smell, the scientific thing to do is to get out!"

405. Dealing with the Book Fair

I have always liked to put up signs in the classroom with good, motivational messages; I think it sinks in. One of my signs one year (a very prominent one) stated "This above all—to thine own self be true."

We had a book fair in our school, and a schedule had been established for each teacher to take a class down to the library where the book fair people had set up many rows of colorful books for perusal and sale, a percentage of the profits going to the school. The children enjoyed browsing through the books, and, frankly, so did I. It was a pleasant period and a nice break from routine.

My class had been down there about ten minutes when there was a shriek from one of my students, and the boy grabbed a book from the table and, bumping into several other students on the way, ran to where I was standing.

"Look!" he exclaimed.

I did, and it was a book of Shakespeare, edited for young readers. What he was pointing to was a passage from *Hamlet* that began, "This above all; to thine own self be true . . ."

"Yes, I see," I said. "What are you so excited about?"

"How can you be so calm?" shouted the boy. "Don't you see? This guy, Shakespeare—he stole your sign!"

406. Examining Career Education

One of the activities we go through in our school is an exercise in career education. Students prepare reports on various careers, outlining the educational requirements, what the duties of the career entail, the salary, and so forth. Many times, we invite members of the community to come to school and speak about their jobs. The kids really get into it, and it's a beneficial activity for everyone.

Therefore, I was somewhat taken aback when I was collecting the reports from one class and a student handed in a paper with his name on it and the name of his father in the center of the page, and nothing else.

"Jim," I asked, "What's this supposed to be? You were to write a report about the career you wanted to follow. How does this qualify?"

"Sir," said Jim with a huge sigh, "you've taught me all year long. You know what my marks are like, and you know how I don't do all the homework, and you know that what I like to do best is nothing."

"Well . . ."

"So, my father has this business. That's his name. I don't even know what he does, but I know enough to realize that if I'm ever going to make it in this world, I'd better get a job someplace where my father is the boss!"

407. Celebrating a Historical Event

The elementary school class was going to celebrate Washington's Birthday by presenting a pageant which included a recreation of Washington crossing the Delaware. Parents had been invited, and it was to be a grand affair.

Harry, who played General Washington, was extremely nervous on the day of the production. Just before the "big scene," he tugged at his teacher's sleeve.

"I can't go on," he whispered. "I have to go to the lavatory!"

"There's no time!" the teacher whispered back. "You're on!" With that, Harry was pushed gently on to the stage and the scene began.

Later, when the pageant had ended and the children were meeting with their parents, Harry's father remarked, "It was wonderful, Son, but how come you didn't come out on stage with the rest of the kids to take a bow at the end?"

"Dad," answered Harry, "I never knew why George Washington stood up during that boatride across the Delaware River, but now I understand.

"He was making sure that when the boat struck ground, he could get a running start to the nearest rest room!"

408. Competing in Sports

An idea was proposed of giving out medals in physical education for those students who excelled in the class. The teachers were asked how many medals they felt should be ordered.

"Let's see," said one teacher, "I have five classes, and we'll have a first, second, and third in each, so . . . fifteen medals should do fine."

"I'll need 132 medals," said another.

"132! For goodness sake, why that many?"

"Look," said the teacher, "how are you going to determine who gets the medals?"

"Well, I'll probably have the kids jump over a stick, and I'll keep raising it until there're only one or two kids who can do it."

"Well," said the teacher, "that's not my philosophy. You see, I'm going to have my kids jump over that stick, too. The only difference is that I'm going to start out with it about five feet high and then keep lowering it until every kid in my class is a winner!"

409. *Teaching and Learning Art*

The art teacher had her elementary art students painting portraits. She told the class that they should try to paint a face they really knew well, and she suggested that they try to paint her.

The teacher was circulating from child to child. Finally, she came to little Natasha who sat with a scowl on her face. The portrait before the child was an unrecognizable blob.

"How are you doing, Natasha?" asked the teacher.

"Not so good," the child answered. "I'm trying to paint you, but I don't think it's going to work."

"So, what are you going to do?"

"Oh, that's easy," answered Natasha, "I'll just take your face, put a tail on it, and make it a dog!"

410. *Teaching and Learning English*

The parent had come in for a conference, and the teacher was showing a test paper to the mother whose daughter sat beside her for the interview.

"You will see," said the English teacher, "that the spelling word was *sugar,* and your daughter spelled it *S-U-G-G-E-R.*"

The mother looked intently, and then she turned her gaze upon her daughter.

"How many times did we go over this?" asked the distraught parent. "And still, you forgot to put in the *H!*"

411. Teaching and Learning a Foreign Language

One of Bobby's courses in seventh grade was French I, and when he returned home from his first day of school, he was bubbling with enthusiasm about it.

"*Bonjour!*" he stated as he came through the door.

"Well, said his mother, "I guess I don't have to ask how your first day in French class went—you're already speaking it."

"*Oui!*" Bobby answered, "I am *parlez*-ing French now!"

"Tell me," Mother asked, "do you think you could carry on a conversation with someone who was born in France?"

"Not exactly, but I know what I could do."

"What's that?"

"I could carry on a conversation in French with anyone who's had one lesson!"

412. Teaching and Learning History

The history teacher always liked to instill a sense of awe in his students about time and age. Toward that end, he had obtained a fossil that had been dated at a million and a half years.

He held up the specimen to his class and stated, "I want you to look closely at this, and then I'd like one of you to guess how old it is."

One boy raised his hand and was recognized.

"I think they are one million, five hundred thousand and five years old," the boy said.

The teacher was amazed. "That's wonderful," he said. "You have it almost exactly. This fossil is a million and a half years old. But, where did you come up with that 'five years' at the end?"

"That was easy!" stated the student. "They were a million and a half years old when you showed them to the class my brother was in, and he had you five years ago!"

413. Teaching and Learning Home Economics

Discussion in the home economics class had turned to the national preoccupation with dieting. The teacher explained the dangers of fad diets, and went on to point out sensible diets for weight loss as well as some dieting tips.

"For example," the teacher told the class, "you should try to slow down your eating. It has been absolutely proven that people who eat slowly have a tendency to eat less, and that would certainly help dieting."

"Wow! I know that's true!" piped in one student.

"Oh," remarked the teacher, "have you tried dieting by eating more slowly?"

"No," replied the child, "but we have seven children in our family, and with six brothers and sisters, if you don't eat fast, you don't eat anything!"

414. Teaching and Learning Math

An elementary teacher announced to her colleagues that she was having difficulty with one of her small charges in the area of math. Arranging a demonstration, she placed a five-dollar bill and a one-dollar bill in front of the child and asked which one he wanted. The child took the one dollar bill.

"Let me try that," said another teacher who performed the experiment with the same results; the child took the one rather than the five. Before long, most of the teachers in the school had performed the small experiment, and no matter how they worded the question, the boy invariably took the one dollar bill.

Finally, they called in a math teacher from the high school to meet with the child and perhaps determine why he could not distinguish between a larger and a smaller amount.

After they had gotten acquainted, the math teacher put five wooden blocks on one side of the table and one block on the other. "Five is more than one," the teacher said.

"Are you crazy?" replied the student. "Of course it is!"

"But, if you know that," stated the teacher, "why do you keep taking the one-dollar bill rather than the five?"

"If I took the five," replied the child, "they'd stop doing the test, and right now, I'm making a fortune!"

415. Teaching and Learning Music

"Remember," the music teacher told her students, "that being able to play an instrument well takes dedication, and that means practice. No one ever got good on an instrument without practice. If it is a beautiful day and you feel like going outside and running around, you must find the inner discipline to stay in and practice. Besides, your parents are paying for these lessons, and you wouldn't want to disappoint them, would you?"

And, that very afternoon, Terry Smith, one of the students, visited every house in his neighborhood and proclaimed, "Look, if my piano playing and practicing bothers you—complain to my parents . . . please!"

416. Teaching and Learning Physical Education

One of the rules of the physical education class is that everyone must dress for the class. This meant wearing sneakers, a tee shirt, and gym shorts.

It was near the beginning of the school year when one P.E. teacher greeted his class and noticed one boy still in regular school clothes.

"You!" yelled the gym teacher. "You're not dressed for gym! Get out there and run four laps of the gym!"

"But . . . but . . . " the student began to protest.

"No backtalk!" asserted the teacher, wishing to establish discipline. "Get out there and do those laps."

The student shrugged and began a slow and leisurely trot around the gym's perimeter. When the four laps had been completed, the boy trotted up to the teacher.

"Sorry to be so hard on you, son," said the teacher, "but everyone has to dress for gym. Do you understand?"

"Sure," said the boy, "I always dress for gym."

"Then why not now?"

"Because," replied the boy, "I'm not in your class; the office sent me in here to deliver a message to you. I've forgotten it by now, but thanks for the workout!"

417. Teaching and Learning Reading

The reading teacher was having her advanced students do a research paper. She explained to them about footnoting and research techniques.

She particularly cautioned her students about using what someone else had written without giving credit. She stated, however, that they might use as many authors as they wished for reference purposes—in fact, the more the better.

When the papers were finally in, the teacher asked, "Well, has this project taught you anything about the literary process?"

"It sure has," said one student. "I learned that if you steal from one author, it's called plagiarism; but if you steal from a whole lot of authors—it's called research!"

418. Teaching and Learning Shop

"Now," said the shop teacher to his class, "are there any questions?"

"Yes," said one student, "do you have any good pieces of wood in here?"

The shop teacher drew a deep breath. He hadn't planned on giving a lecture on the types of wood, but he believed that an honest question deserved an honest answer, so he began to explain the types and variations of wood.

Thirty-five minutes later, he asked, "Now, does that answer your question?"

"Not really," said the student. "See, my desk is wobbling, and I wanted to know if you had a splinter of wood we could stick under the short leg?"

419. Overcoming Obstacles to Learning (I)

"Miss Jones," said the little girl, "I'm having some trouble with the lesson, because I can't read what you write on the board."

"My goodness," said the teacher, "you go sit down, and I'll take care of that right away."

Immediately, the teacher notified the school nurse about the child's poor eyesight. The nurse in turn notified the home. An appointment was made for that afternoon to have the child's vision checked. Just after school was dismissed that afternoon, the child's mother came to the room with the child in hand.

"We've been to the eye doctor," the mother told the teacher, "and he says she has 20/20 vision!"

"I don't understand," the teacher said. Then she turned to the little girl and asked, "Didn't you tell me you couldn't read what I wrote on the blackboard?"

"Sure," said the child, "but that's because that fat Billy Smith sits in front of me, and he won't move his head. The minute I move to another desk, I can see fine!"

420. Overcoming Obstacles to Learning (II)

There are many obstacles to overcome if we want our students to learn. Of course, that is what we all desire, but we should all be aware, as well, that it is going to take a great deal of hard work and dedication.

It's rather like the very bad golfer whose ball rolled to rest on top of an anthill. Several of the ants came out to look at the event and comment about it, when the golfer came up for his next shot. He swung and missed the ball completely, sending up a shower of dirt and a number of ants. His next shot dug a large furrow that buried several of the ant community. His third shot missed the ball but created such a breeze that several more ants were blown away. Finally, one ant turned to another.

"Brother," said the ant, "if we want to survive around here, it looks as if we're going to have to get on the ball!"

The same philosophy applies in education!

421. The Class and Dramatic Ability

The principal was walking past the second-grade classroom when he glanced in the window in the door.

One little girl lay slumped in her desk with her eyes rolled upward and her tongue sticking out the side of her mouth. Another boy lay face down on the floor, his hands formed into clawing fingers. Yet another boy was dragging his legs across the floor, his mouth gaping open and one hand stretched before him, reaching for something only he saw. Still other students gasped and panted and held clutching hands to their throats. It looked like a scene from one of those disaster movies.

The principal burst into the room.

"Good Heavens!" cried the principal. "What's wrong here?"

"Oh, don't pay any attention to them," said the serene and calm teacher. "This is a very dramatic class, and they were just reminding me that I haven't taken them for a trip to the water fountain yet!"

422. The Great Science Experiment

The science teacher was going on at length about the marvels of science. He had even prepared a short experiment to illustrate. As he spoke, he mixed some chemicals together, added a third, and immediately, the mixture hardened, and the scientist scraped it out, moulded it into a ball and bounced it high on the table.

"You see," continued the enthusiastic teacher, "there is nothing which science cannot do. You take anything, and science can do the same thing!"

"Just a minute!" exclaimed one child who ran out the door of the room only to return a few minutes later with a handful of grass, obviously grabbed hastily from the playground.

"Here," said the student, plopping down the grass, "change this into milk! It should be real easy for science; cows have been doing it without thinking about it for centuries!"

423. Using the Library (I)

The student came up to the school librarian and asked, "Where can I find books about sailing?"

"That would be under sports," said the librarian, and she indicated the section of the school library that contained those books and also directed the student to the proper sections of the card catalog.

Half an hour later, the student was back. "I can't find anything about sailing on a red boat," she protested.

"Sailing a red boat?" questioned the librarian. "Could you be more specific?"

"Well," said the girl, "our teacher assigned me to read this book tonight, and she said I could find it here, but I've looked under sailing, under red, and under boat, and there's nothing."

"The story was about a red boat?"

"Yes, I'm sure. I even wrote it down."

"A red boat?" puzzled the librarian.

"Here it is!" exclaimed the student, retrieving a wrinkled scrap of paper from her pocket, "I'm supposed to read a book called *The Ruby Yacht,* by a Mr. Ki Am. Do you have anything about red boats at all?"

424. Using the Library (II)

The school librarian was disappointed that more of the classics were not being signed out of the school library and read. In fact, most of them just gathered dust. The librarian resolved to do something about that situation.

Three months later, the number of classics being taken out of the school library had risen by four hundred percent. Upon looking over a report on this, the principal called the librarian to his office.

"This is wonderful," the principal said. "How did you ever manage to get the kids to start reading the classics like this?"

"I take it you haven't been in the library for a while," stated the librarian.

"Well, no, I . . ."

"I thought not," said the librarian with a grin. "If you had, you would have noticed that I rearranged the library into three sections. Over the first section is a sign which states *'These are the books your teachers want you to read.'* Over the second section the sign states *'These are the books your parents want you to read.'* And over the third section, I put a sign that says, *'These are the books your parents and teachers kept in the back of drawers or in locked trunks or in closets where you couldn't find them.'* That third section is where I put all the classics, and we now have a waiting list!"

425. The Grading of Students (Humorous)

One elementary school had decided to experiment with giving up grades in favor of a written report on each student's progress. So it was that Timmy brought home a report REPORT rather than a report card.

"Well," father said to mother after both had a chance to read it, "what do you think of this new system of reporting?"

"I don't like it," said mother, "it's far too ambiguous."

"Ambiguous? What do you mean?"

"Look here under Choral Music," mother illustrated. "The teacher wrote, 'Timmy really contributes to choral music by being such a good listener.' What does she mean by that?"

426. The Grading of Students (Serious)

In the days before computer printouts, all the report cards we gave out were marked by hand in ink. I recall that I always took care to make the grades legible and neat.

Naturally, the cards had to be signed and returned. One card came back to me, and as I started to file it in a drawer, I noticed that my usual neat and clean writing was blotchy and smeared. Naturally, I investigated.

The student had changed all of his poor and failing grades with the use of ink eradicator and then had obviously changed them back before returning the report card.

I pursued the matter and the boy confessed, but couldn't see why I was so upset. I took my information to his parents, and they told me that they would "speak to him," but that it seemed like youthful mischief, and they didn't think that it was any "big deal." When I spoke at length to the child, his only remorse was that he had gotten caught. It never went any further.

I learned the other day that he has been expelled from a private college he attended for selling the answers to certain final exams. I guess he could change the marks I gave him, but he could never erase the grades he gave himself.

427. *Giving Out the Report Card*

The first time I ever gave out report cards to a class, I called the name of one student, and he stood in the back of the room and addressed me cheerfully.

"Sir," he said, "I bet you can't sail it to me back here!"

I was in a jovial mood, and I smiled and sailed the report card across the room—practically into his outstretched hands.

Later that day, I was standing in the lunch room when I heard that student and a friend of his discussing the incident.

"Why did you want the teacher to throw the card at you?" asked the friend.

"Listen," returned the student, "tonight my father is going to ask me if I got my report card."

"So?"

"Well, I'm going to tell him that the teacher never handed me my report card. After all—I don't want to lie to my father!"

428. *Planning for College*

Three children met around a table.

"I'm going to Harvard;" said the first, "my father insists on that."

"It's Princeton for me;" intoned the second, "Mom's *alma mater* you know."

"I'm headed for Penn State," stated the third, "on a football scholarship."

"Listen," said the first, "before we go any further, there is something we should do."

"What's that?"

"I think we should finish stringing these darn plastic beads so we can get out of this kindergarten class!"

429. *An Educational Misunderstanding*

My wife and I were following behind the hostess to the table where we would be seated in the restaurant. As we passed one table, a young man in his twenties rose up and turned toward me. I recognized him at once as a student I had had a number of years ago. I even remembered his name. I could see that he had recognized me as well.

We stopped and there were introductions all around as well as the pleasantries that one exchanges in situations like that. Finally, I spoke directly to the young man.

"Really," I said, "it is very nice of you to rise and greet us like this, but you really don't have to stand up for me. Please sit down and relax."

"But . . ." he protested, starting to come forward a bit.

"No," I continued, practically pushing him into his chair, "honestly, you don't have to get up for me!"

"OK," he said as he sank into his chair, "but can't I please go to the bathroom first? That's where I was headed five minutes ago when I first spotted you!"

430. The Private Lives of Educators (Humorous)

The teacher came into her second-grade classroom one day and placed a framed photograph on her desk. It was a picture of herself, a man, and two small children, a boy and a girl.

"Mrs. Snyder," said one of the second graders pointing to the photo, "who is that?"

"The man is Mr. Snyder, my husband," she explained, "and the children are Melissa and Harry, my son and daughter."

"You mean . . . you mean . . . you have kids? You're a mommie?"

"That's right," the teacher replied. "Those are my children, and I'm their mother!"

"Gosh, Mrs. Snyder," said the child in obvious amazement, "I never realized that teachers did homework, too!"

431. The Private Lives of Educators (Serious)

When I was a child going to school myself, I honestly thought that the teachers lived in the school. After all, they were always there when I arrived in the morning, and they were still there when I left for home in the afternoon. Teachers and school went together, so, of course, the teachers lived in the school. They ate in the cafeteria; that was obvious. I didn't know where they slept, but I imagined that they probably put up a cot in the classroom and spent the night there, beside their desks.

Then, one day I was with my mother in the supermarket. All at once, I froze. There was Mrs. Novikus, my teacher, and with her were a man and two children. I stared in wonderment at what she was doing outside the school, when she turned and saw me.

She walked over to where we were and spoke to my mother, introducing her husband and her two daughters, and my mother and she chatted sociably for a few moments.

I said nothing. I couldn't; I was too deep in shock to be able to find my voice. A teacher—outside of school! A teacher—married and with two kids! She wasn't just a teacher, she was a mommie, too! I spent the rest of the day in silent wonder.

Gosh! There was just so much to learn!

432. A Personal Introduction to the Drug Problem

I had noticed that his grades were slipping and that his behavior was becoming more and more bizarre, so I kept him one afternoon and tried to talk with him. I got nothing from him except disjointed answers and a feeling that he was hearing about every fourth word I said. I also noticed that his eyes were pinpoints, and he couldn't concentrate.

In my naiveté, I took him to the school nurse, inquiring of her if perhaps this child was ill.

"Not the way you mean," she told me. "He's not sick; he's high!"

Of course I had read about drugs in the schools, but this was the first time in my young life that I had knowingly come into personal contact with drugs. It was a shock, because this was someone I knew, someone who sat in my class each day and laughed and smiled and learned under my direction.

I wish I could report a success story, but I can't. I tried; the nurse tried; everybody in the school tried. Nothing we could say or do, or so it seemed, could penetrate that blank stare.

When I saw him in his coffin, several years later, that blankness was still there. It always is. He was the first student I met with a drug problem. He wasn't the first of my students to die.

God help us—he won't be the last, either!

433. Getting Tough with Drugs

The kid sold drugs. Everybody in the school knew it. The students knew where to go to get whatever they wanted, and the boy all but openly flaunted it. Dozens upon dozens of students had been "turned on" by this boy.

He was arrested one day and taken from the school in handcuffs. There was some legal hassling about improper searches and violation of his rights. On top of that, judges were reminded again and again of his "tender" years. In the end, he was given a "second chance," and he returned to school.

Within a week, sales were back to normal.

A few months later, the boy's family moved out of the area, and I never saw or heard of him again. He did leave me, however, with an opinion that has formed rock hard within me.

When will we realize that drugs not only kill the body, but they destroy the soul as well? Whether it is sold by a forty-year-old career criminal or a sixteen-year-old apprentice pusher, death is still death; drugs are still a cancer which eats away until there is nothing left but death.

And, like any cancer, it needs to be cut out and destroyed!

434. Loving Your Students

Fully half the class had not done the homework assignment, and the teacher was furious.

"Well," the teacher fumed, "you have really disappointed me! You are going to sit here and do that assigned work right now, and this afternoon, those who didn't do it for homework will stay with me so we can do even more practice! I tell you, I am really angry at you!"

Later, the teacher continued, "I really want you to learn this material, and when you don't, it makes me feel really bad. Keep working!"

One child raised his hand and was recognized.

"Do you mean that you're going to keep us after school and make us do all this practice work every time we don't do the homework?" the student asked.

"I want you to learn," answered the teacher, "so, yes, I certainly am!"

The child stood silent for a moment, deep in thought. Then, with the whole class watching, he looked intently at the teacher.

"Gee!" said the student, "you must really love us!"

And the boy sat down.

435. A Career in Education

It was a special event in the elementary school. It was Career Awareness Day, and several parents were visiting the school to talk about jobs and careers in the fields with which they were most familiar.

One of the teachers had volunteered to talk about education as a career. She outlined what was needed to prepare for teaching and the education needed, and then she began telling the students what they would have to do as a teacher. She explained, on their level of understanding, about lesson plans, curriculum work, correcting papers, supervision, and all the other tasks that a career in teaching implies.

Suddenly, one small student stood up and addressed the teacher.

"Gosh, Mrs. Dean," the child stated, "I thought all you had to do was take care of us. I didn't know you had to work, too!"

436. Definition of a Teacher

What is a teacher?

To his spouse, he is someone who brings home a paycheck that doesn't quite reach. He is one who spends an inordinate amount of time worrying about other people's kids.

To the public, he is a cross between an overpaid baby-sitter and an undernourished saint, all at the same time. He vascillates between being the cause and the cure of most of our nation's ills.

To the school administration, he is someone who frequently refuses to understand budget cuts and goes to extremes to get the best for his students, even in the face of economic logic and often at his own expense.

To his students, he is the giver of homework, the grader of papers, enforcer of discipline, dryer of tears, opener of minds, and leader into new and sometimes scary realms.

To himself, he is often one who cannot understand how he ever got into this thankless mess and would never do it again . . . but wasn't it wonderful the way Billy answered that question today, and what a privilege it is to watch Alice's mind begin to mature.

437. Definition of a Principal

What is a principal?

To her spouse, she is the person who spends more time at school than at home. In fact, the spouse has learned that even when she's home, she's at school.

To the public, she is their primary contact with the school. She is the first person to go to when something goes wrong and the last person who will receive credit when the problem is righted.

To the faculty, she is the one who evaluates performance and checks off lesson plans; the final decision-maker in a school who can one moment cancel the plans to shoot off a rocket on the back lawn and the next moment join in an English class with such enthusiasm that every kid in the class catches the fire.

To the students, she is the person you are sent to see when you've done something wrong or the person who sees you when you get an award. She is the one who roams hallways at odd hours.

To herself, she is a person who knows that she can make a difference and is willing to put in the time and effort to do so, because, to her, the education of the students in her school is more important than anything else. She is aware that she does not have a job; she has a calling.

438. Definition of a Student

What is a student?

To his parents, he is a source of constant worry and constant delight, all in the same package. He is the center of his parent's hopes, yet he can't seem to get his homework done.

To the public, he is often the reason for those property tax increases. He is the playing piece in a game of numbers and percentages which, in some mysterious way, equates with the latest tax assessment on their house.

To his teachers, he is the source of a tremendous amount of bookkeeping and a great deal of trouble, all of which suddenly becomes worth it when the kid begins to hand in his homework and his grades start to slowly rise.

To school administration, the student is a source of constant study, constant trouble, and constant joy; he is the opening assembly and the commencement exercise; he is, after all, what the school is all about.

To himself, he is an abused, overworked, and underloved object of pity, at the mercy of practically everybody else in the world, who cannot see any value in the tons of homework and endless papers—until that day when everything falls into place and, with the clarity of a blind man receiving his sight, he sees, and knows that the world will never be the same again.

439. Definition of a Parent

What is a parent?

To his children, he is the solid rock in the center of a world of turbulence and change, the one fixed point to which the child will return again and again for directions on how to get to the next place.

To the school, the parent is the primary source of every reason for their existence. They are the school's first resort and final authority in the process of shaping what the world will call an educated human being.

To the teacher, he is a partner, antagonist, and cause of anxiety all at the same time. He is the tree which the apple doesn't fall far from and the ultimate solution to the lack-of-homework problem.

To the community, the parent is often the object of blame when a kid goes wrong and the figure in the background when a glimmer of hope shines through the darkness.

To all of us, the parent is tomorrow, for his is the precious and delicate and sacred duty of shaping that one who will shape tomorrow.

God be with him.

440. The Teacher Who Believed

He was the worst kid in school, and everyone had given him up for lost. Everyone, that is, except one teacher who truly believed that he might make a difference.

Call it tenacity or call it pig-headedness, but the teacher refused to give up. When the kid failed again and again, the teacher spent countless afternoons and mornings going over, going over, going over, going over. . . .

One day, the kid exploded. "Why are you doing this?" he shouted. "Why don't you just give up on me like everybody else?"

"Because," answered the teacher, "I believe that there is someone inside of you who is worth any amount of time and trouble. If you won't believe in yourself, I guess I'll have to believe for both of us."

Though the incident took place in elementary school many years ago, that teacher recently received an invitation to a college graduation. On it, that same boy had written, "I believe . . . I think I caught it from you!"

441. The Student Who Had Faith

He wanted to make the team; more than anything, he wanted that. Coaches had told him that he was too light, too slight, and too small. Teachers had reminded him that his grades were not the best and he needed more study time. No one seriously believed that he could make the team and sustain his grades. No one believed that—except the kid.

"I can do it," he told me. "I can learn and grow."

Because he believed, he set to work. The PE teacher worked out a program for his physical development, and I agreed to help with the academics. The kid told us both, "I can do it!"

And, he did. Sure, I stayed a couple afternoons and came in early a few mornings, and he was right there with me.

He believed that it would happen. His faith was contagious, and he made me believe that it would happen, too.

When the names of the team members were announced and his was among them, I could not have been prouder had he been my own child.

442. The Anatomy of Success

I give you Bill, a child with average intelligence and no physical impediments to learning.

His parents care, and they prepare him for school by reading to him and telling him how wonderful school will be.

When he brings home papers, they are proudly posted in the home. Each day his parents talk about what happened in school, and they refuse to take "Nothing" as an answer.

They go to church or temple together and put their beliefs into practice. Bill won't cheat, because it is morally wrong; he will do his best, because it is morally right.

The child and the family progress through school together. If there is failure, it is their failure. They all celebrate the child's success.

Given these circumstances, it would take several armies to keep Bill from the success that awaits him.

443. The Anatomy of Failure

I give you Cathy, a child of average intelligence and no physical impediments to learning.

Before she even hits school, her parents have told others how they hated school and how they expect that Cathy will hate the rotten place as well. Of course, there is so little time in their busy lives that they can hardly be expected to read to the child.

When Cathy, on rare occasions, brings home papers from school, they are glanced at casually and returned with comments like, "How are things going?" When Cathy answers, "OK," it is accepted at face value and never challenged.

When Cathy is caught cheating, it is dismissed as "youthful mischief." Hey, all kids cheat, right? Right?

Of course, the family is very busy and there is no time for things like church or temple or family conferences or working things out together. Cathy is expected to get by in school as well as she can.

If she does, it will be by the grace of God.

444. The Hidden Cost of Failure

Let's call him Ron. He wasn't merely a kid who failed; he was a failure.

Ron's family simply did not care, and Ron flat out refused to work. Except for several teachers and administrators, everyone seemed content to let him fail. So what?

So, Ron failed—but that's not all he did.

He proved to be a highly effective negative role model, and he took several other students with him down the path of failure.

He stole the time I and others might have spent with the class or in teaching. We had to spend the time on him, while others in the class sat and waited.

He usurped the time of teachers, counselors and administrators, taking them away, time and again, from positive pursuits that would have benefited many students, to turn their attention and effort to one who challenged and defied at every step.

He took the money that might have been spent on education and was instead used to repair the vandalism he caused and to contain him from causing even more destruction.

He caused pain for everyone he touched.

When a kid fails, it is far from a personal matter. Not many see that it is there, but that hidden cost of failure is lying just below the surface—and it's growing bigger every day.

445. Those Who Want to Learn

If you believe that we should educate every child who wants to learn, then you'd better close down the schools right now. Let me illustrate.

There was a girl who could not get long division. Parents stayed up nights; teachers kept her after school; administrators found extra books and scheduled tutors. Nothing worked. The kid could not do long division.

Finally, one teacher decided to go to the kid. "Why can't you do long division?" the teacher asked.

"Because I'm not interested in it," the student replied. "I don't want to learn it."

"What do you want to do?" asked the amazed teacher.

Said the child, "Play video games!"

Let that be a lesson to us. We in the schools should realize that it is not enough just to present the material with the egotistical expectation that they want to learn what we present. Children want to learn what *they* want to learn.

Our task very often is to get them to want to learn what we have to teach!

446. The Ones We Can't Reach

When he first entered my classroom, he took his seat, crossed his legs, crossed his arms, and set his face into a hard and frozen mask that defied penetration.

We tried, of course. Myself and others poured hours of time into him, sometimes threatening and sometimes cajoling, sometimes being a friend and sometimes being an authority figure. Do I have to tell you that nothing worked? We tried being excited, tried being disappointed, tried being angry, tried being gentle—*nothing worked*. Throughout the ten months I had him, the mask did not move, did not crack, did not shift.

The year ended, and he left.

There were comments, of course, like "Good riddance," and "Forget about him!"

Even so, on more than one midnight hour, my mind has turned to him and those like him. They are the ones who sit behind the mask. They are the ones we can't reach. They are the ones who fill your dreams in the lonely hours.

They are the ones we pray for.

447. The Value of Education (I)

Does the long process of education *really* have value? Let me tell you a story.

Papa Lizard and Junior Lizard were sitting on a branch. Three hours went by, and neither of them moved so much as a millimeter. At the end of the fourth hour, several flies began to buzz around the vicinity. Still Papa and Junior moved not a bit. At the end of the fifth hour, two flies came to rest nearby. Papa Lizard suddenly stood up to his full lizard height, opened his mouth, unfurled a long sticky tongue and zapped the two flies in one lightning stroke.

As Papa Lizard gulped one down and prodded the other toward his son, he said, "So you see, it doesn't matter how long you have to wait while your education seems to be of no practical value, as long as it's there when you really need it!"

448. The Value of Education (II)

The student asked a question in class, and the teacher, grasping the opportunity, sent the child to the school library to "look it up."

The child did not return for the rest of the period. In fact, three periods later, the student had failed to show up for his next three classes. They began a discreet search of the school.

He was found twenty minutes later in a corner of the library, all but completely hidden behind a pile of books.

"We've been looking all over for you," stated the teacher. "Do you realize you've missed the last three periods of school?"

"I just took a book and started to look up the answer to the question," said the student, "but that brought up some other questions, and each of those questions had questions."

The boy looked up at the teacher. "Every street I went down had another street at the end of it. Once I started the trip, I just couldn't stop!"

449. The Ultimate Value of Education

The man was very proud of his son, now a Ph.D. and teaching at a major university.

One day, the father was visiting in his son's office on campus. A topic of conversation came up, and the father asked his son a particular question related to the son's specialty.

The Ph.D. frowned, rose, and went to a floor-to-ceiling bookshelf. He studied the titles for a moment, took one down, paged through it, read, and pronounced the answer to his father's question.

His father quipped, "You mean that your mother and I put you through four years of college and another five years of graduate school for this? All that education just so you could look in a book?"

"I don't think you understand," the young man smiled. "It doesn't take all that education to be able to look in a book; it takes all that education to be able to know which book to look in!"

450. Education and America's Future

There is a future President of the United States who sits in a classroom right now. He or she does homework, cheers at football games, and listens while a parade of teachers expound on subject after subject and shape the content of that young mind as well as the thought processes that will serve it throughout life.

Considering how many lives and future lives will depend upon that President's decisions, the task of preparing the person who will fill the job becomes particularly awesome. When you further consider that this future President could be *any* student in *any* school in our nation, the responsibility it places upon educators is frightening.

Make no mistake about it; the future of the United States of America is being shaped right now in the classrooms of this nation. Truly, it is we who will shape those who will shape tomorrow.

Under the circumstances, how can we do less than try our hardest to educate every child as if he or she will one day decide the fate of our nation? It may just come to pass?

ENDING UP WITH A GOOD BEGINNING—MATERIAL FOR DYNAMIC AND INSPIRATIONAL CONCLUSIONS

As educators, we have all seen students exceed our expectations and accomplish far more than anyone, perhaps even themselves, would have thought possible. Indeed, these success stories help sustain us when we must deal with those who steadfastly refuse to live up to even a percentage of their potential. Quite often, the difference lies in the motivation supplied by home and school. We have seen motivation work miracles; so have you.

So, let's end this book with a section of stories designed to be inspirational, designed to be motivational. After all, if we start out by motivating others, there is no telling whether we, ourselves, may catch the fire!

451. *It Is What You Make of It*

It is what you make of it.

I can honestly say that in all my decades as a teacher, I have never failed a student. Of course, that's not what several of my former students might feel; but it is nonetheless true.

I remember a student who, after report cards had been given out, came pounding up to my desk with wild and indignant eyes and asked, "Why did you fail me?"

"I didn't," I replied.

"Yes, you did!" he asserted, pointing to his report card.

I took out my marking book and showed him the colorful line of failed tests and missing homeworks and uncompleted projects.

"You see," I said, "I didn't give you a failing grade. I merely recorded the failing grade you gave yourself."

In the final analysis, we are responsible for what we do.

It is what you make of it.

452. *Don't Come Back Tomorrow*

Of course, I'm betraying my age, but I remember listening to serial dramas on radio when I was a kid. Superman, the Lone Ranger, Sky King, Sergeant Preston of the Yukon—they filled many an afternoon and evening. Each episode would end with the announcer's injunction to "tune in tomorrow for the next thrilling episode . . ."

Years later, after having faced thousands of "thrilling episodes" in the classroom and school, I'd like to amend that statement.

Kids, don't come back tomorrow. Take what you have learned and get out into the world. Teach others and inspire them to teach others still. Administrators, don't come back tomorrow to the same school you served today. Use your position and your expertise to fashion a new school, one that changes and grows better every day. Teachers, don't come back tomorrow to the same routine you went through today. Make each day a new and exciting experience for everyone, yourself included, as you get those kids ready for the new days that they will face.

Don't come back tomorrow—go out and make tomorrow happen!

453. *What Do You Do For An Encore?*

Be careful what you allow in the classroom, for what you permit today is the precedent that will have to be exceeded tomorrow.

I remember one teacher who allowed her class members to put their heads down on their desks to "rest" whenever they felt tired. "It will refresh them, and they will be ready to learn." That was in October. By May, she had lost the class completely. Students roamed at will, lolled in corners and on bookcases, and paid no attention to the teacher whatsoever.

Even in our society, not so long ago, people argued that movies should be allowed to use "realistic" language. Surely an occasional *hell* or *damn* wouldn't hurt. Today's movies take language once relegated to the sewer and serve it up on the dining room table as the main course.

Be careful what you allow in your classroom today, for what you allow tomorrow will have to be bigger and louder and larger.

When today's class is over, the question remains—what will you do for an encore?

454. *Getting Through the Day (I)*

I had given the homework assignment to the class and written the page numbers on the board, allowing them to get started with it during the few remaining minutes of class.

Most got right to it, but I noticed one boy who was still referring to the single page number and the three words of direction I had written on the board. While all the class was busy doing the assignment, he seemed to be still copying it in what I knew to be his "homework book."

I went over to him and glanced at what he was writing.

"John," I said, "that's not the assignment. You've written five times the amount I gave, adding pages and work I never required!"

"I know," John replied, "but whatever you give, I write down more. Then at night, I cross off some and say, 'I'm not going to do that!' and I cross off some more and say, 'I refuse to do that!' When just your homework is left, I do that."

"Why in the world . . ."

"Hey!" responded the student, "It helps me get through the day!"

455. Getting Through the Day (II)

I knew a teacher who shared her philosophy with me: "I learned early on that I would never be able to reach each student each day; there were just too many variables involved. I discovered, however, that it was entirely possible to reach one student with one new idea every single day.

"Each morning, I would look over my class lists and try to spend some time reflecting on them. Billy needs to learn how to share; Mary could use help in math; Tommy needs to be reassured. Throughout the day, I would go about with that in mind, reassuring myself that I could reach at least one of them and doing my best to do so. I knew that one child would be better off for my having tried.

"Most days, I found that in trying to reach just one, I had touched them all. It's a wonderful way to get through the day!"

456. Facing Each New Day (Humorous)

It was just before the start of school, and I was in my classroom when one of my students stuck his head in the door.

"Excuse me," he said, "but is it true that the teachers are going out on strike?"

"Of course not. Where did you get that idea?"

"Well, did the furnace break down so we have to be sent home?"

"The furnaces are fine."

"How are you feeling? It's the flu season, you know."

"I'm fine," I said and added, "and the other teachers are fine as well."

"Aw, come on!" said the student with a scowl. "Can't you give me some good news? If I don't have a little hope, how am I ever going to be able to face the day?"

457. Facing Each New Day (Serious)

How difficult it would be to face each new day if, for one moment, I allowed myself to believe that what I was doing was not important.

I have seen the results of that. I have seen educators who no longer felt that they made a difference. I have watched as they pulled themselves through the day like a toy whose battery is running down. They have lost the glow. They feel they no longer make a difference, and they don't.

But, if I believe that what I do and say to my students this day will help to shape what they do or say tomorrow and throughout their lives, then I will be bright and alert at all times. I will seek every chance I can find to teach and help and inspire. I will face each new day as an opportunity to help my kids make the difficult transition between childhood and young adulthood.

I believe that I can make a difference, and each new day, I will!

458. Prepared to Teach (I)

I am prepared to teach . . .

I am prepared to teach if my students want to learn.

I am prepared to teach if my students do not want to learn.

I am prepared to teach on bright and shiny days, on wet and gray days, in hot rooms and in freezing rooms, when bees come through the open window, and when the rain falls inside.

I am prepared to teach in spite and because of parents who don't understand, administrators who don't understand, colleagues who don't understand, and students who don't understand—because getting them to understand is what I am all about.

I am prepared to teach with books, without books, with charts or with words alone, with plentiful paper or on the ground with a stick.

I am prepared to teach under any and all circumstances.

I am prepared to teach.

Bring on the kids!

459. Prepared to Teach (II)

It was to be the young man's first teaching assignment, and he was extremely nervous. As the sun was just peeking over the horizon, he awakened his wife and stood at the foot of the bed.

"Well," he said, "I'm ready to teach. Check me out before I leave for school."

"It's too early," his wife muttered.

"Come on, this is important. Look, my shoes are shined; my suit is fresh from the cleaner; my tie is spotless; I have two black pens and one red pen; there's a ruler and glue and extra paper in my briefcase, and I have my schedule taped on the inside cover of my attendance book. I am ready to teach!"

"Not quite," yawned his wife.

"What do you mean?"

"You may be all set to teach," she smiled, "but teaching isn't ready for you. This is Sunday morning; school doesn't start until tomorrow!"

460. Prepared to Learn

The boy was failing every subject except physical education, and even there, he hovered on the brink of disaster. It was a sad situation, and the boy's father was called in for a conference.

When he was advised of his son's grades and continued lack of effort, the father remarked, "I can tell you that the boy's not lazy. Do you know that he has memorized the roster of every Major League baseball team? He has, and he can give you the current batting average of every player in the league!"

"That is impressive," remarked one teacher, "but I have to tell you that he hasn't done that with his schoolwork."

"Of course not," stated the boy's father. "You haven't taught him anything he wants to learn!"

461. The End of Recess

Recess has always been a popular item in the school day. One incident I remember vividly occurred at recess time on a day when we were doing a unit about which I was particularly enthusiastic. We were about three-quarters of the way through the material when the bell rang, and we filed out to the playground.

I was enjoying the fresh air and sunlight when one of my students came up and asked me the time. I told him and he left. Not ten seconds later, another student came to ask the time, then another, and another.

Finally, I said to the student currently before me, "Look, you have to be the eighth kid to ask what time it is. What's going on?"

Looking at me with absolute honesty in her face, she replied, "Nothing's going on. We just want recess to be over so we can get back to what you were doing."

In all the years I have taught, I have never received a finer compliment.

462. The End of the Class

The bell signalling the end of the period did not always signal the end of the class. While many—indeed, most—of the students filed out the door, invariably there would be some who lingered, anxious to talk about the day's lesson. I never had the heart to shoo them away, and consequently a steady stream of kids were arriving late for their next period, having been "detained" by me.

I got in trouble for that. Not horrendous trouble, but my colleagues were disturbed, and I was gently "spoken to" by a sympathetic principal who asked me to try to keep to the schedule.

How could I? Could I tell a kid that I would not explain or comment because a bell had rung, and that meant that learning had ended?

Finally, I hit upon it, and I began ending the class three minutes early! Now, while most students chatted and got books together for the next class, I had time to meet and talk with those who needed to have the class carried slightly beyond the confines of the schedule.

I never had a kid be late to the next class again!

463. The End of the School Day

As a young teacher, I was complaining to an older and respected member of the faculty.

"At the end of each day, I'm exhausted," I told him. "Perhaps when I learn to get things better organized, I won't be so tired."

He looked at me and said, "I hope you never get to that point."

"What do you mean?"

"Just this," he replied. "If you are going to be the kind of teacher you want to be, then you had better be tired at the end of the school day. A good teacher works hard; a great teacher works harder. He puts everything he has into every lesson he teaches. If there comes a time when you are not tired at the end of the school day, perhaps it would be a good time to reassess your career choice."

It was a lesson I have never forgotten, and one that has seen me through the weary end of many a day.

464. The End of the School Year

How volatile and changeable is that period of turbulence we call youth. Emotions and opinions seem to change with a rapidity that is both unparalleled and unprecedented.

Timmy had started at the end of September to tell me how much he anticipated the end of the school year in June. In fact, he had gotten a calendar and counted the school days left in the school year.

"Only 153 days to go!" he would inform me. "Only 116 . . . only 87 . . . only 33 days until freedom!"

Then came the much-heralded last day of school, and in the closing moments, there was Timmy, hugging me fiercely, with tears flowing down his face.

"I'm going to miss you so much!" he sobbed. "What am I going to do?"

I assured him that there was a future, dried his tears, and sent him on his way.

At the doorway, he turned and faced me.

"You know," he said, "there's only 62 days until school begins. Isn't that great?"

465. *The End of School*

"I will be so glad when I graduate and get out of school," the high school senior told his teacher. "I can't wait to get out from under you teachers and the thousand rules this place has. When I graduate, I will never set foot in a school again!"

Graduation came and went, and a number of years passed, when the teacher looked up, saw a young man standing in the doorway of his class, and recognized him as the former student so anxious to be rid of school.

They had a reunion of sorts, and the teacher recalled the student and the young man's greatest wish—to get out of school.

"I never got that wish," said the student.

"Of course you did," returned the teacher. "You graduated from here years ago."

"Oh, I graduated all right," the former student remarked, "but I never got out of school. I just changed one classroom for another. I found that when it comes to life, school never ends. Believe me, the classroom out there is ten times harder than the ones in this building!"

466. *The End of Summer*

What is the end of summer?

To throngs of students it is watching the last days of freedom ebb away as on the horizon the specter of the schoolhouse looms and laughs. It is the countdown to imprisonment!

To parents throughout the nation, it is the unabashed and blessed silence that will be descending upon the house for a few hours each day. It is screen doors no longer slammed, floors untracked with mud—but it is also an emptiness that will not be entirely filled until that yellow school bus rounds the corner. It is a countdown to freedom and to anticipation.

And, to thousands of teachers, the end of summer is a trip to the empty, waiting building to put up bulletin boards in the late August heat and move books and arrange desks for those million kids who won't care anyhow. It is getting out those plans and worksheets that worked so well last year. It is knowing the path and the problems ahead and still wanting to leave the summer behind. It is a countdown to kids and all the joy and heartache that a new school year will bring.

It is the end of summer and the start of school.

It is life.

467. The Night Before Christmas Vacation (Humorous)

'Twas the day before Christmas vacation
　In that place where the schoolchildren roam,
And the students and staff were all busy
　Munching goodies they'd brought in from home.

For the day before Christmas vacation,
　As those who have been there will state,
Is devoted to eating and munching
　Of holiday cookies and cakes.

There are brownies and cookies and candies,
　Each lovingly made in the home,
Which each mother has given to junior
　To present to the teacher alone.

So of course I must sample each offering,
　Though my stomach complains and grows sour;
In the name of good home/school relations,
　I'm gaining three pounds every hour!

468. The Night Before Christmas Vacation (Serious)

'Twas the night before Christmas vacation,
　And the students had finally gone home;
I was the last teacher remaining,
　And I stood in the hallway alone.

I thought of the children that morning
　　Who had shaken the classrooms with glee
And the Christmases they'd be enjoying,
　　With presents 'neath twinkling trees.

Then I thought of some kids in the building
　　And the gifts they had given to me,
Like the gift of their laughter and wonder,
　　And those young eyes that suddenly see.

And I prayed that the gift I had given
　　To them would be blessed from above,
For along with the knowledge and learning,
　　I pray I have given them love.

469. *In the Midst of Winter*

After years of contact with children, I am convinced that there is a decided connection between weather and behavior. In spring, I've seen children literally bouncing like spring lambs when the warm and promising breezes have stirred the young green buds on branches. I have also seen days where leaden gray clouds press close to the earth, and an icy wind blows scraps of paper that skitter across the frozen ground. On those days, I have been witness to solemn-faced children who stared listlessly into empty corners and showed all the enthusiasm of a lump of modelling clay.

That was precisely what I complained about in the teacher's lounge one day, describing the lack of enthusiasm in the kids that parallelled the listless gray day. It was at that point that another teacher glanced my way and remarked, "When it's winter outside, it should be your duty to make it summer inside."

She was right, of course. From that moment, my outlook changed, and I did my best to inspire summertime in my winter children.

It worked, of course, and I learned that we all carry springtime within us.

In the midst of winter, that's not a bad lesson to learn.

470. *Spring Will Come*

"If you wait long enough, spring will come." That was the favorite expression of an older teacher I knew. She would use it three or four times a week at least. It had little meaning to me then. It was just words.

Then there was that child, the one everyone else had given up on; the one who broke my heart and kept me working extra hours and gave me fitful sleep. Soon, I was ready to give up on her as well, and I said as much to my colleagues. Then, that teacher was at my elbow, and she said, "If you wait long enough, spring will come."

I made no reply, but somehow the idea stuck. I refused to let the kid go; I kept working with her; I would not give up. If I could wait long enough . . .

And, she got better. Her behavior improved; her grades rose; her outlook changed . . .

It is one of the sadnesses of my life that that teacher died without my ever having told her what she had done for me.

They were just words about springtime . . . but she helped me to smell the flowers.

471. The Kid Who Loved School

Most kids like school, but I knew one once who really loved school. When I arrived early, as has always been my habit, he would be waiting for the student doors to open and school to begin. Late in the afternoon, as I would be going home after extra help and late calls to parents, I would see him in the halls or in the school library. I was told that he stayed until the custodians finally shooed him away. My goodness, I thought, this kid really loves school.

It wasn't too much later that I found out about his home—the alcohol and drugs, the shouting and screaming, the constant turmoil, the beatings; and the pain—the terrible pain.

Clean, warm, peaceful by comparison, with rules that did not change from minute to minute on a drunkard's whim, school was a haven—if not heaven. Of course he loved it and was there all the time they would let him stay.

The school and its agencies went to work on the family of the kid who loved school.

How I hoped that there would come a day when that boy would have reason just to like the place.

472. Putting Principles into Practice

The superintendent of schools had a reputation far and wide as a very powerful speaker. Indeed, he was often in demand, so much so that he had publically vowed that he would only speak on occasions that related directly to the school or school system.

One day, the superintendent received a telephone call from a woman who informed him that her pet poodle had died, and she wanted the superintendent to deliver a eulogy for the dog at the dog's funeral the next day.

"Madam," huffed the superintendent," I don't give eulogies for dogs, and even if I did, I have publically stated that I will make no speech not directly related to our schools."

Replied the woman, "I have set aside one thousand dollars as the speaker's fee."

"Madam," stated the superintendent, "you didn't tell me that the dog was an alumnus of our system!"

473. Give Me Your Hand (I)

As I taught the lesson, I noticed a boy and a girl in the back of the classroom holding hands. I try never to embarrass anyone, so I waited until the class was totally occupied with work, and I made my way back to them.

"OK, lovebirds," I said gently, "let's save it for the romance novels . . ."

"We're not 'lovebirds'!" the young lady protested indignantly. "I don't even like him!"

"Really?" I said with a smile. "Then what's with the hand holding?"

"You don't understand," said the girl, grimmacing. "I have to hold his hand. It's the only thing that will keep him from cracking his knuckles!"

474. Give Me Your Hand (II)

I'll tell you a story of two boys, although the incidents happened years apart. Both boys were bullies. Both boys picked on others. Both boys made life miserable for those around them. Both boys also finally picked a fight with someone who had had enough, and the bully ended up being knocked to the ground. In both cases, I arrived as the bully was hitting the ground, and I stepped over the prostrate form and offered my hand to help the boy up.

In one case, the boy took my hand, and when he rose, my other hand went around his shoulders, and we talked. He never became an honor student and was never class president, but he was never a bully again, either. At the end of the school year, he shook my hand enthusiastically.

In the other case, the boy slapped my hand away. He scrambled to his feet unaided and scampered from the playground screaming of the revenge he would take. He would not talk to me, and not a week passed afterwards that he was not in trouble. By summertime, his eyes had become twin beacons of hate.

I stand before every child in the school, and I stretch out my arm and ask each one to give me his hand.

The choice is theirs, and so is the future.

475. *The Value of Committment*

The kids called him "Tiny," because he was anything but. He also had the reputation of the boy who could eat the most in our school.

One day, Tiny was challenged by a boy from another grade to see how many chocolate chip cookies each could shove in his mouth at one time.

The other boy crammed eighteen cookies into bulging cheeks and then could do no more. Tiny shoved in eighteen and added a nineteenth to cheers and applause. Then, Tiny added a twentieth and twenty-first and topped it off with three more for an even two dozen. When he finished, he looked as if it would be weeks before his cheeks would shrink back to anything near normal.

"Tiny," I asked, "you had him beaten with the nineteenth cookie. Why did you do the extra five?"

"Sir," he said as he looked seriously at me, "there is no sense in taking on a challenge unless you are totally committed to your cause!"

476. *What Faith Can Do (I)*

Her brother Billy had diagnosable learning problems and was not doing well in his regular classes. Sue understood this and came to me asking what she could do to help.

Frankly, my answer was to be supportive of her brother, but to leave the learning to us 'experts.' Sue was polite, but I think she rejected that suggestion immediately. In her heart, Sue believed that she could help her brother learn, and she set about to do just that.

Sue would come to me and others from time to time, checking on what we were doing in class, assessing her brother's progress, seeking advice on his brother's needs. I know for a fact that she read books on learning strategies that were far beyond her years.

Here's the bottom line: Billy's grades began to rise, and Billy began to learn.

It was easy for the school and us teachers to take credit for that, but I know of a child, content to remain in the background, who loved her brother, believed she could make a difference—and did.

Once again, I had been privileged to witness the miracle that faith can accomplish.

477. *What Faith Can Do (II)*

What can faith do? How can faith help in education? To borrow a phrase, let me count the ways.

I have seen kids who were hell-bent for lives of trouble and pain literally turn around, because a teacher believed that they could be salvaged and refused to give up on them.

I have seen children whom others have labelled as incapable of learning suddenly begin to learn and improve, because teachers and families and the child himself believed that it was possible.

I have seen shy children become happy children, bullies turned into champions of justice, cheaters and thieves discover honesty—I have seen all of that and more accomplished, because people believed that those behaviors could be changed if they only kept trying.

Time and again, I have seen the impossible happen in the lives of children. I have seen what faith can do, and I believe!

478. *Taking the Next Step*

I was going to the dentist to have root-canal work done. At the threshold of the doctor's office, I paused. I became acutely aware that if I did not take the next step into the office, he could not get to the drilling. It took me every ounce of willpower to enter.

. . . Not that teaching children is in any way like pulling teeth, but it is a great deal like standing at the door to the dentist's office. I have seen incident after incident where I have laid out everything I have before a student, opened wide every door to success and happiness and that bright future that the school has to offer, and the student has stood, wavered, and steadfastly refused to take the next step.

Extra help and special tutoring have been offered and never accepted. The same is true of counseling, social services, and the personal sympathy and aid and concern of a legion of educators.

The finest treatment in the world lies fallow if we cannot get the patient to take the next step into the doctor's office!

479. Stepping Into Tomorrow

Even after all these years, I can remember rainy days in my childhood. My mother would scold and warn me not to leave the house without my rubbers in place to protect my good shoes from getting wet and me from catching some horrible rain-related disease.

I think I know how my mother felt, because for years I have been "warning" my students not to step out into tomorrow without their skills and learning in place. I have tried to get them to realize that if they will just "put on" their learning, it will keep their minds and hearts from getting "wet" with discouragement and failure, and it will protect them from many a world-related illness such as apathy and despair.

Sure, I sound like my mother, but maybe Mom had a point.

Learning—don't you dare leave school and step out into the world without it!

480. Accepting the Challenge (I)

Every class that I have ever taught has started with a challenge. Of course I don't mean that some student steps forward and offers to take me on in personal combat. No, that is the stuff of Hollywood, but the challenge is real nonetheless.

There is the challenge to me to do my best to teach this class before me, to guide them into new knowledge, to help them to grow, to work and prepare and agonize and expound and present to the best of my ability.

There is also the challenge to the class to learn what will be taught, to put in the time and effort to work and study and assimilate and apply and take what is offered and make it a part of themselves.

There is a challenge for the class and a challenge for me.

If we both accept those challenges, there is no limit to what can be accomplished.

481. Accepting the Challenge (II)

I have seen them and so have you. They are the kids who sit in our classes on the first day of school with legs crossed, arms folded, jaws set, and eyes hard. Their every look oozes challenge. "Go ahead," they seem to seeth, "teach me if you can!"

That is a challenge which needs accepting and which is accepted as a matter of course by teachers throughout our nation. Time and again I have seen teachers take that deep breath and march into the arena of the classroom, accepting the challenge to dare to teach.

At the end of the school year, those same kids whose once-defiant attitude spurred the conflict would not believe you if you dared to suggest that a few months back they were the essence of resistance in the classroom.

Perhaps that, above all else, bespeaks the challenge accepted and the struggle won!

482. Accepting the Challenge (III)

Our cafeteria had a "how-many-beans-in-the-jar" contest, the prize being free dessert for a week. Students submitted official "entry blanks" with their name, homeroom number, and official guess.

When the winner was announced one afternoon, another student protested. The winning student, it seemed, had missed the exact amount by only two beans, while the disputing student pointed to a page in his notebook where he had jotted down the exact amount.

"I can't seem to find your entry blank," said the contest coordinator.

"I never filled one out," answered the protester, "that's baby stuff!"

That settled it, of course, and the first student, not the challenger, ate free pie and cookies for a week.

Which, of course, points out that no matter how good the solution, you have to be actively engaged in the process for it to be of any value.

In other words, first you have to accept the challenge and enter the fray before you can have a chance to win.

483. *Let Me Help You With That*

"Come on," I said, "let me help you with that." The boy was obviously struggling with the assignment, and I hoped I could make it a bit clearer.

"No!" the kid fumed, "I don't need help. I can do it myself!"

"Admirable," I commented, "but don't you think it might make it a little easier if I explained the part that's causing trouble?"

"No!" he all but shouted, "I'm not stupid. I don't need help. I can do it myself!"

"Of course you're not stupid. No one said you were. But, you don't have to be dumb to need help. Won't you let me help you?"

"No!"

So, the kid failed, and I doubt if he ever properly understood the concept being reinforced. Later, I tried to explain to him that it is a part of wisdom to seek out and accept help when you need it.

I don't think he was listening.

484. *Working for a Goal (Humorous)*

"Set goals for yourself and try to see to it that everything you do works toward that goal," mother explained to her daughter who listened patiently.

Then it was Christmas Eve, and preparations were being made for the arrival of Santa Claus. The three was trimmed, stockings were hung, and cookies and milk were put out so the jolly old elf could have a snack.

A few minutes later, mother saw her daughter carrying the snack back to the kitchen. The child returned with a glass of water and a package of Slim-Fast. The child placed the items next to the fireplace, looked up at the chimney, and smiled.

Mother smiled broadly as well. She had never realized just how goal-oriented her daughter was!

485. *Working for a Goal (Serious)*

It didn't seem to matter how much extra attention I gave him, how much extra help, or how long I stayed with him in the afternoon, the absolute best I could manage was to get enough of the material into his head for him to squeak by with a *D* on a quiz or test before it left his mind for parts unknown.

One day, I opened my plan book before him and showed him the outline of the lesson. I asked, "What would you like to do?"

"Get back home in time to watch my soap operas," he answered.

Well, there it was; it suddenly became amazingly clear. What I wanted most was to have him learn the material; what he wanted most was to get out of school as soon as possible.

Obviously, there would be no substantial progress until we were both working for the same goal!

486. Working Together (Humorous)

One day out on the playground, I chanced to observe two children who were trying to move a wooden box that was obviously very heavy. First, one child would struggle and grunt, barely manage to lift the box a few inches from the ground, stagger a couple of feet, and then let the box thud down as he stood panting. Then, the other child would go through the same process as the other waited.

"Kids," I said, "you're not getting anywhere. Why doesn't one of you take one end and the other take the other end and try doing it together?"

The children looked at each other and bent to the task. In no time at all, they had moved the load.

Both came running back to me.

"That was great!" exclaimed one.

"Yeah!" shouted the other. "Man! You teachers sure come up with some great new ideas!"

487. Working Together (Serious)

There are thousands of success stories I could tell you. If there weren't, I think I would have given up teaching long ago. But, successes do occur, and they happen frequently. Every time a kid shapes up, begins to do the work, gains in maturity, or goes from a classic underachiever to a normal functioning student, it is a success.

And, of all those successes that I have had a part in, the uncounted majority of them have happened because three units have worked together as one—the student, the teacher, and the family. Without all three of those elements, there can be progress, but the goal of success will always be elusive.

However, when the student has come to the decision to learn, when the teacher and the home communicate and work together to accomplish that goal, then success is virtually assured.

It is by working together that the student succeeds, and when that happens, so do we all!

488. *The Power of an Idea (I)*

The little girl came home to show her parents a miracle. In school, the teacher had the class take seeds and plant them in paper cups filled with earth. The planted seeds were tended and watered by the children, and soon little green shoots began to appear. Presently, a small flower valiantly rose from the containers.

The family shared the wonder of growth and the miracle of life.

This scene has been repeated a million times over across this land, since it is an activity very popular in elementary schools everywhere.

It is also a process that is repeated day after day in virtually every classroom of every school. Ideas are seeds that are planted in the fertile soil of the human mind. Throughout the school year, these "idea seeds" will be watered and nourished and given the room to grow. And there is only wonder and exultation at the blossoms these "seeds" produce!

489. *The Power of an Idea (II)*

In the faculty lounge, one teacher was remarking about a system he had developed for grading and recording homework.

"You know," said a second teacher, "I thought of that, too, but I never got around to doing anything about it."

A third teacher then told about a project she was doing that had the kids enthused and was producing some great results.

"I was thinking about that a year ago," said the second teacher, "but I never did anything about it."

Just then, the bell rang for the next class. As the teachers rose, a teacher who had observed the exchange walked over to the second teacher and said, "Listen, if you should get the idea that you should go to the bathroom before class, maybe you'd better get around to doing it and not wait."

The very best of ideas have no power at all unless and until they are acted upon. We must be thinkers, certainly, but we must be doers as well.

490. The Power of an Idea (III)

It's a recipe.

Take an idea about education, share it with some colleagues, and stir well until it produces ten more ideas and each of those produces ten more. Allow to simmer in a classroom until it has been fully tested, ammending here and there as circumstances warrant. Then, serve it up to class after class, allowing them to savor its flavor.

What you will have is an educational success: a process or method or unit or procedure that will stimulate, challenge, make learning fun, and open the minds of countless numbers of students.

Take this as a warning, however. Make certain that you start out with a fresh idea. Old and stale ideas have a tendency to weaken the final punch. But, a new and fresh idea, properly prepared and seasoned, can provide a dish that hides nourishment in its good taste and provides sustenance for years to come.

491. Don't Look Back

An older and respected teacher I once knew told me that there are three demons that particularly enjoy tormenting educators.

The name of the first devil is "Woulda," as in "I 'Woulda' done more if I had only known."

The second demon goes by the name of "Coulda," as in, "I 'Coulda' given the kid extra help if I weren't so busy."

The third is named "Shoulda," as in "I 'Shoulda' spent more time on that."

Of course, the uses of the names change, but the basic idea remains the same. Woulda, Coulda, and Shoulda are demons of regret, and they will paralyze you and destroy your effectiveness if you allow them to.

There is only one way to exorcize these demons, and that is to refuse to look back, to keep your eyes on the future and to build for that future.

Allow Woulda, Coulda, and Shoulda to become stepping stones to new heights for your students.

492. Before We Sleep

It was Robert Frost who wrote that we have ". . . miles to go before (we) sleep." To teachers and administrators everywhere, this strikes home with considerable earnestness. At times it seems that there is just so much to do, so much to be accomplished, so many children to help and teach and watch grow. Indeed, there are endless miles before we rest, before we sleep.

And, what a burden this places on us. For in the journey of those endless miles, what we do *will affect* so many others who will, in turn, affect others still.

William Penn wrote, "I expect to pass through this life but once. If, therefore, there be any kindness I can show or any good thing I can do to any fellow-being, let me do it now and not defer or neglect it, as I shall not pass this way again."

What a beautiful map to guide us through the miles ahead, and what a sweet and lovely sleep at journey's end.

493. Competing for the Prize

He didn't stand a chance. He had no head for science, his grades were pitiful, and he lacked the devotion to a cause to carry through. If he entered the science fair, he'd come in dead last. That was the appraisal given to the student by his parents, most of his teachers, and all of his friends.

I don't know—perhaps it was all that negativism that spurred him on, but when the list of competitors for the Science Fair was published, there was his name.

Since the kid didn't have the remotest possibility of winning, many people thought they should at least help out to "give the kid a fighting chance." Consequently, books were recommended and courses of action suggested and help offered here and there.

Every so often, someone would pass him by and snicker, but all that did was to get him to work harder toward the prize.

He had a reason now; he had a goal. He worked.

When his project won first prize at the science fair, several of his friends and teachers were heard to say, "We knew he could do it. We never doubted for a moment!"

494. *Finishing the Race*

She wasn't a very good athlete, so when she entered the 5K race, the question was not how she'd finish, but if she'd finish. There were serious doubts about that.

In the days before the big event, I doubt that the kid heard anything but discouraging words. Most people blatantly told her that she was crazy. Those who didn't, those who were kinder, reminded her that she could drop out anywhere along the route, and that medical aid would be available.

The day of the race finally arrived, the starting pistol sounded, and a huge group was off. The kid had started at the front of the pack, and rapidly fell behind, until she was dead last.

There was cheering when the winners crossed the line, and a buzz as people began to realize that the kid who was dead last refused to quit and was stumbling along with all the might and courage she had.

When she eventually crossed the line after all the others and fell into the arms of the paramedics, the crowd was on its feet and roaring. She had not won, but she had succeeded. She had finished and given it her all.

Come to think of it, that's not a bad epitaph for any of us.

495. *Who Else But You?*

"If I don't do it, it won't get done," my mother would sometimes say. It was calculated to instill guilt, I suppose, and it certainly had the effect of getting the rest of us pitching in to help.

Years afterward, when I had become a teacher, I remember the electric shock that went up my spine when, one day, I used the exact same phrase. I was discussing my class at the time and talking about teaching them some skill. It occurred to me that for this period in their lives, I was the resident expert in that subject, and if I didn't teach them about it, it probably would not get taught.

Perhaps it was a small revelation, but to me it meant checking myself to make certain that I had given my students all I was capable of giving, because if I didn't do it . . .

Hey, they're your students, they sit in your classroom, all those eyes turn upward to you.

Who else but you?

496. Looking Forward to Tomorrow

I wasn't feeling too well, and I guess it showed, because one of my students came up to me during a quiet moment and asked me straight out what was wrong.

"I have to do some things that I don't want to do," I told him honestly, "and I don't feel good about it."

"Why don't you do what I do?" advised the student. "When I feel like that, I think about something good that's going to happen afterwards."

So, I put my afternoon meeting and the difficulty that would bring into a back corner of my mind, and I thought about how good it would feel to get home to my family.

It worked!

Now, when school and all its problems get me down, when I hear all the reports about how our youth is self-destructing, when there seems nothing to look at but gloom and doom, I start thinking about the thousands of success stories, the thousands of good kids who will turn into good adults and do their best to shape for all of us a good future . . . and I begin to smile.

That student was right—you don't have much inclination to brood over the problems of today when you are looking forward to tomorrow!

497. Believing That There Is a Chance We Can Win

We had practiced for the intra-school spelling bee for some time, and I was especially pleased with one student who had a very good chance in the activity.

The evening of the event, however, the team from the other school arrived. With them, they had a boy who had won virtually every academic award the system had to offer. This student was known not as a "brain," but as a "super-brain."

My student took one look, turned to me, and said, "We can't win! I know that kid; he's a genius. We don't stand a chance!"

"Yes! We do!" I challenged, and I tried to convince my student that she was just as prepared as anyone.

It didn't work. In the eighth round, my student went down on a spelling word I remembered going over just a few days before.

That was years ago, but I still wonder what would have happened if I could have gotten that kid to believe that there was a chance of victory.

498. *Believing That We Can Make a Difference*

I talked to a drug pusher once. He was quite candid and described to me in detail just how he went about the process.

He would start by giving away some "samples." This was good for business, because then the kids would come back to him for more, only this time it would cost them. If the kid didn't have the money, he'd trust him, until the kid owed a great deal of cash, was desperate, and really wanted the merchandise. Then, there was no more credit and no delivery until the money was paid. Where or how the kid got the cash was of no concern; he got it or there was no delivery.

This pusher was instrumental in shaping the lives of dozens and perhaps hundreds of students.

He believed that he could make a difference in the lives of those about him. He worked at it, and he succeeded.

He was twelve years old.

Got the point?

499. *Where Do We Go From Here?*

We were out in the middle of the woods with a group of our kids, and we were lost. When we came to the clearing, there were no less than five roughly beaten paths leading off in all directions. The kids looked at us, and one small sage inquired, "Where do we go from here?"

Thankfully, we never had to answer that question, because at that moment a guide appeared shouting, "Follow me! It's this way!"

Now, at the end of one century and the beginning of another, the question of "Where do we go from here?" becomes operative in education once more. It is not that we are lost in the woods; we know full well where we are and how far we have come. There are, however, a multitude of pathways before us, and the paths we take will determine where we will be headed as the new century unfolds.

It will be interesting to see what guides emerge from the woods.

Will it be one of you who steps forward, beckons, and says, "Follow me! It's this way!"

500. You Do Not Go Alone

Have you ever walked the halls of a school after everyone else has gone home? In the silence, the click of your heels sounds loud and comes at you from all angles, almost as if there were others walking with you. It is, of course, the effect produced from sound waves echoing from metal lockers and terrazzo floors.

Or is it?

It doesn't take much in the alien quiet to make you wonder. Could it be the phantom sound of all those other feet that have trodden through this place and laughed and learned in its classrooms? Could it be the voices and chalk scratchings and paper rustling and page turning of countless generations of educators who have walked these halls before you and in whose steps you walk now?

Listen! Are those whispers the fading voices of all those who, like you, have faced the best and worst that life had to offer and lit the torch of love and learning in the darkest of ignorant nights?

Pause again and listen, for the generations who have gone before are with you now. They are the bedrock on which each path in education is forged.

We do not stop. We do not look back. We do go on.

But . . . we do not go alone!

IN CONCLUSION . . .

501. Sometimes You Laugh, Sometimes You Cry

Sometimes you laugh. Sometimes you throw back your head, and the laughter flows from you in great rolling peals—as you hug your kids, and they laugh with you; as you join with parents and roar over the vagaries of youth and incidents that only an adult perspective can enjoy; as you set the teacher's lounge in an uproar with the story of what happened in your class that day; as you let tears roll down shimmering cheeks as the joy of the gift we call life is reflected and enlarged in the young lives of which you have become a part and, for a while at least, have made your own.

Sometimes you cry. Sometimes your stomach turns hard, and it rises in your throat and flows out your eyes unbidden and hot and salty—as you watch your failures step out, smiling arrogantly, into a swamp that waits to eat them alive; as you sit at funerals of kids who sat and learned at your hands only months before; as you watch the effects of the horrors of child abuse and the gnawing cancer of drugs chip away at children's futures; as you deal in a "civilized" manner with parents who don't care, children who don't care, and a system that often seems just as uncaring; as the sorrow engulfs you when you experience the helplessness of having to sit back and watch the self-imposed destruction of those for whom you care so much.

Of course we go on; of course we don't stop; of course we keep trying—we are educators; we do not give up.

But, just the same. . . .

Sometimes you laugh, sometimes you cry.

INDEX OF TOPICS

The index that follows is arranged by topic. The numbers that follow each topic refer to the number of the anecdote or story, not to page numbers. If a search of the Table of Contents does not yield what you desire, try thinking in terms of the topic you wish to cover. Look it up in the index, and the chances are that you will find something to meet your needs.